# Wilson County, Tenneessee

# TAX LISTS

## 1830-1832

Comiled by:
Thomas Partlow

**Southern Historical Press, Inc.**
**Greenville, South Carolina**

Copyright 2010
By: Southern Historical Press, Inc.

All rights reserved. No part of this publication may be reproduced, stored in a retrieval system, transmitted in any form, posted on to the web in any form or by any means without the prior written permission of the publisher.

Please direct all correspondence and orders to:

**www.southernhistoricalpress.com**
or
**SOUTHERN HISTORICAL PRESS, Inc.
PO BOX 1267
375 West Broad Street
Greenville, SC   29601
southernhistoricalpress@gmail.com**

ISBN #0-89308-837-4

*Printed in the United States of America*

## PREFACE

This book contains the tax lists for Wilson County for the years 1830-1832. They are found in a book which was located in the attic of the old Court House. This book was not transferred to the new Court House. It, like others in the attic, was to be destroyed. It was saved, and is now in private hands. It serves as an excellent census for the years covered.

Thomas E. Partlow
April, 1995

## CAPTAIN SILAS CHAPMAN'S COMPANY 1830

| | |
|---|---|
| Anderson, Patrick heirs | |
| Aston, James | |
| Allgain, John | |
| Aston, Daniel | 100 acres |
| Ashworth, Jasper R. | 200 |
| Atkins, Joel | 640 |
| Allen, Mary | 75 |
| Allen, William | 130 |
| Allcorn, Prudence | 500 |
| Allcorn, James | |
| Chapman, Silas | 250 Barton's Creek |
| Chandler, Robert | 110 |
| Cox, Thomas | |
| Caruthers, Robert L. | 194 |
| Chandler, Ekilles | 100 |
| Chandler, Henry | 100 |
| Carter, William W. | 36 |
| Campsey, John | |
| Cummings, George D. | 323 |
| Clark, Joshua | 113 |
| Calhoon, John | 598½ |
| Conyers, William | |
| Cherry, Daniel | 938 |
| Cherry, Wiley heirs | 300 |
| Cook, Samuel A. heirs | 87 |
| Chapman, Benjamin | 100 |
| Crutcher, Thomas, Jr. | |
| Crutcher, Foster G. | |
| Cox, John | |
| Conyers, John | |
| Barton, Ann | 180 |
| Barton, John | |
| Barkley, Robert | |
| Boyd, Charles H. | |
| Burns, Brantley | 106 |
| Brown, Samuel | |
| Burk, Edward Capt. | |
| Bradley, John | |
| Bradley, Charles | 400 |
| Brown, Jordan H. | |
| Barbee, Joseph | |
| Buck, Elias | |
| Burton, Robert M. | 685 |
| Bonner, Thomas E. | 46 |
| Buchanan, John | 1200 |
| Dixon, Thomas | |
| Davis, John H. | |
| Douglass & Page | 482 |
| Dew, John H. | |
| Douglass, Norval | |
| Dew, Davis | |
| Dew, Arthur | 121 |
| Douglass, H. L. | 218 |

1830

| | |
|---|---|
| Davis, John | |
| Davis, Robert C. | |
| Davis, Elijah | 72 |
| Davidson, John | 140 |
| Dew, Matthew | |
| Douglass, Burchett | 396 |
| Elington, Green | |
| Edwards, Thomas | |
| Everly, Adam | |
| Finley, O. G. | 742 |
| Frazer, James | 155 |
| Frazer & Brown | |
| Gibson, Jesse | 161 |
| Garrison, Person | |
| Gibson, John | |
| Golladay, Isaac | |
| Holman, John B. | 135 |
| Hartsfield, William | 135 |
| Holderfield, Jacob | |
| Hibbitts, David C. | 230 |
| Hearn, John Sheriff | 140 |
| Harrison, Steth | |
| Harris, Alexander C. | |
| Hubbard, Peter | |
| Hallum, William | 50 |
| Harris, Furgus S. | 300 |
| Harris, John heirs | 220 |
| Holman, Thomas P. | 334 |
| Hallum, Robert | 69 |
| Harrison, Joshua | 224 |
| Hill, John | |
| Hubbard, Thomas | |
| Hegerty, Dennis | |
| Holiman, German T. | |
| Irvin, James M. | |
| Irby, James | |
| Jones, Henry H. | |
| Jarrott, Frances A. | |
| Johnson, James H. | 217 |
| Johnson, John | 100 |
| Johnson, Joseph | 3474 |
| Irby, John | 100 |
| Kennedy, David | |
| Killingsworth, James | |
| Ligon, Joseph | 72 |
| Laughton, L. G. S. W. | |
| Lytle, William | 3840 |
| Miller, Beverly J. | |
| Mabry, Ben S. | 40 |
| Minick, Avery | |
| Mitchell, William | |
| McConnell, John | |
| Martin, James | 55 |
| Muirhead, John | 150 |
| McConnell, David | 11 |

1830

| | |
|---|---|
| Meazle, Wiley | |
| Mosely, Asa | |
| Matthews, William E. | 70 |
| Newman, John | |
| Nailor, James | |
| Rye, Henry | 50 |
| Rucks, James | 284 |
| Petty, Henry | |
| Randolph, Grieff | |
| Rutledge, Alexander | 140 |
| Rhodes, Frederick L. | |
| Smith, William B. | |
| Swindle, Pillage | |
| Stone, John | 40 |
| Seawell, William | 1215 |
| Searcy, William | |
| Searcy, Mitchell | |
| Seawell, Hardy H. | |
| Seoggins, George W. | |
| Scoby, David | 50 |
| Swindle, Isaiah | |
| Sypert, William L. | 113 |
| Trout, Adam | 50 |
| Tapp, Stone, & Mottley | 115 |
| Thompson, Thomas J. | |
| Traylor, Edward | 123 |
| Tolliver, Zachariah | |
| Tapp, John S. | 197 |
| Tapp, John | 400 |
| Vick, Allen W. | 100 |
| Vinson, David | |
| Wilson, Joseph L. | 170 |
| White, Cader | 86 |
| White, Littleberry | |
| White, E. A. | 161 |
| White, E. & J. B. | |
| White, Jesse B. | |
| Woods, James | |
| Woolard, John B. | 71 |
| White, John W. | 100 |
| White, James | |
| Weir, Elizabeth | 17 |
| Yerger & Golladay | 26 |
| Yerger, Michael | |
| Yerger, Samuel | |

## CAPTAIN TRUETT'S COMPANY

| | | |
|---|---|---|
| Bagwell, Lunsford | 75 acres | |
| Brewer, Morris | 117 | |
| Bland, Arthur | | |
| Billingsley, John | | |
| Bone, Amos M. | | |
| Clemmons, Samuel T. | 70 | |
| Clifton, Lovin | 140 | 1830 |

| | |
|---|---|
| Chance, Alexander | 75 acres |
| Clemmons, Etheldred | 112 |
| Clemmons, Jeptha | |
| Crutchfield, George W. | |
| Caraway, Moses | 100 |
| Caraway, Merritt | |
| Caraway, Willis | |
| Castleman, Jacob | 378 |
| Comer, William | 103 |
| Clemmons, Jeptha heirs | 15 |
| Freeman, Obediah | 647 |
| Fullerton, Robert | |
| Grissim, Elijah | |
| Green, Isham | |
| Goodwin, Jesse A. | |
| Guthrie, Thomas B. | 132 |
| Grissim, John | 89 |
| Green, Thomas S. | |
| Hawks, John | 150 |
| Hickman, John | 162 |
| Hancock, Hope | |
| Hancock, Lesley | |
| Harris, Edward | 120 |
| Hancock, Dawson | 530 |
| Hancock, Simon | 253 |
| Hancock, Samuel minors | 30 |
| Hancock, Nelson D. | 17½ |
| Hickman, Samuel | |
| Hancock, Martin | 180 |
| Hancock, Samuel | |
| Harris, Alfred | 166 |
| Hallum, P. A. R. | 33 |
| Hancock, Verlinda | 38½ |
| Hancock, Matilda | 23 |
| Hearn, George W. | |
| Holloway, Levi | 358 |
| Holloway, John | |
| Holloway, Richard | |
| Holloway, Ezekiel | |
| Hickman, Snoden | 126¼ |
| Hickman, Snoden, Jr. | |
| Hickman, Wright | |
| Harrison, Thweat heirs | 120 |
| Hickman, William | |
| Hancock, Henry M. | |
| Hickman, Lemuel T. | |
| Hancock, Lee | 170 |
| Justice, Samuel | 120 |
| Justice, John | |
| Johnson, Robert | 218 |
| Johns, John | |
| Jackson, Jesse | |
| Knight, James | |
| Link, James A. | 140 |

1830

| | |
|---|---|
| Merritt, John | |
| Moore, Jesse L. | |
| McWhirter, George F. | 140 |
| McCullock, Benjamin | 264 |
| Nickens, Mark | |
| Ozment, Alfred | |
| Ozment, James | |
| Pool, Giles B. | |
| Richmond, James | 851 |
| Rogers, Micajah | |
| Richmond, Alexander P. | 246 |
| Reed, Henry, Sr. | 170 |
| Reed, Robert | |
| Reed, Henry, Jr. | 46 |
| Reed, William | 50 |
| Rhodes, Elisha | |
| Reed, Elum | 54 |
| Reed, Robert B. | 130 |
| Shorter, Berry | 50 |
| Skean, John | 160 |
| Shannon, Robert, Jr. | 130 |
| Shannon, Robert, Sr. | 300 |
| Shannon, Henry, Sr. | 300 |
| Shannon, John | |
| Shannon, James | 350 |
| Swain, Caleb | |
| Truett, Elijah | 601 |
| Truett, Henry | 77 |
| Tarver, Thomas B. | |
| Thomas, James | |
| Thomas, Henry | 100 |
| Warnick, James | 126 |
| Wade, Charles | |
| Wall, Bird, Sr. | 205 |
| Wall, Burrell | 140 |
| Wall, Benjamin | 100 |
| Wall, Bird, Jr. | |
| Wall, Evan | |

## CAPTAIN HORN'S COMPANY

| | |
|---|---|
| Anderson, Richard | 85 acres |
| Arnold, Butler | |
| Atkinson, Rial | |
| Ames, William | 42 |
| Ames, Elizabeth | 56 |
| Arnold, Thomas | 53 |
| Avery, John | |
| Bettes, Alfred | |
| Babb, Thomas | 250 |
| Clay, Arthur | 70 |
| Cartmell, Nathaniel | 109½ |
| Cook, Green B. | 73 |
| Cook, Jesse | 140 |
| Coppage, Charles | |
| Conyers, Thomas, Sr. | 320 |

1830

| | |
|---|---|
| Corvin, James | |
| Dew, Nancy | 240 acres |
| Dean, James | 320 |
| Dickens, Samuel | |
| Davis, Benjamin | |
| Davis, Archum L. | 114  Barton's Creek |
| Enochs, Alfred | 158 |
| Estes, Benjamin | 136 |
| Estes, George A. | |
| Estes, Samuel | |
| Estes, Mary | 44 |
| Echols, Joel heirs | 290 |
| Hobson, Henry | 197 |
| Hicks, Alfred | |
| Hawk, Matthias | 107 |
| Hunt, Thomas | 40 |
| Hunt, John | 28 |
| Hunt, Alfred M. | |
| Hunt, Benjamin | 220 |
| Hunt, James H. | |
| Hunt, Hardy B. | |
| Hunt, Jesse | 123 |
| Horn, Matthew | 428 |
| Horn, E. P. | 373 |
| Jolly, William | 40 |
| Jarrell, Fountain | |
| Jarrell, Boswell | |
| Jones, Thomas | |
| Johnson, Henry | 67 |
| Lambert, Warner | 100 |
| Morris, Thomas E. | |
| Harris, Edward | 234 |
| McWhirter, George B. | |
| Mitchell, Henry | |
| Mitchell, Elizabeth | 315 |
| Mitchell, Zadock | |
| Mitchell, Thomas R. | 50 |
| Maddox, Elijah | 50 |
| Mitchell, Robert | 50 |
| Manier, James D. | 108 |
| McConnell, John M. | 81 |
| Oaks, William | |
| O'Neal, John | |
| Prim, Kinzie | 104 |
| Proctor, Edmund guard for | 180 |
| Mrs. Hill's heirs | 132 |
| Perry, Mitchell | |
| Peak, John | |
| Ross, George | 405 |
| Rutledge, Elijah | 107 |
| Rogers, William | |
| Rotramel, Fed F. | |
| Riggan, Daniel | |
| Riggan, Samuel N. | |
| Sypert, Lawrence | 251 |

1830

| | |
|---|---|
| Scruggs, Gross | 173 acres |
| Sanderlin, Samuel | |
| Sypert, Hardy | 75 |
| Sypert, Thomas, Sr. | |
| Turner, John | |
| Tarver, William | 269 |
| Wherry, Simeon | 69 |
| Walker, Henry | 360 |
| Walker, Tabitha | 76 |

## CAPTAIN WILSON'S COMPANY

| | |
|---|---|
| Allen, Isaiah | |
| Adams, Greenberry | |
| Anderson, John | |
| Adams, William | 274 acres |
| Adams, James | |
| Brashears, John | 500 |
| Bryan, Richard | |
| Blair, William | |
| Bryan, Nelson | |
| Cummings, Sinclair | |
| Candler, John | 30 |
| Dennis, Henry | 70 |
| Dodd, John | |
| David, Susanah | 33 |
| David, Isaiah heirs | 66 |
| Dodd, Joseph | |
| Dodd, James | |
| Dodd, Richard | |
| Davis, James N. | |
| Ewing, James | 685 |
| Gossett, John | 250 |
| Fuston, Joel | 50 |
| Fuston, Leroy | 50 |
| Hancock, Lewis | 126 |
| Hollandsworth, William | |
| Hollandsworth, Isaac | 25 |
| Hollandsworth, John | 70 |
| Hollandsworth, Jacob | 50 |
| Hancock, Richard | 213 |
| Hancock, Charles | 35 |
| Hays, Nathaniel | |
| Holland, William | 320 |
| Johnson, Coleman | 322 |
| Keaton, Abraham | 45 |
| Keaton, Mary | 50 |
| Keaton, William | |
| King, Robert | 50 |
| Keaton, Cornelius | 51 |
| Lewis, John, Sr. | 17½ |
| Lewis, John, Jr. | |
| Lewis, Thomas | |
| Leek, William | |
| Leek, Mask | |

1830

| Name | Acres |
|---|---|
| Lening, Isaac | |
| Michie, James | 220 |
| McDoogle, Arch | 25 |
| Matthis, Alfred | |
| Matthis, Nathan | 25 |
| McAdow, William | 440 |
| Moore, Lemuel | 100 |
| McAdow, James, Jr. | 152½ |
| McAdow, Jehu | 520 |
| McAdow, James | 269 |
| Oran, Thomas | |
| Owens, Josiah | 263 |
| Owens, Fountain | 100 |
| Owens, Anthony | |
| Philips, Thomas | |
| Rich, Charles, Sr. | 640 |
| Rhea, John | |
| Rhea, Robert | |
| Rich, Allen | |
| Reeves, Burrell | |
| Spurlock, John | 100 |
| Spurlock, Frances | 40 |
| Shaw, John L. | |
| Sharp, Benjamin | |
| Standley, Thomas | |
| Smith, Hector | |
| Sneed, John, Sr. | 170 |
| Sneed, William | 560 |
| Sneed, Abraham | |
| Sneed, John | |
| Tunage, Isaac | |
| Turner, Jonathan | |
| Williamson, Auston | |
| Wilson, Robert | |
| Wilson, Matthew | |
| Willard, Beverly heirs | 80 |
| Williamson, Zachariah | 50 |
| Wilson, James | |
| Williamson, William H. | |

## CAPTAIN EDDINGS' COMPANY

| Name | Acres |
|---|---|
| Armstrong, James M. | 124 acres |
| Ayers, James | 257 |
| Alsup, Samuel | 160 |
| Belcher, John | 50 |
| Boswell, William F. | |
| Bumpass, Robert H. | 300 |
| Bone, Thomas | 143 |
| Barnsfield, George | |
| Beadle, Henry | |
| Blankenship, Ganes | 155 |
| Beadle, Osburn | 156 |
| Bone, Azer | 98 |
| Bone, A. W. Esqr. | 313 |

1830

| | |
|---|---|
| Buckley, Sally | |
| Bailey, Jonathan | |
| Bumpass, Robert  agt. | 95 |
| Baird, James | 60 |
| Cook, William R. | 85 |
| Campbell, James | 132 |
| Craddock, John | |
| Campbell, Wilson | |
| Cock, ( eons | |
| Couch, Thomas | |
| Chumney, Beverly | 30 |
| Coleman, Linsey | |
| Cross, James | 100 |
| Dillon, John | 260 |
| Dejornet, John | |
| Davis, William | 162 |
| Cason, James R. | |
| Eands, John | |
| Eddings, Ozburn | |
| Eddings, William | 20 |
| Guthrie, Beverly | |
| Godfrey, James | 85 |
| Garrison, Samuel J. | |
| Hubbard, William | 257 |
| Hubbard, Hiram C. | |
| Hubbard, Clark | 75 |
| Hearn, Wallace | |
| Hill, Samuel | 650 |
| Jennings, Jesse | 115 |
| Jennings, William, Jr. | 225 |
| Jennings, Jacob | 2500 |
| Jennings, Elijah | |
| Jones, Isaiah | |
| Johnson, James | 308 |
| Jennings, Robert, Jr. | 130 |
| Jennings, John A. | 88 |
| Jennings, William W. | 162 |
| Jennings, Jose | 120 |
| Jennings, John | 160 |
| James, Buchanan | 53 |
| Jackson, William | |
| Jennings, Asel | |
| Jennings, Robert, Sr. | 192 |
| Jennings, Rial C. | |
| Jennings, Uriah | |
| Jordan, Jer R. | |
| Kelly, Dennis | 470 |
| Knox, John | 150 |
| King, Dennis | |
| Kelly, Daniel | 200 |
| Lester, William | 144 |
| Lanum, William | |
| Lester, James L. | |
| Lester, Joshua | 103 |
| Lester, William D. | |

1830

| | |
|---|---|
| Martin, James | 257 acres |
| McDaniel, William | |
| McCaffrey, James | 146 |
| McHaney, Oney | 62 |
| McCaffrey, John | 44 |
| McIntire, William | |
| Merritt, Fleming | |
| Moore, William | |
| Morris, Richard W. | |
| Oakley, William | 189 |
| Patton, Andrew | 57 |
| Pane, Henry | 100 |
| Pane, James | 111 |
| Porterfield, Samuel H. | 130 |
| Patterson, Lewis | 150 |
| Patterson, Newsom | |
| Porterfield, James | |
| Pickett, Edward | 63 |
| Patton, John, Jr. | 42 |
| Patton, John | |
| Patton, Samuel | |
| Patton, Thomas | 100 |
| Porterfield, John | 25 |
| Patterson, E. S. | |
| Perriman, Alexander | |
| Pemberton, Richard | 43 |
| Pemberton, John | 73 |
| Philips, George | 75 |
| Richmond, Thomas | 211 |
| Ricketts, William G. | |
| Rich, Joel | |
| Smith, Shadrach | 210 |
| Sugg, Solomon | 33 |
| Short, Thomas | |
| Shores, Philip | 60 |
| Spradley, Tavner | 112 |
| Shores, Jonathan | 54 |
| Scott, Leander | |
| Shearl, William | |
| Stewart, Samuel | 144 |
| Sloan, Jer N. | 12 |
| Smith, George | 48 |
| Smith, David B. | |
| Sadler, William | |
| Sadler, Jane | 120 |
| Sanes, Abraham | |
| Smith, Bird | 57 |
| Smith, John A. | 57 |
| Tally, Spencer W. | |
| Tribble, Isaiah | 154 |
| Thompson, And R. | |
| Thompson, James, Sr. | 200 |
| Thompson, James, Jr. | 126 |
| Thompson, Samuel | |

1830

| Name | Acres |
|---|---|
| Thompson, William | |
| Thompson, James B. | |
| Thompson, Andrew | 210 |
| Thompson, James | 245 |
| Thweatt, William | 90 |
| Williams, Isaac | 125 |
| Whitlock, John | |
| Whitlock, Thomas | 100 |
| Ward, Hosea | |
| Williams, Joseph | 100 |
| Wrae, Hiram S. | |
| Williams, James J. | |
| Williams, Mas | |
| Word, James | 146 |
| Ward, John | 260 |
| Webb, John | |
| Whitlock, James | |
| Wilson, James R. | |
| Whitlow, Henry | 300 |
| Webb, George | 115 |
| Whitlock, Thomas, Jr. | |
| Wade, Willis W. | |
| Young, J. D. | 300 |

## CAPTAIN L. C. ANDERSON'S COMPANY

| Name | Acres |
|---|---|
| Anderson, James | 178 acres |
| Anderson, Sam C. | |
| Bennett, James | |
| Barratt, William | |
| Bennett, Drury | |
| Bond, Elisha | |
| Bond, Samuel | |
| Bond, David | 200 |
| Bond, William | 30 |
| Bond, John | 440 |
| Bennett, John | 110 |
| Bennett, Jacob | 25 |
| Baird, James | |
| Baird, William | 684 |
| Baird, Seldon | 95 |
| Baccus, Minchey | 50 |
| Bennett, Thomas | |
| Cummings, William | 400 |
| Comer, John | |
| Cummings, G. W. | |
| Clemmons, James | |
| Daniels, Black | 15 |
| Edwards, Henry | |
| Edwards, Robert | 488 |
| Edwards, Edward | 190 |
| Edwards, Hugh | |
| Edwards, Crawford | |
| Edwards, Eli | 117 |
| Edwards, John | 42 |
| Edwards, Eaton | |

1830

| Name | Acres |
|---|---|
| Edwards, Stokes | |
| Edwards, Green B. | |
| Fields, Richard | 95 acres |
| Fields, Reddin | 123 |
| Guest, John | |
| Grissom, Stephen | |
| Gibson, John | 80 |
| Gibson, Aaron | |
| Gibson, Jeremiah | 107 |
| Harris, Isham | 57 |
| Hudson, William | 50 |
| Howard, Bradford | 100 |
| Huddleston, George A. | 250 |
| Knight, David | |
| Merritt, Harris | |
| Merritt, Mark | |
| Melton, Thomas | |
| Merritt, Sherwood | |
| Merritt, Silvanus | |
| Merritt, Obediah | |
| Merritt, Silas | |
| Merritt, Lewis | 378 |
| Martin, Lindsay | 125 |
| Ozment, Jonathan heirs | 178 |
| Ozment, Sarah | 89 |
| Ozment, Samuel | |
| Ozment, Armstrong | |
| O'Neal, Asa | 40 |
| Patterson, Peter | |
| Patterson, Lewis | |
| Quesenberry, James | 100 |
| Rogers, Tobias W. | |
| Ragsdale, Lovin | |
| Reynolds, Zebba | |
| Rogers, Henry | |
| Rogers, Samuel | |
| Simmons, Alexander | |
| Sanders, Mrs. heirs | 567 |
| Scott, John | 50 |
| Steed, Steth F. | |
| Townsend, Richard | |
| Warren, Solomon | |
| Warren, Charles heirs | 100 |
| Warren, Sina | 100 |
| Warren, William | |

## CAPTAIN VIVRETT'S COMPANY

| Name | Acres |
|---|---|
| Atherly, Warren | 223½ acres |
| Atherly, James | 126½ |
| Bradshaw, Wilson | 47½ |
| Bridges, Brinkley | 25 |
| Baird, William heirs | 150 |
| Bates, James | 192 |
| Bridges, Allen H. | 205 |

1830

| | |
|---|---|
| Brown, John | 150 acres |
| Bass, Solomon | 111 |
| Bass, (Sion) | 380 |
| Briant, John | 45 |
| Bates, John | |
| Crenshaw, William | 81 |
| Cooley, Henry | |
| Drake, Britain for Joseph Crabtree's heirs | 310 |
| Davis, Nathaniel | 415 |
| Donaldson, Robert, | 150 |
| Donaldson, James | 130 |
| Everett, John | 100 |
| Ellis, Isaac | |
| Ellis, Thomas | |
| Ellis, James | 114 |
| Freeman, Edward | 83 |
| Freeman, Dorrell | 100 |
| Glanton, John | 137½ |
| Howell, Mary | 130 |
| Howell, Edward | |
| Hutcherson, William | |
| Hester, Benjamin | |
| Hill, Luke | |
| Hill, Jesse | 100 |
| Howell, Joseph | |
| Hunter, William heirs | 100 |
| Hill, Isaac W. | 232 |
| Jennings, Anderson | 113 |
| Jennings, Clement | 623 |
| Ingram, Joseph | 127 |
| Ingram, Samuel | |
| Jones, Samuel | |
| Jarrott, John G. | |
| Kimbrell, Nicholas | 81 |
| Kemp, Burrell | 75 |
| Little, John | |
| Little, James | |
| Lunsford, Eaton | |
| Murray, Abraham | 14 |
| Murray, John | 150 |
| Martin, Pascal | |
| Madlin, John | |
| Madlin, Littleton | |
| Martin, Peyton | 123 |
| Maddox, Richard | 120 |
| Martin, Brice | 441 |
| Pitner, Michael | 235 |
| Pitner, Archibald | |
| Pitman, John B. | 50 |
| Perry, Richardson | |
| Sands, William heirs | 170 |
| Right, Thomas A. | |
| Reace, Alsey | 107 |

1830

| | |
|---|---|
| Rice, Coleman | |
| Rutherford, John B. | 254 |
| Young, Stephen | 100 |
| Smith, John | 500 |
| Smith, Samuel | |
| Smith, Hiram H. | |
| Smith, Reuben | 180 |
| Thomas, Ann | 50 |
| Thomas, John | 158 |
| Thomas, David | |
| Taylor, Abraham | |
| Tipton, Barnaby | |
| Vivrett, John | |
| Walker, Drusila | 391 |
| Whitson, John D. | |
| Williams, Jeremiah | |
| Williams, Thomas | 75 |
| Williams, Nathaniel | |
| Wynne, Daniel | 222 |
| Webb, Sarah | |
| Williams, Turner P. | |
| Young, Adnah | |
| Young, James H. | |
| Young, Demetrius | 60 |
| York, James | 63 |
| Young, William | |
| Young, Beverly | |

## CAPTAIN PITMAN'S COMPANY

| | |
|---|---|
| Anderson, Richard | 55 acres |
| Andrews, Gray | 100 |
| Adkison, Thomas | |
| Aust, Joseph | 200 |
| Ames, Elizabeth | 80 |
| Aust, Thomas | 70 |
| Aust, Henry | |
| Aust, Elizabeth | 265 |
| Bay, Andrew | 216 |
| Brown, Jackson N. | 80 |
| Brown, Matthew | |
| Bloodworth, Web | 156 |
| Brown, George | 130 |
| Brown, Richard | |
| Bunderant, Robert | 251 |
| Blalock, Charles W. | |
| Briant, Samuel heirs | 89 |
| Briant, Hiram | |
| Brown, John H. | |
| Britain, James H. | 61 |
| Coles, William T. | 95 |
| Cocke, Fleming | |
| Cocke, William | |
| Cocke, Henry | 214 |
| Coppage, Elias | 40 |

1830

| | |
|---|---|
| Coppage, John | |
| Coles, Robert | 190 |
| Caniers, Thomas | 66 |
| Campbell, Robert | 305 |
| Cartmell, Nathan | 103 |
| Clendenon, Joseph | |
| Coles, Samuel | 48 |
| Creswell, Miner | |
| Creswell, May | |
| Claton, Pheba | 40 |
| Cooper, Margaret | 80 |
| Dill, Joel | 236 |
| Downey, heirs | 130 |
| Davis, John | |
| Drake, William B. | |
| Davis, John | |
| Davis, Thomas | 610 |
| Davis, Henry | 120 |
| Davis, William | |
| Davis, James H. | 325 |
| Edwards, Nicholas | 152 |
| Eagan, William heirs | 103 |
| Eagan, Barnaba | 45 |
| Eagan, Hugney | 174 |
| Eddings, James | |
| Eagan, Jesse | 90 |
| Eagan, Reace | |
| Eagan, James | 100 |
| Gray, Samuel, Sr. | 140 |
| Gray, John | |
| Glenn, Daniel | |
| Gray, William | 120 |
| Gray, Samuel M. | |
| Green, Isaac | 125 |
| Gregory, Thomas | 148 |
| Garden, Obediah | 207 |
| Howell, Caleb | |
| Harrison, Answorth | 508½ |
| Harris, John D. | |
| Henry, Samuel | 440 |
| Hunt, Benjamin | |
| Hill, Lewis | |
| Hunt, Matthew | |
| Harris, William F. | 150 |
| Hayworth, Micajah | |
| Hays, Harman A. | 173 |
| Johnson, William B. | 50 |
| Johnson, James | |
| Johnson, Samuel | 185 |
| Johnson, Samuel M. | 6 |
| Kirkpatrick, Anderson | |
| Kirkpatrick, Alexander | 108 |
| Kirkpatrick, David heirs | 133 |
| Kirkpatrick, John | 108 |
| Kirkpatrick, Joseph | 596 |

1830

| | |
|---|---|
| Lambert Anderson | 17¼ acres |
| Lawrence, Robert | 100 |
| McHaffrey, Robert | 50 |
| Martin, George B. | |
| Motheral, Samuel | 480 |
| Motheral, Robert | |
| Mays, James | 220 |
| McWhirter, Charles | |
| Michael, John | |
| McHaffrey, Henry | |
| Mays, William heirs | 45 |
| Mays, Jacob | 93 |
| Moore, Israel | 104 |
| Mosely, Thomas | 250 |
| Pitman, Henry M. | 220 |
| Puffer, Samuel | |
| Parker, John K. | |
| Ray, Joseph | 50 |
| Ray, Simpson | 127½ |
| Ray, Alsey | 110 |
| Ross, Allen | 221 |
| Ross, Henry P. | |
| Ray, Willis | 66 |
| Rieff, John | 210 |
| Right, Anderson | 50 |
| Right, Isaac | 140 |
| Right, John | |
| Ray, William | |
| Roach, Alexander | 170 |
| Rider, Reuben | 20 |
| Ray, John | 55 |
| Rieff, Torres | 92 |
| Ross, John | 210 |
| Rieff, Henry heirs | 304 |
| Ray, Thomas heirs | 202 |
| Sanders, Nathaniel | |
| Smith, William | 140 |
| Stewart, Cyrus | 160 |
| Sanders, Joseph F. | |
| Sanders, Richard | 367 |
| Tomlinson, Major | |
| Taylor, Hughey | |
| Tipton, James | 145 |
| Tipton, William | |
| Tompkins, James | 96 |
| Wood, Josiah | 148 |
| Wood, John | 157 |
| Wood, Thomas | |
| Wynne, Citiva | 40 |
| Wood, Isham | |
| Walker, James D. | 282 |
| Whitson, Abram heirs | 150 |
| Webb, John | |
| Whitson, John | |
| Tatum, Dabney | 124 |

1830

| | |
|---|---|
| Vaughan, Thomas | |
| Vaughan, Mary J. | 156 |
| Vaughan, Turner | |
| Vaughan, Malijah | |
| Young, Joseph | |
| Willis, Thomas | 106 |

## CAPTAIN F. ANDERSON'S COMPANY

| | |
|---|---|
| Anderson, Paulden | 65 acres |
| Archer, Jacob | 114 |
| Archer, Hisekins | 33 |
| Alexander, George | 50 |
| Alexander, John | |
| Bowers, Sopan | |
| Bone, Enos | 50 |
| Beckers, James | |
| Bundy, Nathan | 35 |
| Barksdale, Thomas W. | |
| Carlin, Mrs. Patsey | 142 |
| Carter, Leroy C. | |
| Carruth, James S. | |
| Carruth, Samuel C. | |
| Carruth, William R. | 50 |
| Carruth, James | 100 |
| Clary, John | |
| Chamberlin, Thomas | |
| Clifton, Thomas | 150 |
| Clifton, Benjamin | 330 |
| Cates, John | |
| Coe, John | |
| Clark, Parsons | |
| Donnell, Robert | 238 |
| Furguson, Robert | |
| Graves, Joseph | |
| Graves, Lorenso | |
| Guthrie, Thomas | 160 |
| Henry, Alexander | |
| Hearn, Thomas | 158 |
| Harris, Thomas | |
| Hartsfield, Solomon | 216 |
| Harrison, Sterling | 100 |
| Hearn, Pernel | 230 |
| Hearn, William | |
| Hearn, Milby | 200 |
| Hearn, Stephen L. | |
| Jones, James | |
| Johnson, Robert | 244 |
| Jones, John Parson | 180 |
| Jones, John, Jr. | |
| Jones, Elisha | |
| Johnson, Philip | 130 |
| Johnson, Jeremiah | 270 |
| Jones, Allen | |
| Johnson, Littleberry | |

1830

| | |
|---|---|
| Lane, Woodson | 78 acres |
| Loyd, Jarrott | 273 |
| Lester, Henry | 27 |
| Lindsay, Philip | 2560 |
| Lash, Harman | 160 |
| Morris, Isham | 175 |
| Morris, Patrick | |
| Morris, Patterson | |
| Martin, James M. | 250 |
| Moore, George D. | 200 |
| Nickens, Prescoat | 50 |
| Nickens, James | 100 |
| Newby, John | 162 |
| Palmer, John | |
| Pemberton, Josiah | |
| Sweatt, William | 60 |
| Smith, Mary | 200 |
| Standley, Benjamin | 23 |
| Sims, James | 20 |
| Standley, David | |
| Smith & Barksdale | |
| Smith, Henry F. | 20 |
| Sims, Matthew | 114 |
| Stembridge, Matley | 100 |
| Smith, Josiah, Sr. | 120 |
| Thomas, Robert | 70 |
| Tally, James | |
| Tucker, Priscilla | 75 |
| Todd, John | 171 |
| Turner, James | 600 |
| Vinson, David | |
| Woolard, Alligood | 35 |
| Woolard, Alfred | |
| Walsh, James | 74 |
| Walsh, Norman | |
| Williams, Elijah | |
| Whorton, Joseph | 912 |
| Wynne, William | |
| Yates, John B. | 110 |

## CAPTAIN DILLARD'S COMPANY

| | |
|---|---|
| Allgood, William | 656 acres |
| Allgood, Joel | |
| Avery, John W. | |
| Allen, Willas | 65 |
| Bell, Benjamin T. | |
| Bennett, Simpson | |
| Bell, Joseph G. | 42 |
| Bradley, George | 134 |
| Browning, Thomas P. | |
| Bell, John | 50 |
| Browning, James | 100 |
| Corley, Alfred | |
| Corley, Nathaniel | 50 |
| Corley, William | 150 |

1830

| | |
|---|---|
| Corley, Austin | 63 acres |
| Corley, Samuel | |
| Dice, Jacob | 200 |
| Duncan, George A. | 112½ |
| Dillard, William B. | |
| Dillard, Edward | 70 |
| Dillard, William M. | 50 |
| Douglass, Ennes | 72 |
| Dillard, William B. | 160 |
| Grubbs, William | 16 |
| Goald, Pleasant | |
| Goald, Thomas | |
| Hay, William | 1444 |
| Harris, Sneed | 74 |
| Holder, B. S. | 137½ |
| Harrison, Samuel R. | 147 |
| Harris, John | 122 |
| Jones, Elijah | 130 |
| Jackson, Coleman, Jr. | |
| Jackson, Purnel | |
| Jackson, Coleman, Sr. | 91 |
| Jackson, Robert | |
| Joplin, Thomas Esqr. | 296 |
| Lyon, Richard | |
| Lyon, Thomas | |
| Lowe, Green B. | 474 |
| Massee, Henry | 40 |
| Motsinger, Jefferson | 40 |
| McDonald, Randel | 90 |
| Martin, George | 246½ |
| McDonald, And J. | 347 |
| Martin, Pleasant, Jr. | |
| McDonald, Elias | |
| Powell, William | |
| Palmer, John W. | 21 |
| Shaw, Solomon | |
| Shaw, Jeremiah | 40 |
| Shaw, Alsey | |
| Shaw, William | 111 |
| Standifer, William | 96 |
| Swan, Andrew | 234 |
| Swan, James | |
| Sea, Beverly | 50 |
| Taylor, Mary | |
| Terry, Peter G. | |
| Terry, Elijah | 108 |
| Warren, Boothe | |
| White, George | 136 |
| Wheeler, Edward B. | 200 |
| Whitehead, James | |
| Woodcock, Mary | 80 |
| Woodcock, Henry | |
| Williams, George | 50 |
| White, Samuel | 55 |
| Woodard, Hezekiah | 180 |

1830

| | |
|---|---|
| Woodward, H. W. | |
| Woodcock, Jesse | 136 |
| Williams, John | 88 |
| Williamson, Littleberry | |
| Warren, Lucy | 25 |
| Warren, Benjamin | |
| Ward, Henry | 180 |

## CAPTAIN ALLEN'S COMPANY

| | |
|---|---|
| Alexander, Gideon | 200 acres |
| Allen, James | |
| Allen, Mary | 110 |
| Allen, William E. | 28 |
| Afflax, John | 158 |
| Anderson, John | |
| Bell, John | 640 |
| Bell, Amzi | |
| Boyd, John | 100 |
| Borum, Richard | 612 |
| Baker, William | 23 |
| Borum, James | |
| Borum, John | 145 |
| Borum, William | |
| Bradley, Jonas | 450 |
| Bradley, Samuel B. | |
| Bradley, Everett | |
| Bell, Robert D. | |
| Bradley, David | 200 |
| Belcher, Sutton E. | |
| Balue, James | 165 |
| Calhoon, Thomas | 225 |
| Carson, Henry | 100 |
| Calhoon, James | 88 |
| Chappel, Thomas B. | |
| Calhoon, Samuel | 312 |
| Clary, James | |
| Crenshaw, Garland C. | 220 |
| Donnell, George | 60 |
| Ellis, Robert | |
| Ellis, Hicks | 82½ |
| Ellis, Nathan | 122½ |
| Evans, William | |
| Elliott, Samuel | 460 |
| Ellis, Moses | 215 |
| Ellis, James | 15 |
| Eason, Ira E. | |
| Falkner, Edward P. | |
| Ferrell, William | 130 |
| Franklin, George | 120 |
| Foster, Robert | 95 |
| Graves, Rice | 100 |
| Harland, Samuel | |
| Hatcher, William | |
| Harris, Magee | 165 |
| Harris, Eli | 215 |

1830

| | |
|---|---|
| Harris, Catharine | |
| Hamilton, Thomas | 250 |
| Harland, Thomas | 160 |
| Harland, John | 64 |
| Johnson, Robertson | 320 |
| Johnson, William | 500 |
| Jones, Michael | 41 |
| Johnson, Daniel | 174 |
| Johnson, Samuel | 108 |
| Johnson, James | 220 |
| Keas, heirs | 90 |
| Lyon, William | |
| Lyon, John | 226 |
| Motley, Benjamin | 1253 |
| McSpadden, Thomas | 109 |
| McSpadden, William | 147½ |
| Mooningham, Elijah | |
| Martin, David | |
| Martin, John M. | 228 |
| Martin, Pugh | 72 |
| Martin, Thomas | |
| McMurray, David | 350 |
| McMurray, James B. | |
| Organ, Woodford | |
| Organ, Simpson | |
| Owens, Watkins | 50 |
| Owens, John F. | 100 |
| Owens, William P. | 150 |
| Owens, Richard | |
| Peace, William H. Esqr. | 564 |
| Kisa Walker | 51 |
| Philips, Barkley | |
| Philips, Henry | 174 |
| Provine, Alexander | 223 |
| Pully, Robert | |
| Pemberton, Jesse, Jr. | |
| Pilkinton, Henry B. | |
| Provine, Samuel F. | |
| Pursley, William B. | 2 |
| Provine, John | 190 |
| Pully, John | |
| Pully, William, Jr. | |
| Pully, William, Sr. | |
| Pemberton, James | |
| Richardson, Loyd | |
| Roane, Hannah | 200 |
| Rutherford, G. W. | 405 |
| Steele, William Major Esqr. | 378½ |
| Scoby, James | 400 |
| Scoby, John B. | 100 |
| Sullivan, Lea, Jr. | 243 |
| Sullivan, Lea, Sr. | |
| Sherrill, Hugh | 100 |
| Stephens, Sanders | |
| Stephens, James | 1830 |

Swindle, Joel             100 acres
Smith, Benjamin
Trout, Joseph             136
Trout, John
Tomlinson, William
Tomlinson, Allen          40
Tomlinson, Irvin          50
Vaughan, David
Vaughan, Abram            126
Waters, Shelah, Jr.       170
Weir, James, Sr.          587
Wilson, William           80
Young, David              230
Samford, James
Simmons, John A.
Sanders, George

## CAPTAIN COX'S COMPANY

Abanatha, Mark
Andrews, Rowland
Bennett, William F. heirs    49½ acres
Bartlett, William
Andrews, Pernel
Andrews, Asa              127
Bundy, David
Bundy, John               143
Bass, Sion                110
Belcher, Alexander
Belcher, Isaac
Badgett, John
Bass Cader                65
Briant, Mary O.           273
Burge, Peterson
Bundy, James
Belcher, Richard
Belcher, Pleasant
Belcher, Thomas
Buchanan, William         1000
Cartwright, Elizabeth     200
Cropper, James            100
Cartwright, Benajah       100
Crutchfield, Samuel       225
Carter, Frederick         100
Cox, William, Sr.         127
Cox, William, Jr.
Cox, Henry
Cox, James
Cox, John                 120
Carter, Bernard           114
Donnell, Levi             125
Edwards, John             137
Edwards, Granville
Foster, Emsley D.         39
Foster, John S.           100
Forbes, Thomas W.

1830

22

| | |
|---|---|
| Grindstaff, David | 60 acres |
| Gates, James | |
| Green, John | 160 |
| Green, John G. | |
| Green, William | 49 |
| Hankins, John | |
| Hall, Benjamin B. | |
| Hearn, Wilson | 186 |
| Hearn, James W. | 130 |
| Harvey, John | 50 |
| Hankins, William | |
| Hearn, Ebenezer | 300 |
| Long, Alexander M. | |
| McBride, Daniel | 171 |
| Maholland, John | 138 |
| Maholland, William | 200 |
| Motheral, James | 280 |
| McBride, Abraham | 50 |
| Mayo, Stephen | |
| Moxley, Joseph | 197 |
| New, William | 308 |
| New, Nelson | 30 |
| Oakley, John | |
| Powell, Abram | |
| Philips, Alpha | 130 |
| Parham, Thomas | 100 |
| Parmer, John | 154 |
| Routon, William | |
| Routon, Richard | 130 |
| Sims, Caswell S. | |
| Sims, Chesty | 100 |
| Spears, Lewis P. | 50 |
| Steele, Miner | |
| Steele, William | |
| Spears, William | |
| Spears, Sarah | 60 |
| Williford, James C. | 65 |
| Whitworth, James | |
| Williford, William H. | 12 |
| Williford, George A. | |
| Taylor, John | |
| Tippitt, John C. | 230 |
| Turner, Thomas D. | 89 |
| Vaughan, Thomas | 87 |

## CAPTAIN LANNOM'S COMPANY

| | | |
|---|---|---|
| Adams, James | 100 acres | |
| Alsup, William | 280 | |
| Alsup, Asap | | |
| Alsup, Samuel J. | | |
| Alsup, Richard | 225 | |
| Alsup, William H. | 149 | |
| Alsup, Joseph | 285 | |
| Ashley, James | 75 | |
| Borke, Thomas Esqr. | 116 | 1830 |

| Name | Acres |
|---|---|
| Burke, Arnold | 200 acres |
| Burke, Fielden | 100 |
| Baird, John Capt. | 140 |
| Baird, Hiram | |
| Baird, Lindsay | |
| Bell, Robert | |
| Bell, James  heirs | 285 |
| Baskin, Robert M. | 250 |
| Baskin, William | |
| Barker, Richard | |
| Baird, Hardy H. | 100 |
| Cluck, William | 100 |
| Cluck, Henry, Jr. | |
| Cluck, Henry, Sr. | 60 |
| Gibson, David | |
| Gray, James Esqr. | 321 |
| Goodwin, William, Jr. | |
| Goodwin, Allen H. | |
| Howard, Hiram | |
| Haynes, Herbert | |
| Hedgpeth, Silas | |
| Holland, Edward | 81 |
| Jackson, James | 100 |
| Jones, John C. | |
| Johnson, Charles | 20 |
| Johnson, Garrett | 100 |
| McCulloch, William | 110 |
| Lannom, John | 56 |
| Lovin, John | 10 |
| Leath, Peter | 207 |
| Martin, Jacob | 100 |
| Miles, Thomas, Sr. | 100 |
| Miles, Thomas, Jr. | 232 |
| McHenry, Jesse | 102 |
| Nelson, William | |
| Nelson, Garrett | |
| Roberts, March | |
| Ragsdale, Sarah | 50 |
| Ragsdale, Richard | |
| Reynolds, Thomas | |
| Ricketts, John S. | 30 |
| Richardson, Martin | 50 |
| Robertson, Andrew | 62 |
| Stewart, William | |
| Sanders, Richard | |
| Thompson, Henry | |
| Thomas, Jacob | 150 |
| Vaughters, Ludwell | 25 |
| Woolen, Joshua | 85 |
| Woolen, Edward | 50 |
| Woolen, Moses | 50 |
| Wood, James | 100 |
| Zachry, Allen | 50 |
| Zachry, Stokes | |
| Underwood, Perry  heirs | 115 |
| Jackson, Larkin | 140 |

1830

| Name | Value |
|---|---|
| Abernatha, Charles | |
| Allison, Samuel | 90 |
| Allison, John L. | 30 |
| Almore, Solomon | |
| Barnett, Isaac | |
| Brocherton, Henry | |
| Brocherton, John | |
| Bailey, James S. | |
| Bond, John | |
| Barker, William | |
| Bond, James | 140 |
| Bond, Margaret | 263 |
| Cain, George | 1500 |
| Craddock, William C. | |
| Calhoon, Moses P. | |
| Cocke, John | 100 |
| Clopton, Walter, Sr. | 204 |
| Clopton, Jesse B. | 147 |
| Clopton, William | 125 |
| Clayton, Benjamin | 120 |
| Clopton, Walter, Jr. | 373 |
| Collins, William C. | |
| Drew, Edward | 34 |
| Dance, John E. | 390 |
| Doak, Nelson | |
| Fouch, John | 35 |
| Florida, Patrick | 80 |
| Harris, Arthur | 350 |
| Hodges, James W. | |
| Hight, Joab W. | |
| Hight, Alfred M. | 86 |
| Harris, Thomas R. | |
| Harris, Allen | 225 |
| Harris, John R. | |
| Heard, George W. | |
| Heard, John A. | |
| Hutchings, William | 677 |
| Hutchings, Stephen | 126 |
| Huddleston, Anthony | 207 |
| Jarman, Robert | 390 |
| Jones, David, Jr. | |
| Jenkins, Nathan | 50 |
| Jenkins, Turner | |
| Jarman, Shadrach | |
| Jones, William | |
| Lasater, Jonathan | |
| Lasater, Jacob B. | 90 |
| Lasater, Elizabeth | 100 |
| Leach, George | 50 |
| Lewis, Edgecomb | |
| Lasater, Alexander | |
| Lasater, Hardy | 40 |
| Matthews, Samuel | 25 |
| Matthews, Matt | 100 |
| Matthews, James | |

1830

| | |
|---|---|
| Medling, John | 90 acres |
| Martin, James | |
| Martin, Amos | |
| Osburn, Thomas | |
| Piercy, Boswell | 140 |
| Piercy, Sherwood | 80 |
| Pickett, Isham | |
| Piercy, Frances W. | |
| Pryor, John | |
| Patterson, Burwell | 225 |
| Puckett, Isham | 142 |
| Puckett, William | 30 |
| Piercy, Williamson | |
| Puckett, Francis | 320 |
| Puckett, Patrick | |
| Puckett, Washington | |
| Powell, Allen | |
| Quarles, John B. heirs | 550 |
| Smith, William H. | |
| Sellars, Alfred | |
| Sellars, Alvis | |
| Sellars, Joseph H. | |
| Upchurch, Abner | |
| Winston, Isaac | 288½ |
| Wood, William | 580 |
| Wood, John | 175 |
| Woodward, John | |
| Winston, John J. | 120 |
| Williams, William | 381 |
| Williams & Cain | |
| Woodward, Baker | 87½ |

## CAPTAIN HUGHLEY'S COMPANY

| | |
|---|---|
| Atherly, Jonathan | 375 acres |
| Anderson, Whitwell | |
| Ames, Thomas | 50 |
| Atherly, John | 213 |
| Atherly, Robertson | 150 |
| Bridges, Sampson | |
| Bridges, David | 110 |
| Barton, Eleanor | 196 |
| Baird, David | 200 |
| Bass, Cader | 170 |
| Boothe, Samuel | 250 |
| Bridges, John A. | |
| Blackburn, Washington | |
| Bridges, Joel C. | |
| Brown, John C. | 110 |
| Bilbro, William | 250 |
| Brown, Elizabeth | 110 |
| Baird, Andrew | 380 |
| Bridges, Alexander | |
| Curd, Price | 34 |
| Curd, William | |
| Curd, Elizabeth | 140 |

1830

| | |
|---|---|
| Carter, Jacha | |
| Carver, Isaac | |
| Curd, Elizabeth, Jr. | 38 |
| Curd, James | 30 |
| Curd, Thomas | 50 |
| Cawthon, Thomas F. | |
| Cawthon, James H. | |
| Carver, William | 140 |
| Cawthon, John | 417 |
| Chandler, William | 33 |
| Chappell, Robert | |
| Chappell, William | 44 |
| Cawthon, Lawson | |
| Chandler, Green | 33 |
| Clay, Sidney | |
| Cannon, John A. | |
| Davis, Isham F. | 160 |
| Davis, John | 385 |
| Donaldson, William  heirs | 200 |
| Donaldson, Robert | 434 |
| Elliott, Robert | |
| Graves, John G. | 200 |
| Graves, John B. | |
| Gains, Anthony | 75 |
| Gains, William H. | 52½ |
| Gains, Gideon | 91 |
| Graves, Benjamin | 170 |
| Hughley, William | |
| Hardy, William | 544 |
| Hamilton, William | 875 |
| Haralson, Alexander | |
| Hughley, George W. | 55 |
| Hamilton, Joseph | 204 |
| Hughley, Charles | 147 |
| Hooser, Valentine | 160 |
| Holland, Levi | 70 |
| Hughley, Abram | 208 |
| Hobson, Nicholas | 100 |
| Hubbard, Merritt | |
| Kneel, Joseph | 100 |
| Jones, Willerford | 80 |
| Ligon, Henry | 160 |
| Ligon, James H. | 100 |
| Ligon, John H. | 395 |
| Lane, William | 50 |
| Lane, Armstead | 150 |
| Lane, William | 50 |
| Lane, William F. | |
| Lumpkin, Obediah | 191 |
| Loyd, James | |
| Lane, David | |
| McGregor, Flower | 979 |
| McGregor, John | 640 |
| Moss, John | 220 |
| McDerman, Brien | 130 |
| Martin, John | |

1830

| | |
|---|---|
| Mosely, Littleton | 45 acres |
| McGregor, William | 265 |
| Moss, John W. | 60 |
| Moss, Dandridge | 449¼ |
| Puckett, Charles | |
| Rutland, Rutherford | 320 |
| Rowland, Richardson | |
| Reeves, Peter | |
| Randolph, Peyton | |
| Shane, John | 165 |
| Stevenson, Benjamin F. | 160 |
| Sullivan, Joab | |
| Sullivan, Edmund | 100 |
| Spickard, John | 100 |
| Sullivan, John | |
| Shepherd, William | 180 |
| Shepherd, John | 120 |
| Shepherd, Samuel | |
| Shepherd, James M. | |
| Smith, Malcomb | |
| Stone, William N. | 50 |
| Sullivan, Asel | 155 |
| Swingley, Jonas | 95 |
| Tilman, Jacob | |
| Tate, Zachariah | 170 |
| Tomlinson, William | 221 |
| Wray, Thomas | 173 |
| Walker, Samuel | 100 |
| Willis, Edward | 169 |
| Willis, James M. | |
| Walker, Mary for son | 47 |
| Williamson, James | 427 |
| Yarnell, Lyda | 62 |
| Young, William L. | |
| Young, William, Sr. | 100 |
| Woodson, Washington M. | |

## CAPTAIN CHANDLER'S COMPANY

| | |
|---|---|
| Baker, John E. | 554 acres |
| Binkley, Henry J. | 85 |
| Barr, Silas | 65 |
| Barr, Joseph | |
| Barr, William H. | 200 |
| Brown, Samuel | 95 |
| Brown, Robert | |
| Barr, William | 75 |
| Bond, Robert | 113 |
| Blankenship, Allen | 130 |
| Curray, A. B. | 70 |
| Curray, John | 50 |
| Crutchfield, James | |
| Clemmons, John | 440 |
| Chandler, Andrew | 175 |

1830

| Name | Acres |
|---|---|
| Clemmons, Allen | 100 acres |
| Clemmons, Alfred | 100 |
| Clemmons, William L. | |
| Chambers, Thomas | 150 |
| Crage, Abner J. | |
| Chandler, Jordan | 85 |
| Chandler, Josiah | |
| Chandler, Widow | 100 |
| Curray, James | 20 |
| Curray, Ezekiel | |
| Carter, Gideon | |
| Cawthon, John H. | |
| Crutchfield, O. F. | 60 |
| Clay, Wadkins | |
| Drennan, Delphy | |
| Dobson, William R. | 160 |
| Dobson, Benjamin | 260 |
| Drennan, Thomas | 400 |
| Drennan, William | |
| Devault, Henry | |
| Davis, heirs | 156 |
| Drennan, James | 250 |
| Edney, John | 116 |
| Ford, Paskel | |
| Ferrell, Wiley | 37 |
| Gwynn, Robert | 80 |
| Gwynn, Ransom | 185 |
| Gibson, Isaac | 100 |
| Gibson, Thomas | 8 |
| Golden, Thomas | 50 |
| Gwynn, Andrew | 100 |
| Goodman, Coleman | 200 |
| Hobson, Benjamin | 95 |
| Hooker, Joshua | 148 |
| Hughley, Enoch | 113 |
| Hamilton, George | 690 |
| Hooker, Benjamin | 150 |
| Hooker, Benjamin, Jr. | 147 |
| Hooker, John | 250 |
| Horton, Lee | 382 |
| Horton, Ephraim | |
| Hobson, Joseph | |
| Jones, Thomas | |
| Kirkpatrick, Thomas | 554 |
| Leach, C. | |
| Lane, Augusta | 60 |
| Lindsay, Taylor | 225 |
| Leath, William E. | 134 |
| Logue, Carn | 350 |
| Miles, Patterson | 370 |
| Mires, Peter | |
| Mitchell, John | 60 |
| Murray, William | 150 |
| McDerman, Wiley | 75 |
| Moss, John | 69 |

1830

| | |
|---|---|
| Matlock, George | 200 acres |
| Nipper, Ambrose | |
| Nicholas, Benjamin | 20 |
| Piner, John O. | 100 |
| Posey, Alexander | 100 |
| Partlow, Thomas | 200 |
| Posey, Alison | 62 |
| Philips, Benjamin F. | |
| Puckett, Ship A. | 200 |
| Patterson, Elijah | |
| Quinley, Owen | |
| Rice, Nathaniel | |
| Rice, Benjamin | 144 |
| Rice, William | 420 |
| Rice, James | |
| Rutland, Joseph | |
| Rutland, Abednego | 85 |
| Rice, Nancy | |
| Rice, Thomas | |
| Robertson, Jordan | 170 |
| Richmond, Joseph | |
| Rice, John | 70 |
| Roach, John, Jr. | 217 |
| Roach, John, Sr. | 140 |
| Ray, John | 220 |
| Sherrill, heirs | 40 |
| Sullivan, Holland | 200 |
| Sullivan, Reuben | |
| Sharon, Thomas | |
| Sherrill, Archibald | 114 |
| Swanner, John | 100 |
| Terrill, William | 349 |
| Telford, John | 150 |
| Thonton, Seth | 100 |
| Telford, Thomas | 104 |
| Telford, Hugh | 299 |
| Telford, Robert heirs | 72 |
| Townsend, Onswell | 640 |
| Woodrum, Jacob | 640 |
| Wood, Reuben | 220 |
| Whitaker, Mark | |
| Wynne, James | 108 |
| Wynne, Ridley | 202 |
| Welch, John | 30 |
| Welch, Thomas | |
| Ward, Andrew | |
| Young, Samuel | |

## CAPTAIN HARPOLE'S COMPANY

| | |
|---|---|
| Arrington, James | 100 acres |
| Adams, James W. | |
| Bradley, Thomas | 756 |
| Blacknell, Charles | |
| Burnett, John | |
| Bettes, James | |

1830

| | |
|---|---|
| Briant, David | |
| Click, Matthias B. | 86 |
| Carr, Richardson | 108 |
| Carr, John | 150 |
| Carr, Walter heirs | 144 |
| Carr, Dabney | |
| Cox, James | 60 |
| Cowger, Adam | 150 |
| Cowger, John | 233 |
| Compton, John, Sr. | 111 |
| Compton, Robert | 16 |
| Compton, Nancy | 16 |
| Compton, John, Jr. | |
| Casy, John | |
| Chandler, John | 75 |
| Crocker, Jesse | 50 |
| Corum, Eli | |
| Davis, Isham | 630 |
| Davis, Zachariah | 200 |
| Davis, William | 100 |
| Dorch, Isaac | |
| Dedman, Robert R. | |
| Davis, Hezekiah | |
| Dill, John | |
| Dorch, John | |
| Dorch, Abel | |
| Estes, Bartlett | |
| Furguson, John | 230 |
| Gilbert, Ebenezer | 175 |
| Harpole, Daniel | |
| Hunter, Isaac | 200 |
| Hunter, Jacob | 130 |
| Hunter, Nancy | |
| Harpole, Adam | 84 |
| Harpole, Adam, Sr. | 193 |
| Halbrook, William | |
| Harpole, George | 226 |
| Huse, Robert | 100 |
| Holman, Thomas | 334 |
| Hobson, Benjamin | 150 |
| Hill, Braxton | 58 |
| Harpole, Sampson | |
| Horsley, John | |
| Horsley, Tolbert | 40 |
| Holt, Jesse | |
| Horn, William | 21 |
| Horn, Richard | |
| Horn, Samuel | |
| Hail, Jeremiah | |
| Hartsfield, Sion | |
| Irby, Joseph | 120 |
| Jarrott, John | 181 |
| Jackson, William | 200 |
| Jarrell, J. | |
| Jolly, Frederick | |

1830

| | |
|---|---|
| Jarrell, Hiram | |
| Jarrell, William | |
| Kindred, Thomas | 56 |
| King, George | 50 |
| Martin, William L. | 220 |
| Murphy, John | 55 |
| Moser, Daniel | 160 |
| McDaniel, James   for | 150 |
| Nancy | 88 |
| Mansfield, Granville | 100 |
| Moss, Thomas | |
| Melton, Thomas | 150 |
| Melton, Richard | |
| Moss, William | 107 |
| Moss, James C. | 28 |
| Nowlin, Bird | |
| Prim, William | 137 |
| Pullum, Bird | |
| Proctor, Edmund   for | 130 |
| Hill's heirs | 132 |
| Rochel, James | |
| Riggan, Henry | |
| Right, Berry | 90 |
| Robb, John | 316 |
| Right, James | 107 |
| Robb, John, Jr. | |
| Steele, William | 50 |
| Scurlock, Dudley | 40 |
| Scurlock, Thomas | |
| Sutton, Toliver | |
| Sutton, Nicy | 130 |
| Shepherd, Thomas | |
| Swan, John | 114 |
| Summerhill, William | |
| Travillian, Edward | 289 |
| Tucker, Green | 202 |
| Travillian, James | |
| Tailor, Paterson | 131 |
| Tailor, Benjamin | 16 |
| Sypert, Thomas | 200 |
| Sypert, Robert | 235 |
| Miles, William | |
| Mosely, John | |
| Mosely, William | |
| Freeman, Daniel | |
| Walker, William | 200 |
| Walker, Milner | 446 |
| Walker, Radford | |
| Walker, William, Jr. | |
| Lain, John J. | |
| Joplin, Elihu | |
| Yonce, Patrick | 100 |
| Nicholas, Murphey | |

## CAPTAIN LAWRENCE'S COMPANY

| | | |
|---|---|---|
| Atwood, Edwin | 40 acres | 1830 |

| | |
|---|---|
| Allen, Archibald | 174 acres |
| Booker, William L. | 50 |
| Burke, Samuel | |
| Belcher, James | |
| Belcher, Isaac | |
| Campbell, Hugh | 90 |
| Campbell, Thomas | |
| Campbell, Harrison | |
| Compton, Matthew | 70 |
| Davidson, James | |
| Grindstaff, Isaac | 187 |
| Hodges, Ephraim | |
| Jackson, David | |
| Jenkins, Joseph | |
| Lawrence, William, Jr. | 433 |
| Lawrence, Turner M. | 220 |
| Lawrence, William, Sr. | 214 |
| Lawrence, Joseph | 213 |
| Moody, James | |
| Mabry, William | 43 |
| Moore, James | |
| Moore, Tilford | |
| Mullinax, Zadock | 178 |
| McKee, Robert | 50 |
| Neal, Claborn W. | 100 |
| Neal, William | 435 |
| Neal, Charles | 50 |
| Neal, Isaac | |
| Neal, Madison | |
| Neal, Elizabeth | 250 |
| Neal, Pallis | 420 |
| Smith, Daniel | 203 |
| Tally, Hailey | 222 |
| Tally, Richard | |
| Tally, Payton | |
| Tally, Archibald | |
| Turner, James | 163 |
| Turner, Jeremiah | |
| Vantrease, William | |
| Wheeler, Nathan | 34 |
| Wood, James | 115 |
| Walker, William | |
| Walden, John | |
| Walden, Fielden | 64 |
| Vantrease, Jacob | 267 |
| Vantrease, John | |
| Kelly, Samuel | |

## CAPTAIN MOORE'S COMPANY

| | |
|---|---|
| Atkinson, Joseph | 90 acres |
| Bowden, Bennett | 52 |
| Babb, Bennett | 400 |
| Bettes, William | 50 |
| Bettes, John | |

1830

| | |
|---|---|
| Baxter, George | 157 acres |
| Baxter, John | |
| Beel, Nathaniel | |
| Blaze, George | |
| Campbell, David | 299 |
| Campbell, Joseph W. | |
| Cook, Thomas | 186 |
| Cole, Sarah | 350 |
| Duke, William | 98 |
| Duke, Uriah | |
| Denton, Edward | 200 |
| Duke, John | 109 |
| Duke, Sion | |
| Eddings, William | 250 |
| Eddings, William, Jr. | |
| Estes, Thomas | 16 |
| Gholdson, John | 212 |
| Guthrie, James | 29 |
| Guthrie, John | 100 |
| Grant, William | |
| Holly, Alex P. | |
| Holland, John M. | |
| Holly, Joseph | |
| Hicks, Thomas | 75 |
| Irby, Carter | 108 |
| Johnson, Henry | |
| Jarrott, Devereaux | 200 |
| Jolly, Isham | 114 |
| James, Rial | |
| King, John W. | |
| Kennedy, Isaac | 150 |
| Loyd, Andrew | 137 |
| McFarland, John | 259 |
| Moser, James W. | |
| McFarland, James | 800 |
| Moore, Warren | 165 |
| McWherter, George M. | 44 |
| McWherter, George F. | 100 |
| McWherter, Sam C. | 75 |
| Norman, Thomas | |
| Proctor, Green | |
| Proctor, David | |
| Proctor, Thomas | 515 |
| Payton, John W. | 335 |
| Payton, John M. | |
| Pane, Jesse | 100 |
| Perkins, John | |
| Powell, John | 400 |
| Robertson, Higdon | 320 |
| Robertson, Lewis | |
| Rotramel, Henry | |
| Sheron, Wood H. | |
| Smith, James | 184 |
| Sherrill, Newman | 145 |
| Standfield, Thomas | |

1830

| | |
|---|---|
| Sherrill, Ephraim | |
| Simmons, Joseph | |
| Tarver, Benjamin | 196 |
| Tucker, Benjamin | 154 |
| Tucker, John W. | |
| Tarver, Silas | 135 |
| Vivrett, Henry | 98 |
| Vivrett, Micajah | |
| Winford, William | |
| Winter, Ambrose V. | 205 |
| Winter, William | |
| Winford, Alexander | 190 |
| White, William | 297½ |
| Wynne, A. H. | 104 |
| White, Edward | 200 |
| Wynne, John K. | 1205 |
| Watkins, Joel | 70 |

### CAPTAIN LESTER'S COMPANY

| | |
|---|---|
| Aston, Alexander | 144 acres |
| Aston, Joseph | |
| Bonner, Williamson | 50 |
| Bonner, Benjamin T. | 80 |
| Burdine, Weston | |
| Burdine, Penelope | 100 |
| Beasley, Josiah | 160 |
| Beasley, Gabriel | |
| Brown, Henry | 85 |
| Bonner, John | 150 |
| Bonner, John L. | |
| Bonner, Thomas L. | 96 |
| Beasley, Benny B. | |
| Carruth, James | 90 |
| Carruth, Joseph W. | |
| Chambers, Lewis | 260 |
| Chambers, John | 81 |
| Chambers, Nicholas | |
| Carruth, William S. | 100 |
| Carruth, Alexander | 200 |
| Carruth, Eli S. | |
| Carruth, Walton | |
| Carruth, Alexander C. | 150 |
| Carruth, James C. | |
| Carter, John T. | |
| Dyer, Lewis H. | |
| Eason, Eli E. | 36 |
| Figures, Mary | |
| Fulks, Alfred F. | |
| Figures, Bart | 564 |
| Fulks, And J. | |
| Glenn, Giles | |
| Grooms, John | |
| Glenn, Ben | |
| Glenn, William | |

1830

| | |
|---|---|
| Glenn, Martha | 246 acres |
| Hamilton, Thomas J. | |
| Harris, Richard | |
| Hunter, Wright | |
| Holman, Robert | 50 |
| Jackson, Mark | 186 |
| Jackson, Henry | |
| Jackson, Dolly | |
| Jackson, John M. | 152½ |
| Johnson, James C. | |
| Johnson, Samuel | |
| Jackson, Daniel | |
| Locke, Charles | 70 |
| Locke, Thomas | 150 |
| Lyon, Merritt | |
| Lyon, James | |
| Lyon, Richard | 150 |
| Lyon, Valentine | |
| Locke, William | 110 |
| Mitchell, Thomas | 100 |
| Mitchell, Everett | |
| Mitchell, Taswell | 180 |
| Murphy, William | |
| Melton, John | |
| Motsinger, Elijah | |
| McDonnell, Stephen | 107 |
| Moser, Adam | |
| Moser, Peter | 442 |
| New, William | 300 |
| New, William O. | |
| Newsom, A. B. | 200 |
| Petway, William | 96 |
| Pearson, William | |
| Prestley, Halum | |
| Pugh, George | 63 |
| Ramsey, Thomas | |
| Ramsey, Richard | |
| Ray, Martin B. | |
| Southworth, James | |
| Sims, Edward | |
| Sims, Robert | |
| Sims, Christopher | |
| Stephens, Littleberry | |
| Tarpley, Sterling | 500 |
| Taylor, James N. | 91 |
| Tarpley, John | 55 |
| Thompson, Swan | |
| Underwood, Joel | |
| Underwood, Thomas | 42 |
| Underwood, Milton | |
| Warren, Benjamin | 278 |
| Vaughan, James | |
| Walton, James | |
| Woodrell, George | 70 |
| Woodrell, Henry | |

1830

## CAPTAIN DANIELS' COMPANY

| | |
|---|---|
| Birthwright, Williamson | 209 acres |
| Balentine, Coster F. | 130 |
| Baird, John | 390 |
| Crabtree, L. D. | 25 |
| Chandler, James | |
| Carroll, John | 400 |
| Carter, Nathaniel G. | 186 |
| Crabtree, Rebecca | |
| Carroll, William | |
| Davis, Samuel | 249 |
| Daniel, James | |
| Deloach, Jerusha heirs | 32 |
| Deloach, Samuel | 30 |
| Eatherly, Isaac | 227 |
| Eatherly, John R. | |
| Grundy, Felix | 300 |
| Goodman, John J. | 100 |
| Hide, Richard | 400 |
| Hooper, John J. | |
| Hill, Thomas | |
| Hill, Isaac | |
| Hodge, William C. | |
| Hogg, John | |
| Johnson, William | 170 |
| Johnson, Isham | 116 |
| Jackson, Dabney | |
| Jones, Wood | 215 |
| Ingram, Shadrach | |
| Ligon, John G. | |
| Mason, Ramsey L. | 170 |
| Medlin Gray | |
| May, Craddock H. | |
| Medlin, Wilson | |
| McClain, Josiah S. | 170 |
| McClain, Alfred | 220 |
| McClain, Alexander F. | 66 |
| McClain, William P. | |
| McClain, William heirs | 143 |
| McClain, John A. | |
| Moore, Whitfield | 90 |
| Mosely, Peter | |
| Neighbours, John | |
| Norris, Samuel | 140 |
| Nooner, John | |
| Puckett, Charles R. | 80 |
| Perry, Albert | |
| Quigley, George | |
| Rowland, James | |
| Rowland, Benjamin | |
| Robertson, Hugh | 88 |
| Rowland, Isaac | 100 |
| Sanderson, Wade | 330 |
| Stevenson, Isaac F. | 106 |

1830

| | |
|---|---|
| Smith, William D. | |
| Smith, Henry | 100 |
| Smith, George | 238 |
| Sanders, James | 1700 |
| Taylor, Caleb | 150 |
| Thrift, Drewry | |
| Taylor, Solomon, Jr. | |
| Taylor, John D. | |
| Vick, Samuel | |
| Williams, Thomas | |
| Watson, Thomas | 278 |
| Wright, E. | |
| Willis, William | 269 |
| Watson, Joseph | 463 |
| York, Edmund | |

### CAPTAIN PATTERSON'S COMPANY

| | |
|---|---|
| Alexander, Nelson G. | 40 acres |
| Bass, Archibald | 137 |
| Barkley, Benjamin G. | |
| Bass, Ezekiel | 390 |
| Bass, John | 339 |
| Bridges, Ann heirs | 37 |
| Bass, Etheldred | 218 |
| Berry, Nathaniel | |
| Belt, Polly | 30 |
| Cartwright, Richard | 117 |
| Cartwright, John | 137 |
| Cunningham, Moses | 155 |
| Carlock, Eber | |
| Compton, Alexander J. | |
| Compton, Charles | |
| Campbell, Archibald | 150 |
| Compton, Rebecca | 30 |
| Campbell, William | 150 |
| Campbell, Hugh | |
| Ellis, Radford | |
| Dowell, John | |
| Garner, Wiley | |
| Garner, Jeremiah | 35 |
| Gaddy, Ezekiel | 16 |
| Garner, John | 116 |
| Gaddy, Elizabeth | 26 |
| Hudson, William | 30 |
| Hammer, John | 30 |
| Holbert, Joel B. | 45 |
| Henson, Lasorius | |
| Hearn, Matthew | 100 |
| Hearn, Jacob | 200 |
| Hearn, George | 612 |
| Hancock, Nancy | 200 |
| Hearn, Thomas | |
| Jones, William F. | 153 |
| Jacobs, Edward G. | 30 |

1830

| | |
|---|---|
| Jennings, Samuel | |
| Long, Robert | |
| Maxwell, William | 138 |
| McKinney, heirs | 60 |
| Moore, George | 80 |
| Morgan, William | |
| Morgan, William | |
| Massey, Abram A. | 125 |
| Maxwell, Milton M. | |
| Nooner, Nathan | |
| Nettles, William | 228 |
| Nettles, Benjamin | 8 |
| Nettles, John | |
| Neal, Ashley | 125 |
| Philips, William | 270 |
| Philips, Joseph | 101 |
| Patton, Jonathan | 89½ |
| Philips, Benjamin, Sr. | 160 |
| Philips, Benjamin, Jr. | |
| Philips, David | 108 |
| Patterson, Samuel F. | 57 |
| Patterson, Julian | 180 |
| Patterson, Esther | 63 |
| Patterson, William | 245 |
| Patton, Joseph | 251 |
| Philips, Josiah | 84 |
| Pemberton, John | |
| Patterson, Samuel | 68 |
| Philips, John | 257 |
| Scott, Wyatt | |
| Read, Robert | 82 |
| Reeder, Harris | 43 |
| Reeder, Benjamin | 360 |
| Reeder, Edwin | |
| Smith, Jacob | 48 |
| Shanks, William | 100 |
| Smith, Nicholas | 200 |
| Smith, John T. | 110 |
| Scott, heirs | 69 |
| Young, Doak | 50 |
| Thompson, Eli M. | 46 |
| Taylor, Thomas | |
| Taylor, John | 48 |
| Williams, Martha | 86 |
| Vaught, Elijah | 46½ |
| Vowell, James L. | 110 |
| Wamack, Richard | 170 |
| Wamack, Elijah | 30 |
| Wamack, Rachel | 160 |
| Wood, Jesse | |
| Waters, William | 125 |
| Williams, Anderson | 47 |
| Waters, Wilson T. | 162 |

CAPTAIN MADDOX'S COMPANY                1830

| Name | Acres |
|---|---|
| Andrews, William | 134 acres |
| Alexander, William S. | 116 |
| Alexander, John | 150 |
| Alexander, Isabel | 75 |
| Bingham, Thomas W. | |
| Bond, James | 130 |
| Bond, William | |
| Booker, Samuel | 160 |
| Booker, John | 65 |
| Berry, Jesse | 140 |
| Boothe, Mary | 75 |
| Bingham, Thomas | 106 |
| Bingham, John | |
| Bradshaw, Amzi | 85 |
| Braden, Charles | 500 |
| Boothe, John | |
| Boothe, James | |
| Coker, Valentine | |
| Comer, Reuben C. | 100 |
| Comer, Samuel R. | |
| Cannon, James | 167 |
| Cunningham, John | 150 |
| Cunningham, James | |
| Cox, Robert | |
| Donnell, James | 200 |
| Donnell, Josiah | 211 |
| Davis, Terrill | |
| Drollander, William S. | |
| Donnell, George | 580 |
| Doak, Martha | 130 |
| Doak, A. F. | 70 |
| Donnell, William | 274 |
| Donnell, Edney | 245½ |
| Davis, Robert | |
| Donnell, William | |
| Donnell, Robert | |
| Donnell, William | 193 |
| Donnell, Jane | 160 |
| Donnell, William | 250 |
| Davis, Elizabeth | 168 |
| Davis, Thomas | |
| Donnell, John | 120 |
| Doak, John F. | 180 |
| Doak, Rufus P. | |
| Donnell, Thomas | 200 |
| Donnell, Martha | 200 |
| Foster, Alexander | 300 |
| Foster, James | 250 |
| Foster, John D. | 285 |
| Foster, Albert | 100 |
| Foster, Alfred H. | |
| Graves, Asa | |
| Graves, Bachelor | |
| Griffis, William | |
| Hudson, Obediah | 193 |
| Hudson, Paskal W. | |

1830

| Name | Acres |
|---|---|
| Henderson, M. D. | |
| Hancock, Westly | 60 |
| Hancock, John heirs | 100 |
| Hearn, Stephen | 130 |
| Hearn, Pernell | 130 |
| Jones, Richard | |
| Jones, Edward | 79 |
| Jones, Isham | |
| King, Edward | 25 |
| Lea, Samuel | |
| Lea, Hiram | |
| Lea, Benjamin | 109 |
| Marrs, Martin | 240 |
| Maddox, Notley | 330 |
| Maddox, William | |
| Maddox, Sims | |
| Massey, Eli | 155 |
| Massey, Louis | |
| Marrs, Alexander | 170 |
| Major, John | 465 |
| Major, John W. | 100 |
| Marrs, William | 75 |
| Marrs, Mary | 200 |
| Morrison, Hugh | 50 |
| Moser, Henry | 180 |
| Nickens, John | |
| Quesenberry, John | 150 |
| Ragsdale, Asa | 150 |
| Sherrill, Ephraim | 160 |
| Smith, John C. | |
| Smith, David | |
| Scott, Ann | 60 |
| Sparks, Nathan | 200 |
| Smith, Thomas S. | |
| Scott, James | |
| Thompson, Moses | 384 |
| Thompson, Moses H. | 34 |
| Thompson, William A. | 100 |
| Tinsley, Josiah B. | 153 |
| Trice, Edward | 76 |
| Thorn, John H. | |
| Thorn, David | |
| Vowell, William A. | |
| Vowell, Jesse J. | |
| Williams, Thomas R. | |
| Williams, Nathaniel | 130 |
| Wiley, Mary Ann | 90 |
| Wiley, James | 100 |
| Young, John | |

## CAPTAIN ODUM'S COMPANY

| Name | Acres | |
|---|---|---|
| Alexander, Abner | 208 acres | |
| Alexander, Ezekiel | 218 | |
| Arnold, Henry heirs | 150 | |
| Arnold, Nancy | 73 | 1830 |

| | |
|---|---|
| Armstrong, Elijah | 50 acres |
| Bumpass, Robert, Sr. | 425 |
| Bryson, Samuel, Jr. | |
| Bryson, John | 56 |
| Bryson, John, Jr. | |
| Bogle, George | 340 |
| Bryson, Samuel, Sr. | 100 |
| Bogle, Thomas | 100 |
| Bryson, Joseph | |
| Bryson, Joseph, Jr. | |
| Bryson, William | |
| Bogle, Joseph heirs | 100 |
| Cooper, Abraham | |
| Cooper, Christopher | 357 |
| Cooper, Frances | |
| Corn, John A. | 170 |
| Cooper, Benjamin B. | |
| Devenport, Edmund | 40 |
| Devenport, Reuben | 27 |
| Devenport, Wiley | |
| Devenport, Warren | |
| Devenport, Hardy heirs | 20 |
| Devenport, Absolum | 20 |
| Francis, E. | |
| Francis, Armstead | 320 |
| Francis, Mary | |
| Gunn, Amey | 220 |
| Higgans, William | 50 |
| Higgans, John | 50 |
| Howard, George | |
| Howard, Mary | 179 |
| Jewell, Elihu | |
| James, Enos | |
| Johnson, William | |
| Ingram, Martin | |
| Ingram, Sidney | |
| Kennedy, William | 116 |
| Keaton, Larkin | |
| Leach, Thomas | 120 |
| Leach, James | 70 |
| Leach, John heirs | 711 |
| McMinn, Jediah | 237 |
| McKee, Daniel | 75 |
| McMinn, Jehu | 144 |
| McGahee, Samuel | |
| Morrison, Andrew | |
| Montgomery, Alexander | 157 |
| Montgomery, James | 157 |
| Montgomery, Elizabeth | 179 |
| Moore, Abner | 410 |
| Moore, T. C. | |
| Marshall, Robert | 250 |
| Marshall, Carson | 175 |
| Miligan, David | |
| Miligan, James | 24 |

1830

| | |
|---|---|
| Odum, James S. | 34 acres |
| Odum, James | 290 |
| Odum, Samuel | |
| Owen, Jesse | 88 |
| Owen, John | |
| Owen, Nelson | |
| Odum, William | |
| Patterson, John | 260 |
| Reed, James | |
| Reed, Hailey | |
| Reed, Levi | |
| Railey | |
| Richardson, Brice | |
| Sauls, Henry | |
| Summers, James | 233 |
| Summers, Matthew | 250 |
| Shelton, William | 118 |
| Summers, Anthony | 229 |
| Sandley, John | |
| Tittle, Anthony | |
| Travis, Solomon | |
| Williford, Wiley | |
| Wilson, Charles | 25 |
| Willard, John | 80 |
| Hight, Landson | 180 |
| Jones, Erasmus | 226 |
| Jones, Tolbert | |
| Witherspoon, Alexander heirs | 50 |
| Bryson, James | 247½ |
| Somers, John | 90 |
| Jones, Michael | 16 |
| Jones, Erasmus | |

Taken by Christopher Cooper, age 80 years

## CAPTAIN YOUNG'S COMPANY

| | |
|---|---|
| Allison, Elizabeth | 160 acres |
| Arnold, John | 43 |
| Arnold, William | 50 |
| Arnold, Noel | |
| Adams, Parker | |
| Baxter, John | 78 |
| Briant, John | 100 |
| Briant, Richard | 123 |
| Browning, Gilford | |
| Belt, Jeremiah | 100 |
| Bradley, Sarah | 400 |
| Cloyd, James M. | 128 |
| Caffy, James D. | |
| Edwards, Warren | |
| Gunn, Sarah | 73 |
| Gunn, Samuel | |
| Gunn, John M. | |
| Garmany, Margaret | 132 |
| Garmany, William | |

1830

| | |
|---|---|
| Goodman, Edward | 80 acres |
| Green, James | 416 |
| Green, Ezekiel C. | |
| Holland, Alexander G. | 300 |
| Hooper, George | 160 |
| Jones, Thomas | |
| Johns, William M. | |
| Lansden, Susannah | 200 |
| Lester, Bennett | |
| Lasater, Federick | 62 |
| Lasater, Abraham | 70 |
| Lackey, Cela | 50 |
| Lansden, Thomas D. | 100 |
| Morrison, Robert | 70 |
| Martin, George W. | 330 |
| Putman, Jehu | 61 |
| Pennybaker, Samuel W. | 61 |
| Puckett, Coleman | 84 |
| Quarles, Milton W. | 200 |
| Quarles, Elizabeth | 300 |
| Reynolds, John | 50 |
| Rhodes, Claborn H. | 318 |
| Sims, Matthias | 100 |
| Sublet, William S. | 61 |
| Sims, Thomas | 80 |
| Sharpe, Joseph | 570 |
| Sharpe, Ezekiel | 130 |
| Sims, Benjamin | |
| Stephens, Elisha C. | |
| Smith, Sampson | 310 |
| Smith, William H. | |
| Smith, George | 150 |
| Smith, William P. | 37 |
| Thomas, Jacob H. | 200 |
| Thomas, John F. | 32 |
| Thomas, Jacob | 177 |
| Thomas, John C. | |
| Thomas, James | 143 |
| Thomas, Wilson B. | |
| Tubb, John | 132 |
| Willy, Ezekiel C. | 120 |
| Williams, Mahala | 100 |
| Williams, Thomas G. | |
| Young, Charles | 240 |

## CAPTAIN CARLOCK'S COMPANY

| | |
|---|---|
| Bone, Adnah | |
| Bone, James C. | 130 acres |
| Bone, Henry F. | 125 |
| Bond, James | 188 |
| Bone, John | 100 |
| Bacon, Edmund P. | |
| Bandfield, John | 140 |
| Clemmons, Samuel   heirs | 126 |
| Carpenter, Conrod | 552 |

1830

| | |
|---|---|
| Cock, Jarrett | 200 acres |
| Cason, Jeremiah | |
| Cason, Joseph | 420 |
| Carlock, Epenetus | 70 |
| Coapland, Samuel | 245 |
| Donnell, David K. | 185 |
| Donnell, John | 133 |
| Edwards, Hiram   heirs | 125 |
| Etheridge, Matthew | 50 |
| Foster, William P. | 40 |
| Gillam, William | |
| Gillam, Ann | 150 |
| Goard, William | 50 |
| Gillam, Edmund | 150 |
| Hazlewood, John | |
| Hackney, Seth | |
| Henderson, Preston | 35 |
| Hudson, Richard | 50 |
| Jones, David | 120 |
| Leman, Henry | |
| Merritt, James P. | 242½ |
| Merritt, William P. | 371 |
| Merritt, John W. | 185 |
| Mount, Alfred | |
| Merritt, Thomas J. | 215 |
| Mount, Matthias | |
| McMinn, Samuel N. | |
| McMinn, Elihu | 320 |
| Moore, Robert R. | |
| Mount, Richard | 213 |
| Norval, James | |
| O'Neal, Asa | 40 |
| Patterson, Burrell | |
| Polk, John | 45 |
| Porterfield, Samuel C. | |
| Pound, Daniel | |
| Pasale, Hiram | |
| Rhea, Archibald | 104 |
| Rhodes, William | |
| Smith, John | 150 |
| Simpson, Hannah | 100 |
| Smith, Aley | 125 |
| Smith, Charles | 150 |
| Smith, George | 169 |
| Sanders, Jordan | 400 |
| Sellars, Lard | 428 |
| Smith, William | 600 |
| Smith, Samuel | |
| Sherrill, Abel | 125 |
| Trigg, William H. | |
| Trigg, Daniel | 1200 |
| Trigg, Lucy | 1300 |
| Thomas, William | 40 |
| Teague, William | 200 |
| Teague, Joshua | |

1830

Warren, John
Whitton, Robert J.
Whitton, Jonathan
Williams, Edward
Williams, Henry B.
Williams, Jonathan
Williams, Julias H.          106
Warren, William              176
Ware, Dudley                 130
Word, Fanny                  280
Williams, Jeptha
Williams, Elbert             123
Weatherly, Denny
Williams, Washington         110
Wallis, Cary

## CAPTAIN BARBEE'S COMPANY

Askew, Franklin
Anderson, James
Branch, Thomas               104 acres
Boyd, William                194
Barbee, Joseph               164
Barbee, Thomas
Branch, Fanny                173
Branch, Jackson              94
Branch, Robert C.            20
Branch, James H.             94
Barbee, John, Jr.
Baker, Jeremiah              85
Baker, John
Boon, John
Barbee, John, Sr.            400
Brittle, Milton
Barbee, William
Biles, Jane                  150
Baird, David                 125
Barbee, Donnell              150
Bartlett, Benjamin F.
Clark, George                310
Casy, Jesse                  70
Cartwright, Hezekiah
Compton, Margaret            160
Corder, Benjamin
Dearing, Alben J.            164
Donnell, Leo L.
Doss, Samuel
Davis, Solomon               138
Daughty, Robert              221
Edge, Elem                   79
Ellis, David
Fonce, Elizabeth             80
George, John                 100
Grindstaff, John             100
Gore, Joseph

1830

| | |
|---|---|
| Hailey, James | 139 acres |
| Hofter, Joab | |
| Holms, James | 116 |
| Humphrey, John | 57 |
| Johnson, Margaret | 200 |
| Kelly, Dennis  heirs | 100 |
| Lawrence, John, Sr. | 220 |
| Lawrence, John, Jr. | 157 |
| Neal, George | 40 |
| Moore, James | 85 |
| Marks, John | 50 |
| Odum, Britain | 70 |
| Odum, Moses | 35 |
| Philips, Thomas | 190 |
| Pritchett, George | 75 |
| Pendleton, Abraham | |
| Pendleton, James | |
| Pritchett, Nathaniel | 33 |
| Rains, John | |
| Sanders, Joseph | |
| Searcy, Hiram | |
| Smith, Daniel | 211 |
| Smith, John | |
| Taylor, Joshua V. | |
| Taylor, Joshua | 140 |
| Turner, James | 110 |
| Taylor, John | 110 |
| Taylor, Richard | 125 |
| Taylor, John | 300 |
| Taylor, Fanny | 85 |
| Tracy, Evans | 150 |
| Taylor, Joseph | |
| Taylor, Robert | 36 |
| Taylor, James B. | 72 |
| Waters, Lansy P. | |
| Waters, John | |
| Waters, William | 200 |
| Waters, Shelah | 220½ |
| Young, James | 125 |
| Adamson, Simon | 262 |
| Alexander, Isaac | |
| Adams, John | 210 |
| Brogan, Armsted | 125 |
| Borum, Jones | |
| Bailey, Samuel | |
| Chumley, William | 80 |
| Chumley, Denny | |
| Chumley, Daniel | 41 |
| Chumley, Richard | |
| Coleman, Theophilus | |
| Candler, Winsor | |
| Dunn, William | |
| Edge, Edward | 50 |
| Fite, Leonard | 200 |
| Fite, Joseph | 247 |

1830

| | |
|---|---|
| Fowler, John F. | |
| Fuston, James G. | 203 |
| Gallon, Joseph | 55 |
| George, James | |
| Green, Abraham | |
| George, Henry | |
| George, Charles | |
| George, James | |
| Harvey, Isaac | |
| Hutcherson, Bailey | |
| Hass, John | 160 |
| Hass, Simon | |
| Hughes, John | |
| Hass, Henry | |
| Hays, James | |
| Hays, Nathaniel | |
| Jones, Thomas | 28 |
| Johnson, Hartwell | |
| Kelly, Nathaniel | |
| Moore, Lemuel | 100 |
| McMullin, John | 20 |
| Moren, Uriah | |
| Neighbours, William | 75 |
| Nowlin, Thomas | |
| Oliver, William | |
| Pernel, N. L. | |
| Parson, Elijah | |
| Pugh, Royley | |
| Pugh, Jesse | |
| Perriman, James | |
| Pugh, George | 120 |
| Ruyle, Aaron | 200 |
| Robinson, James | 175 |
| Rogers, Robert | |
| Rowen, Hughey | |
| Rutledge, Daniel | |
| Robinson, Edward | |
| Stoneman, Jack | |
| Smith, Fanny | |
| Smith, William | |
| Sneed, Abraham | |
| Underwood, Joseph | |
| Williams, Barnett | 30 |
| Williams, Nathaniel | |
| Rowen, Robert | |
| Parker, Frances | |
| Blythe, Frances | |
| Williamson, Robert | |
| Wilson, Allen | |
| Dunn, Elizabeth | 25 |
| Kelly, Nathaniel | 44 |
| Rowen, Robert | |
| Hathaway, John | |
| Smith, Bird | 62½ |
| Walton, Archibald C. | |

1830

## CAPTAIN WRIGHT'S COMPANY

| | |
|---|---|
| Alexander, Benjamin | 142 acres |
| Alford, Wiley | 322 |
| Alford, Lodwich B. | |
| Alexander, George | 316 |
| Askew, Russell | |
| Bernard, Horatio | |
| Bullard, William | |
| Brooks, Moses | 10 |
| Breedlove, Aylette B. | 90 |
| Brown, John C. | |
| Cloyd, Ezekiel | 220 |
| Cloyd, Joseph | 74 |
| Cloyd, David | 70 |
| Cloyd, Newton | |
| Crutchfield, James | 96 |
| Cowgill, John | 10 |
| Cloyd, Alexander | 92¼ |
| Cloyd, John M. | 150 |
| Crudup, Elisha P. | |
| Crudup, John | 65 |
| Drollinger, John  heirs | 200 |
| Drennan, Jonathan | |
| Drennan, William | |
| Earheart, Nimrod | |
| Earheart, Joseph | |
| Earheart, Moses | 144 |
| Evans, Anderson | |
| Ford, Paskel | |
| Green, Joshua | 50 |
| Gleaves, Absolum | 130 |
| Guill, Bernett | |
| Green, John | |
| Guill, Josiah | 120 |
| Hessey, James | |
| Hessey, John | 352 |
| Hamilton, Thomas | 153 |
| Heralson, Zarey | 10 |
| Hamilton, Joseph | 200 |
| Hughley, Samuel | 223 |
| Hooker, Matthew | 79½ |
| Harrison, Answorth | |
| Hager, Jonathan | 61¼ |
| Hurt, Henry | 75 |
| Hays, James | 68 |
| Hays, Preston | 65 |
| Hays, Jane | 45 |
| Hays, Elizabeth | 68 |
| Hays, William | |
| Hays, Hugh | 420 |
| Jackson, Obediah | 150 |
| Jackson, Abraham | |
| Jackson, Josiah | 152 |
| Jackson, William | |
| Jenkins, William | 100 |

1830

| | |
|---|---|
| Jenkins, John | |
| Jackson, Archibald | |
| Jackson, Obediah | |
| Johnson, Jesse W. | |
| Land, Edward | |
| Lantern, Henry | |
| Lane, Tyre | 75 |
| Ligon, Josiah | |
| Lantern, Joseph | 60 |
| More, Joseph | 2 |
| McCulley, John | 70 |
| McCulley, David | |
| Murray, John | |
| Murray, Jeremiah | |
| Martin, Rebecca | |
| Parham, Mary | 80 |
| Pride, Shelton | 200 |
| Radford, Edward | |
| Rutland, Henry | |
| Rutland, Isaac | 263 |
| Seabourn, Isaac R. | 235 |
| Seabourn, John H. | |
| Seabourn, Christopher | |
| Smith, Mary R. | 76 |
| Sperry, Samuel | |
| Sperry, Thomas | 317 |
| Steward, Joseph | 132 |
| Searcy, Reuben | 380 |
| Sharp, James | 130 |
| Sullivan, Jesse W. | |
| Sullivan, Gilbert | |
| Sullivan, Parker | |
| Sullivan, Joel | |
| Thompson, William | 147 |
| Tate, Robert S. | 237½ |
| Thompson, Osburn | 130 |
| Tate, John W. | |
| Tate, Zachariah | 114 |
| Tate, Richard D. | 78½ |
| Thompson, James P. | 225 |
| Thompson, John heirs | 112 |
| Thompson, Margaret | |
| Thompson, Elizabeth | 200 |
| Wilson, John | 150 |
| Wright, Charles | |
| Wright, Thomas | 230 |
| Williamson, Thomas | 215 |
| Williamson, John A. | |
| Wilson, James heirs | 108 |
| Williamson, John | 295 |
| Wood, Archibald | 183 |
| Williamson, Margaret | |
| Williamson, William | 582 |
| Williamson, George | 217 |
| Wilkerson, Meredith | 120 |

1830

| | |
|---|---|
| Wright, Lewis | 37 acres |
| Williamson, Joseph | |
| Whitworth, Daniel | |
| Wright, Solomon D. | |
| Wright, Joseph | 200 |
| Wright, Jonathan | |
| Wright, Lemuel | 183 |

## CAPTAIN CAPLINGER'S COMPANY

| | |
|---|---|
| Anderson, William | |
| Bell, James | 100 acres |
| Bell, Benjamin | |
| Bone, Henry P. | 125 |
| Bradley, John, Sr. | 156 |
| Bradley, Barnett | |
| Cartwright, Hezekiah | 240 |
| Cartwright, Samuel | 133 |
| Chick, Hamblin | |
| Cathcot, Midget | |
| Cawnthey, George | 60 |
| Colewick, William | |
| Chastain, Elisha | 166 |
| Caplinger, Solomon | 200 |
| Caplinger, William | |
| Cutheral, Joseph | 63 |
| Dice, William | 35 |
| Duff, Robert | |
| Davis, Enoch | 107 |
| Davidson, William | 197 |
| Davidson, Francis | 116 |
| Dudley, Woodson | 45 |
| Edwards, James | 332 |
| Echols, Joseph | |
| Foster, Elisha | 211 |
| Fisher, Philip | 124 |
| Goodall, Hardin | 100 |
| Goens, Shadrach | |
| Gill, William B. | |
| Goodall, William | |
| Grissom, Rowlin W. | 160 |
| Goodall, John S. | 116 |
| Harrison, William | 271 |
| Harrison, Sanders | |
| Huffman, Leonard | 153 |
| Huffman, Robert | |
| Huffman, Archibald | |
| Huffman, Burrell | |
| Hobbs, Joseph C. | 89 |
| Henry, Charles | 88 |
| Hobbs, James | |
| Hearly, William | |
| Henry, Jeremiah | |
| Jones, Elizabeth | 126 |
| Jenkins, Wiatt | |

1830

| | |
|---|---|
| Lindsay, Elizabeth | 164 acres |
| Mannon, Lewis | |
| Motsinger, Joshua | |
| Mannon, John | 60 |
| Mannon, Caty | 60 |
| Marks, James | 106 |
| Midgett, George | |
| Marks, Thomas | 125 |
| Murphy, Robert | |
| Murphy, Tilson | |
| Murphy, Aaron | 85 |
| Pitmore, William | 150 |
| Pride, Freeman | |
| Philips, John | 160 |
| Rather, Elizabeth | |
| Reese, Thomas B. | 265 |
| Sweatt, Joseph | 100 |
| Swan, John W. | 35 |
| Swan, William | |
| Swan, John, Jr. | 90 |
| Swan, George L. | |
| Steele, Miner | 50 |
| Spring, Abner | 191 |
| Spring, Moses | 100 |
| Spring, Benjamin | |
| Swan, James | 130 |
| Swan, William & John | 75 |
| Sweatt, William, Jr. | 400 |
| Sweatt, Edward | 400 |
| Sweatt, Robert | |
| Sweatt, Asariah | |
| Spring, John | 142 |
| Standfield, Robert | |
| McWherter, William | |
| Turner, William | |
| Henry, Philip | 40 |
| Coe, Isaiah | 100 |
| Bell, John | |
| Philips, William | 226 |
| Philips, A. | |
| Moore, Thomas | 73 |
| Sweatt, George heirs | 160 |
| Burge, William | 20 |
| Seay, John, Jr. | 106 |
| Hadkins, Matthew | |
| Moore, William | 80 |
| Pembleton, John | |

## CAPTAIN RAGLAND'S COMPANY

| | |
|---|---|
| Brown, Poindexter | |
| Brevard, Thomas | 187 |
| Bradshaw, James C. | |
| Billings, David | 600 |
| Billings, Ben H. | |

1830

| | |
|---|---|
| Bell, Jefferson | 60 |
| Barton, Gabriel | 103 |
| Carlin, Hugh | |
| Coe, William | 220 |
| Cox, Anderson | 40 |
| Delapp, Thomas | 3 |
| Dillis, Robert | 90 |
| Edwards, William | 163 |
| Hankins, Matthew | |
| Hankins, John | |
| Hankins, Richard | 1020 |
| Hale, Thomas | |
| Joyner, William | |
| Johnson, Zealous | 40 |
| Johnson, Matthew | 100 |
| Johnson, Jordan | |
| Jones, Wiley | |
| Jackson, Thomas R. | 111 |
| Irby, Pleasant | 79 |
| Lampkins, Charles | |
| Martin, Robert H. | |
| Mason, Thomas | |
| McNeely, Enoch | 150 |
| Organ, Ennis | 107½ |
| Owens, Robert | |
| Patterson, S. | |
| Pemberton, William | |
| Powell, Seamore | |
| Powell, Nathaniel | |
| Pemberton, Jesse | 100 |
| Stone, Thomas | 180 |
| Swinney, William | 40 |
| Satterfield, Reuben | 224 |
| Ragland, Pettes | 300 |
| Russell, John | |
| Weir, James J. | 112 |
| Weir, James C. | 115 |
| Weir, Joseph | 170 |
| Weir, John | |
| Tally, Ephraim | |
| Tally, Henry | |
| Walls, Alexander | |
| Williams, Robert | |
| Walker, John | 1830 |

The aggregate amount of taxable property and polls for the year 1830:

| | |
|---|---|
| 281,166 acres of land at 37½¢ per 100 | $1054.35 |
| 2305 free polls at 25¢ each | 526.25 |
| 2282 black polls at 50¢ each | 1141.00 |
| 75 town lots at 50¢ | 37.50 |
| 59 stud horses at 1.00 each | 59.00 |

## CAPTAIN HOLMAN'S COMPANY 1831

| Name | Acres |
|---|---|
| Adkins, J. heirs | 640 acres |
| Allgin, John | |
| Allen, William, Sr. | 130 |
| Allen, Larkin | |
| Ashworth, Jasper R. | 350 |
| Allcorn, James | 20 |
| Allcorn, Prudence | 250 |
| Allen, Mary | 75 |
| Acles, Joseph | |
| Alexander, Daniel | 430 |
| Burton, Robert M. | 690 |
| Bonner, Thomas E. | |
| Bullard & Tapp | |
| Boyd, Charles H. | |
| Brown, John C. | 110 |
| Brown, Elizabeth | 110 |
| Brown & Land | |
| Barksdale, Thomas W. | |
| Bettes, Samuel | |
| Burke, Edward | |
| Bettes, Alfred | |
| Bullard, George H. | 200 |
| Brown, Jordan | |
| Cummings, George D. | 100 |
| Chapman, Silas | 150 |
| Chapman, Benjamin | 100 |
| Chandler, Robert | 110 |
| Campsey, John | |
| Chandler, E. A. | 100 |
| Chambliss, Henry | 45 |
| Clay, John | |
| Chandler, Henry | 100 |
| Cummings, Charles W. | 123½ |
| Cate, Thankful | 200 |
| Cage, Claiborn C. | |
| Cox, John | |
| Calhoun, Samuel | 320 |
| Cryer, William | |
| Clark, Joshua | |
| Campbell, David | 160 |
| Campbell, David, Jr. | 150 |
| Cherry, Daniel | 400 |
| Cherry, William heirs | 700 |
| Cook, Samuel A. heirs | |
| Cain, Elisha G. | |
| Douglass, Burchett | 408 |
| Douglass, Norvall | |
| Davidson, John | 190 |
| Dew, John H. | |
| Douglass, H. L. | 110 |
| Dew, Matthew | |
| Dew, Arthur | 121 |
| Evans, G. A. | |

1831

| Name | | | |
|---|---|---|---|
| Eastland, N. W. | 200 | | |
| Evrett, Joel D. | | | |
| Edwards, Thomas | | | |
| Everly, Adam | | | |
| Frazer, James | 155 | Barton's Creek | |
| Finley, O. G. | 742 | | |
| Freeman, Joseph | | | |
| Frazer & Brown | | | |
| Golladay, Isaac | | | |
| Garrison, Person | 130 | Spring Creek | |
| Gillespie, David | | | |
| Ganter, John | | | |
| Hibbitts, David C. | 230 | Spring Creek | |
| Holman, Robert | 50¼ | Barton's Creek | |
| Hicks, A. W. | | | |
| Holman, Thomas P. | 334 | Spring Creek | |
| Hickman, William, Jr. | | | |
| Hearn, John | 140 | Barton's Creek | |
| Hegerty, P. H. | 20 | | |
| Harrison, Joshua | | | |
| Holman, John B. | 140 | Barton's Creek | |
| Hartsfield, Jacob | | | |
| Horn, Richard | | | |
| Horn, Thomas | | | |
| Hubbard, Peter | | | |
| Hunt, Britain | | | |
| Hegerty, Dennis | | | |
| Irvin, James | | | |
| Ingram, James | | | |
| Johnson, Hicks & Company | | | |
| Johnson, Joseph | 3530 | | |
| Johnson, James H. | 98 | Barton's Creek | |
| Johnson, Henry F. | | | |
| Johnson, Rawlings H. | | | |
| Jopling, Thomas | 500 | | |
| Jones, Henry H. | | | |
| Killingsworth, James | | | |
| Kimbrell, Benjamin | | | |
| Loyd, Anderson | | | |
| Loyd, Charles | 172 | | |
| Ligon, Joseph | 72 | | |
| Little, William | 3400 | | |
| Loyd, Samuel | 105 | | |
| Laughlin, L. G., Jr. | | | |
| Miller, Beverly | | | |
| Muirhead, John | 271 | | |
| Mosely, Asa | | | |
| Mottley, Stone & Tapp | 115 | | |
| Martin, Robert | | | |
| Martin, Wesley | | | |
| Milton, Thomas | 150 | Cumberland River | |
| McConnell, David | 10½ | | |
| Matthews, William E. | 70 | | |
| Mabry, G. | 10 | | |
| Mabry & Gillespie | | | |
| Nowlin, Mary | 28 | Barton's Creek | 1831 |

| | | |
|---|---|---|
| Netherland, George W. | | |
| Blair, William R. | | |
| Chaver, David | 228 | Barton's Creek |
| O'Brion, Mary | 130 | |
| Petty, Henry | | |
| Prim, William | 135¼ | Spring Creek |
| Perkins, John | 50 | |
| Page & Douglass | 400 | Barton's Creek |
| Rutledge, Alexander | 140 | Barton's Creek |
| Russell, William | | |
| Rhodes, Elizabeth | | |
| Ragland, Pettes | 300 | Spring Creek |
| Swindle, Isaiah | | |
| Smith, Elisha | | |
| Scroggins, Giles H. | | |
| Sypert, Lawrence | 188 | Barton's Creek |
| Sypert, William L. | | |
| Spradlin, James | 11 | |
| Swindle, Pillage | | |
| Stone, John | 60 | |
| Smith & Barksdale | | |
| Smith, Henry F. | 20 | |
| Searcy, William W. | | |
| Seawell, William | 1315 | |
| Sherrill, Mrs. Eve | 15 | |
| Seawell, Hardy H. | | |
| Tapp, John | 187½ | Barton's Creek |
| Truett, Adam | 50 | Spring Creek |
| Traylor, Edward | 60 | Barton's Creek |
| Tapp, John | 400 | Barton's Creek |
| Thompson, Thomas J. | | |
| Tulliston, Robert | 30 | |
| Tolliver, Zachariah | | |
| Usry, Henry | 50 | Spring Creek |
| Vick, Allen W. | | |
| Vaughan, John S. | 30 | |
| Vinson, David | | |
| White, Little B. | 18½ | |
| White, Edward A. | 152 | Barton's Creek |
| White, John W. | | |
| White, Isaac B. | | |
| Wynne, Manerva | 210 | |
| Woolard, John | 142 | Spring Creek |
| Woolard, Simeon | 63 | |
| Wherry, William A. | 69½ | |
| Wilson, Joseph L. | 170 | |
| White, Cader | 86 | |
| Yerger & Golladay | 25 | |
| Yerger, Michael | | |

## CAPTAIN PREWETT'S COMPANY

| | | | |
|---|---|---|---|
| Bland, Arthur | | | |
| Billingsley, John | | | |
| Bagwell, Lunceford | 75 | Barton's Creek | 1831 |

| | | |
|---|---|---|
| Brewer, Morris | 137 acres | Barton's Creek |
| Bone, Amos | | |
| Caraway, Willis | | |
| Comer, William | 103 | Barton's Creek |
| Clemmons, Elizabeth | 120 | Pond Lick |
| Clemmons, Jeptha  heirs | 15 | |
| Caraway, Moses | 170 | Barton's Creek |
| Casselman, Jacob | 330 | Barton's Creek |
| Clemmons, James | 178 | Pond Lick |
| Clemmons, Elizabeth | 140 | Pond Lick |
| Clemmons, Jeptha | | |
| Craig, Abner J. | | |
| Caraway, Merritt | | |
| Crutchfield, George | | |
| Freeman, Obadiah | 117 | Barton's Creek |
| Guthrie, James | 132 | Barton's Creek |
| Grissom, John | 89 | Barton's Creek |
| Green, Thomas L. | 183 | Barton's Creek |
| Green, Thomas B. | | |
| Grissom, Asa | | |
| Goodwin, Jesse A. | | |
| Gholston, Charles | | |
| Holloway, Levi | 390 | |
| Hancock, Dawson | 500 | Pond Lick |
| Hickman, Lemuel | 79 | Barton's Creek |
| Holloway, Ezekiel | | |
| Holloway, John | | |
| Holloway, Richard | | |
| Hancock, Nelson D. | 190 | Barton's Creek |
| Hancock, Lesly | | |
| Hickman, Wright | | |
| Hickman, Snoden, Sr. | 126 | |
| Hickman, Snoden, Jr. | | |
| Hickman, John | 142 | Barton's Creek |
| Hawks, John | 130 | Barton's Creek |
| Hancock, Melisha | 28 | |
| Hancock, Henry | | |
| Horn, Charles | | |
| Hickman, William | | |
| Harrison, Thweatt  heirs | 120 | |
| (Hill), Jeremiah H. | 107 | |
| Hancock, Lemon | 170 | |
| Harris, Alfred H.  guard for  Polly S. R. Hallum | 33 | |
| Harris, Alfred H. | 89 | |
| Hallum, Robert | 47 | |
| Justice, Samuel | 120 | |
| Justice, John | | |
| Johns, John | | |
| Justice, Ebenezer | | |
| Johnson, Robert | 218 | |
| Knight, Jesse | | |
| Knight, James | | |
| Link, James | 148 | 1831 |

| | | | |
|---|---|---|---|
| Lancaster, Levi | | | |
| Moore, Jesse | | | |
| Moore, James | | | |
| McWherter, George F. | 60 | | |
| McGrehey, Daniel | | | |
| Ozment, Armstrong | | | |
| Ozment, James | | | |
| Ozment, Alfred | | | |
| Ozment, Sarah | 89 | | |
| Ozment, Jonathan heirs | 178 | | |
| Ozment, Samuel | | | |
| Pool, Giles B. | | | |
| Richmond, James | 861 | | |
| Robins, Lemuel | | | |
| Reed, William | 50 | | |
| Reed, Henry, Sr. | | | |
| Reed, Robert | | | |
| Reed, Henry, Jr. | | | |
| Reed, Robert D. | 130 | | |
| Reed, Elam | | | |
| Rummels, Libby | | | |
| Rogers, Henry | | | |
| Rummels, John | | | |
| Rhodes, Elizabeth | | | |
| Shannon, James | 350 | | |
| Steed, Seth | | | |
| Shannon, Robert, Sr. | 300 | | |
| Shannon, Robert, Jr. | 130 | | |
| Shannon, Henry | 300 | | |
| Shannon, John | | | |
| Skein, John | 160 | | |
| Sullivan, Price | | | |
| Thrower, Eli | | | |
| Tucker, Abbot | | | |
| Tarier, Thomas | | | |
| Thweatt, Margaret | | | |
| Thweatt, Elijah | 540 | | |
| Thweatt, Henry | | | |
| Tune, Thomas | | | |
| Wade, Charles | 60 | | |
| Wood, Tandy | | | |
| Wall, Bird, Jr. | | | |
| Wanick, James | 124 | | |
| Wall, Burrell | 140 | | |
| Wall, Bird, Sr. | 205 | | |
| Wall, Benjamin | 100 | | |
| Wall, Evans | | | |
| Wall, Adam | | | |

## CAPTAIN HORN'S COMPANY

| | | | |
|---|---|---|---|
| Ames, William | 42 | Barton's Creek | |
| Ames, Elizabeth | 56 | Barton's Creek | |
| Atkinson, Rial | | | |
| Bettes, William | | | |
| Babb, Thomas | 140 | Barton's Creek | 1831 |

| | | |
|---|---|---|
| Bettes, John | 250 acres | Barton's Creek |
| Cowan, James | | |
| Conyers, Thomas | 320 | Barton's Creek |
| Conyers, Andrew | | |
| Cartmell, Nathaniel | 165 | Spring Creek |
| Clay, Archy | 122 | Spring Creek |
| Caraway, John | | |
| Cook, Green B. | 73 | Spring Creek |
| Cook, Jesse | 140 | Spring Creek |
| Dickens, Samuel | 85 | Spring Creek |
| Duke, Sion | | |
| Duke, Alfred | | |
| Dean, James | 407 | Barton's Creek |
| Davis, Wilson C. | | |
| Davis, William | | |
| Davis, Benjamin | 55 | Spring Creek |
| Davis, Arthur L. | 114 | Barton's Creek |
| Enoch, Alfred | 158 | Spring Creek |
| Estes, George A. | | |
| Estes, Benjamin | 154 | Spring Creek |
| Echols, Turner | | |
| Estes, Benjamin H. P. | | |
| Estes, Mary | 47 | Barton's Creek |
| Echols, Mary | 45 | Barton's Creek |
| Horn, Etheldred P. | 373 | Barton's Creek |
| Horn, Matthew | 428 | Barton's Creek |
| Hudson, Richard | | |
| Hunt, Thomas | 40 | Barton's Creek |
| Hunt, John | 38 | Barton's Creek |
| Hicks, Alfred | | |
| Hunt, Jesse | 170 | Spring Creek |
| Hawk, Matthias | 107 | Barton's Creek |
| Hunt, James H. | | |
| Hunt, Benjamin | 220 | Barton's Creek |
| Holly, Joseph E. | | |
| Hunt, Alfred | | |
| Jarrell, Boswell | | |
| Jarrell, Wesley | | |
| Jarrell, Fountain | | |
| Jolly, William | 40 | Barton's Creek |
| Kennedy, Ann | | |
| Lambeth, Warner | 100 | Barton's Creek |
| Lewis, James | | |
| McWherter, George B. | | |
| Mitchell, Robert | 50 | Spencer's Creek |
| Mitchell, Thomas R. | 50 | Spencer's Creek |
| Morris, Edward heirs | 234 | Barton's Creek |
| Morris, Thomas E. | | |
| Mitchell, Henry | 82 | Spencer's Creek |
| Norman, Thomas | 100 | Spencer's Creek |
| Perry, Mitchell | | |
| Payne, George | | |
| Phimm, Kinzie | 104 | Spencer's Creek |
| Ross, George | 405 | Spencer's Creek |
| Ross, Samuel N. | | |

1831

| | | |
|---|---|---|
| Rutledge, Elijah | 107 acres | Barton's Creek |
| Sheron, Wood H. | | |
| Scruggs, Gross | 173 | Barton's Creek |
| Stanfield, Thomas | | |
| Sypert, Thomas | 200 | Barton's Creek |
| Sypert, Sarah | | |
| Sypert, Elison A. | | |
| Sypert, Hardy H. | 75 | Barton's Creek |
| Tarver, William | 249 | Barton's Creek |
| Tarver, Calvin | | |
| Wier, Absolom for Echols heirs | 290 | Spencer's Creek |
| Walker, Tabitha | 76 | Barton's Creek |

### CAPTAIN WILSON'S COMPANY

| | |
|---|---|
| Adams, William | 274 acres |
| Anderson, John | |
| Blair, William | 30 |
| Bryan, Nelson | 520 |
| Brashear, John | 50 |
| David, Susannah | 33 |
| David, Isaiah heirs | 67 |
| Davis, James N. | |
| Dillon, Jesse | 20½ |
| Dennis, Henry | |
| Dodd, Richard | |
| Ewing, James | 777 |
| Fustus, Lee Roy | 50 |
| Gossett, John | 150 |
| Hollandsworth, William | |
| Hollandsworth, John | 50 |
| Hollandsworth, Isaac | 50 |
| Hancock, Richard | 290 |
| Hancock, Lewis | 126 |
| Hays, Samuel | 50 |
| Hancock, Charles | 35 |
| House, Joshua | |
| Haas, Simeon | 85 |
| Johnson, Williamson | |
| Johnson, Coleman | 325 |
| King, Robert | 50 |
| Keaton, Mars | |
| Keaton, William | |
| Keaton, Cornelius | 41 |
| Lewis, John, Sr. | |
| Lewis, John, Jr. | |
| Moore, Littleberry | |
| Matthews, Alfred | |
| Matthews, Nathaniel | 25 |
| McDougle, Archibald | 25 |
| McAdow, James, Sr. | 269 |
| McAdow, James, Jr. | 152 |
| McAdow, William | 350 |
| Michie, James | |
| McAdow, Jehu | 566 |

1831

| | |
|---|---|
| Owens, Thomas | |
| Owens, John | |
| Owens, Anthony | |
| Owens, Fountain | 1200 |
| Phillips, Thomas | |
| Rich, Charles | 640 |
| Reeves, Burwell | |
| Rich, Curtis | |
| Rich, George | |
| Stanley, Thomas | |
| Stoneman, John H. | |
| Smith, Hector | |
| Skurlock, John | 100 |
| Skurlock, Francis | 40 |
| Sneed, John, Jr. | |
| Sneed, John Esqr. | 170 |
| Sneed, William | 275 |
| Sneed, Abraham | |
| Shaw, John J. | |
| Smith, John | |
| Turner, Jonathan | |
| Tittle, Samuel | 75 |
| Turnage, Isaac | 10 |
| Wilson, Robert | |
| Wilson, Matthew | |
| Williams, Nathaniel | |
| Wilson, James | |
| Williamson, William | |
| Williamson, Austin | |
| Willard, John | 42 |

## CAPTAIN EDDINS' COMPANY

| | | |
|---|---|---|
| Alexander, P. M. | | |
| Ayres, James | 257 acres | Smith's Fork |
| Alsup, Samuel | 210 | Smith's Fork |
| Armstrong, J. M. | 124 | Smith's Fork |
| Bumpass, Garrett Robt. | | Statesville |
| Bumpass guardian | | Smith's Fork |
| Branch, James | | Statesville |
| Baird, James | 70 | |
| Boswell, William F. | | |
| Byrn, R. L. | 80 | |
| Belcher, Pleasant | | |
| Belcher, Thomas | | |
| Bumpass, Robert H. | 300 | Smith's Fork |
| Belcher, John | 50 | |
| Belcher, Woodford | | |
| Boyd, James | | |
| Bone, Thomas | 143 | |
| Bone, John | | |
| Bone, A. W. | 314 | |
| Bone, J. P. | | |
| Bailey, Washington L. | | |
| Bailey, William | | |
| Bone, Auger | 98 | |

| | | |
|---|---|---|
| Crowder, David | | |
| Campbell, James, Jr. | | |
| Campbell, James, Sr. | 88 | Smith's Fork |
| Cocke, L. | | |
| Coleman, Lindsey | | |
| Chumley, Beverly | 46 | Smith's Fork |
| Campbell, Wilson | | |
| Cross, James | 145 | Smith's Fork |
| Cross, William | | |
| Dillon, John | 261 | |
| Dillon, James | | |
| Dillon, William | | |
| Dejarnette, J. M. | | |
| Eason, J. R. | | |
| Eddings, O. | | |
| Eddings, William | 25 | Smith's Fork |
| Eddings, L. | | |
| Fowler, John F. | | |
| Gilliam, L. S. | | |
| Guill, John H. | | |
| Hays, George | | |
| Hubbard, William | 257 | Smith's Fork |
| Hubbard, Clark | 75 | |
| James, Buchanan | 53 | Smith's Fork |
| Jennings, John | 160 | Smith's Fork |
| Jennings, John A. | 88 | Fall Creek |
| Jordan, Jesse R. | | |
| Jones, Josiah | | |
| Jennings, William C. | 100 | Smith's Fork |
| Jennings, B. C. | 40 | Smith's Fork |
| Jennings, William, Jr. | 162 | Smith's Fork |
| Johnson, William B. | | |
| Jennings, Rial | | |
| Johnson, James | 386 | Smith's Fork |
| Kennedy, John S. | | |
| Kelly, Daniel | 200 | Smith's Fork |
| Kelly, Dennis | 497 | Smith's Fork |
| Knox, John | 150 | Smith's Fork |
| Lester, J. L. | | |
| Moore, William | | |
| McIntire, William | | |
| McCaffrey, John | 44 | Smith's Fork |
| Martin, James | 250 | Smith's Fork |
| McDaniel, William | | |
| McElyea, H. D. | | |
| Merritt, Flemmin | | |
| McHaney, Oney | 60 | Fall Creek |
| Parrish, William | | Smith's Fork |
| Pemberton, Richard | 43 | Smith's Fork |
| Pickett, Edward | 63 | Smith's Fork |
| Pickett, H. W. | | |
| Payne, Henry | 100 | Smith's Fork |
| Payne, James | 121 | Smith's Fork |
| Pemberton, John, Sr. | 73 | Smith's Fork |
| Pemberton, Thomas | | |

1831

| | | |
|---|---|---|
| Patton, John | 42 acres | Smith's Fork |
| Pemberton, George | | |
| Patton, Andrew | 57 | Smith's Fork |
| Rich, Joel | | |
| Richmond, Thomas | 26 | Smith's Fork |
| Rowen, Robert | | |
| Scott, Lander | | Statesville |
| Smith, David B. | | |
| (    lin, L. C. | | Fork Smith's |
| Smith, George | 48 | Smith's Fork |
| Stroud, O. B. | | Smith's Fork |
| Scruggs, Solomon | 33 | Smith's Fork |
| Scott, William H. | | |
| Smith, Bird | 57 | Smith's Fork |
| Smith, J. A. | 51 | Smith's Fork |
| Stewart, Samuel | 144 | Smith's Fork |
| Sloan, J. N. | | |
| Shors, Jonathan | 54 | Smith's Fork |
| Scott, Eli | | |
| Tally, Spencer W. | | |
| Thompson, James, Sr. | 200 | Smith's Fork |
| Tally, Richard | 20 | Smith's Fork |
| Tarpley, H. | | |
| Thweatt, William G. | 90 | Smith's Fork |
| Tarpley, Thomas | | |
| Thomas, S. T. | | |
| Thomas, James, Sr. | 150 | Smith's Fork |
| Thompson, James M. | 245 | Smith's Fork |
| Tribble, Isaiah | 154 | Smith's Fork |
| Thompson, James B. | | |
| Thompson, Andrew, Sr. | 220 | Smith's Fork |
| Thompson, Andrew, Jr. | | |
| Wilson, J. R. | | |
| Webb, John | | |
| Wade, W. W. | | |
| Wroe, H. L. | 123 | Smith's Fork |
| Walker, W. B. | | |
| Walton, A. C. | | |
| Ward, John, Jr. | 40 | Smith's Fork |
| Ward, John, Sr. | 200 | Smith's Fork |
| Whitlock, John | | |
| Ward, James | | |
| Whitlock, Thomas | 100 | Smith's Fork |
| Webb, George | 115 | Smith's Fork |
| Williams, Isaac | 125 | Smith's Fork |
| Williams, James, Jr. | | |
| Williams, Joseph | 155 | Smith's Fork |
| Whitlock, James | | |
| Word, James | 146 | Smith's Fork |

## CAPTAIN SAMUEL C. ANDERSON'S COMPANY

| | | | |
|---|---|---|---|
| Anderson, James heirs | 178 acres | Hurricane Creek | |
| Anderson, Samuel C. | | | |
| Bennett, Thomas | 150 | | |
| Bond, William | 30 | | 1831 |

| Name | Amount | Location |
|---|---|---|
| Bond, Samuel | | |
| Bond, David | 200 | |
| Baird, William | 348 | Hurricane Creek |
| Baird, James | | |
| Barrett, William | | |
| Baccus, Minchey | 50 | |
| Bond, John, Sr. | 441 | |
| Bennett, Jacob, Jr. | 25 | |
| Bennett, John | 110 | |
| Baird, Seldon | | |
| Donnell, Samuel | 30 | |
| Edwards, Edward | 190 | Hurricane Creek |
| Edwards, Crawford | | |
| Edwards, Henry, Jr. | | |
| Edwards, Robert | 406 | |
| Edwards, Hugh | | |
| Edwards, Henry, Sr. | | |
| Edwards, Stokes | | |
| Edwards, Eaton | | |
| Edwards, John, Sr. | | |
| Edwards, Eli | 117 | |
| Edwards, John, Jr. | 62 | |
| Fuston, John | | |
| Fields, John | | |
| Fields, Redding | 143 | |
| Fields, Richard | 195 | |
| Garrison, Elijah | | |
| Guest, John | 150 | |
| Grissom, Stephen | | |
| Gibson, John | 80 | |
| Gibson, Aaron | | |
| Howard, Hiram | | |
| Huddleston, G. A. | 350 | |
| Merritt, Silvanus | | |
| Merritt, Silas | | |
| Merritt, Obadiah | 70 | |
| Merritt, Sherwood | | |
| Milton, Jacob | | |
| Milton, Joseph | | |
| Merritt, Lewis | 178 | |
| Merritt, Mark | 5 | |
| Partain, Henry | | |
| Patterson, Peter | | |
| Patterson, Lewis | | |
| Phipps, W. R. D. | 628 | |
| Quesenberry, Daniel | 15 | |
| Rogers, Tobias | | |
| Ragsdale, Luvan | | |
| Rogers, Samuel | | |
| Spain, Laban | 200 | |
| Scott, John | 50 | |
| Swain, John | | |
| Stacy, Joseph | | |
| Townsend, Richard | | |
| Warren, William | | |

1831

| | |
|---|---|
| Warren, Linai | 99 acres |
| Warren, Solomon | |
| Warren, Charles heirs | 200 |

## CAPTAIN VIVRETT'S COMPANY

| | |
|---|---|
| Atherly, Warren | 223 acres |
| Atherly, Robertson | 151½ |
| Atherly, James | 126½ |
| Batts, John | |
| Briant, John | 45 |
| Bridges, Allen H. | 203 |
| Brown, William | 120 |
| Brown, John | 150 |
| Bradshaw, Wilson | 117½ |
| Bradshaw, Thomas | 160 |
| Bradshaw, Thomas, Jr. | |
| Bass, Cader | 170 |
| Bass, Sion | 380 |
| Bass, Solomon | 111 |
| Bass, Harmon | |
| Bass, James | |
| Burton, Edmund | 44 |
| Bridges, Brinkley | 54 |
| Criswell, Robert B. | |
| Crenshaw, William | 196 |
| Crabtree, Joseph heirs | 90½ |
| Davis, Isham F. | 200 |
| Donaldson, Robert, Sr. | 130 |
| Donaldson, Daniel | |
| Deloach, Samuel | 30 |
| Davis, Nathaniel | 515 |
| Drake, Britain | 336 |
| Estes, Micajah | |
| Ellis, James L. | 114 |
| Ellis, Thomas W. | |
| Escue, Robert C. | |
| Evrett, John | 100 |
| Freeman, Dorrell | 100 |
| Freeman, Edward | 73 |
| Glanton, John | 133½ |
| Grimes, Jesse | |
| Harrison, Steth | 100 |
| Harrison, Answorth | 412½ |
| Howell, Edward | |
| Hightower, Steth | |
| Howell, Caleb | 127 |
| Hester, John | |
| Hickman, Lemuel | |
| Hill, Jesse | 100½ |
| Hester, Benjamin | |
| Hunter, William heirs | 100 |
| Howell, Ransom | 130 |
| Jennings, Anderson | 113 |
| Jackson, Dabney | |
| Jennings, Clem | 623 |

1831

| | | |
|---|---|---|
| Kemp, Burwell | 75 acres | |
| Ligon, John J. | 150 | |
| Lunceford, Eaton | | |
| Moore, Alfred | 68 | |
| Medlin, Littleton | | |
| Marlow, Payton | 123 | |
| Martin, Brice | 461 | |
| Murray, Abram | 18 | |
| Murray, John | 150 | |
| Pitman, John B. | | |
| Pitner, William | | |
| Pitman, Hutchins M. | | |
| Partain, Archibald | | |
| Perry, Richardson | | |
| Pitner, Michael | 230 | |
| Partain, William N. | | |
| Rice, Anderson C. | | |
| Rowland, Richardson | | |
| Rutherford, John R. | 254 | |
| Rieff, Torris | 92 | |
| Richardson, Kinchen | | |
| Reese, Alsy | 107 | |
| Smith, Reuben | 130 | |
| Smith, John | 500 | |
| Smith, Samuel | | |
| Smith, Frank | 127 | |
| Thompkins, James | 96 | |
| Thomas, John | 150 | |
| Taylor, Abraham | | |
| Thomas, Anna | 50 | |
| Vivrett, John B. | | |
| Willis, Thomas | 106 | |
| Willis, James | 160 | Head of S. Creek |
| Williams, Elijah | 123 | |
| Williams, Thomas | 72 | |
| Wright, Thomas A. | 300 | |
| Williams, Roger | 80 | |
| Williams, James | 427 | Silver Springs |
| Walker, Drucilla | 390 | |
| Young, William | 100 | |
| Young, Delia | 60 | |
| Young, Joseph | | |
| Young, James H. | | |
| Young, Stephen | 100 | |
| York, James | 68 | |
| Young, William, Jr. | | |
| Young, Beverly | 122½ | |
| York, Robert | | Cedar Lick Creek |

## CAPTAIN PITMAN'S COMPANY

| | | | |
|---|---|---|---|
| Anman, John H. heirs | 8 acres | Spencer's Creek | |
| Andrews, Gray | 100 | Spender's Creek | |
| Ames, Elizabeth | 205 | Spencer's Creek | |
| Aust, Thomas | 73 | Spencer's Creek | |
| Aust, Joseph | 200 | Spencer's Creek | 1831 |

| Name | Acres | Location |
|---|---|---|
| Ames, Elizabeth | 80 acres | |
| Anderson, Richard, S. | | |
| Anderson, Richard, Jr. | 85 | B. Creek |
| Adamson, William, Sr. | | |
| Adams, William, Jr. | | |
| Bay, Andrew | 216 | Spencer's Creek |
| Brown, Jackson N. | 80 | |
| Briant, Samuel heirs | 84 | Spencer's Creek |
| Brown, Matthew | | |
| Bloodworth, Webb | 156 | Spencer's Creek |
| Brown, George | 130 | Barton's Creek |
| Brown, Richard | | |
| Bunderant, Robert | 251 | Spencer's Creek |
| Bandy, Richard | | |
| Blalock, Charles, Jr. | | |
| Blalock, Charles, Sr. | | |
| Briant, Archibald | | |
| Briant, Hiram | | |
| Bandy, Epson | 146 | |
| Brown, John H. | | |
| Britain, James H. | 68 | |
| Brown, David | | |
| Blackburn, John | | |
| Bradberry, James | | |
| Cooper, Margaret | 80 | Spencer's Creek |
| Clayton, Phebe | 40 | Barton's Creek |
| Criswell, Eli | | |
| Criswell, Minor | 50 | |
| Coles, Samuel | 45 | |
| Cledemen, Joseph G. | | |
| Cartmell, Nathan | 105 | |
| Campbell, Robert | 324 | |
| Carmus, Thomas | 66 | Cumberland River |
| Coles, Robert N. | 120 | Barton's Creek |
| Coppage, Thomas | | |
| Coles, Isaac G. | | |
| Coppage, Charles, Sr. | 40 | |
| Clay, Charles | | |
| Clay, John | | |
| Cocke, William | | |
| Cocke, Flemming | | |
| Coles, William T. | 104 | Cumberland River |
| Coles, John | | |
| Coppage, Charles | | |
| Coppage, James | | |
| Carr, Wilson | 170 | Cumberland River |
| Cowan, William M. | 200 | Spencer's Creek |
| Dill, Joel | 236 | Barton's Creek |
| Drake, William B. | 93 | Cumberland River |
| Davis, Jack | | |
| Davis, Thomas | 478 | Spencer's Creek |
| Davis, Harvey | 129 | Cumberland River |
| Davis, William | | |
| Davis, James H. | 645 | Spencer's Creek |
| Dorch, Isaac | | |

1831

| Name | Acres | Location |
|---|---|---|
| Eagan, John | 14 | Spencer's Creek |
| Edwards, Nicholas | 152 | Barton's Creek |
| Eagan, Barna | 65 | Spencer's Creek |
| Eagan, Hugh | 189 | |
| Eagan, Jesse | 70 | |
| Eddins, James | | |
| Eagan, Reese | | |
| Eagan, James | 100 | |
| Eagan, James | 100 | |
| Eagan, William heirs | 103 | |
| Frazer, Alexander | 67 | Barton's Creek |
| Frazer, Joel | | |
| Gray, Samuel, Sr. | 167 | S. Creek |
| Gray, John | | |
| Gann, Daniel | 130 | |
| Gray, William | 157 | Cumberland River |
| Green, Isaac | 120 | S. Creek |
| Gregory, Thomas | | B. Creek |
| Gordon, Obadiah | 207 | Cumberland River |
| Gray, Samuel, Jr. | | |
| Gleaves, John heirs | 300 | Cedar Lick Creek |
| Harris, John D. | | |
| Henry, Samuel | 640 | Spencer's Creek |
| Hunt, Benjamin | | |
| Harris, William F. | 150 | Spencer's Creek |
| Hays, Harmon A. | 174 | |
| Higgason, Samuel D. | | |
| Hammons, Thomas | | |
| Hitchcock, William | 15 | Spencer's Creek |
| Hayworth, Micajah | | |
| Johnson, James | | |
| Johnson, Samuel | 273 | B & S Creeks |
| Johnson, Samuel G. | 6 | S. Creek |
| Jolly, Frederick | | |
| Kirkpatrick, Alfred | 54 | Cumberland River |
| Kirkpatrick, Anderson | 83 | Barton's Creek |
| Kirkpatrick, Joseph | 769 | |
| Kirkpatrick, David heirs | 100 | |
| Lambert, Price | | |
| Lawrence, Robert | 100 | Barton's Creek |
| Mays, William heirs | 44 | S. Creek |
| Mahaffy, Isaac | | |
| Martin, Bird B. | | |
| Motheral, Samuel | 480 | |
| Motheral, Robert | | |
| Mahaffy, Henry | | |
| Mays, Jacob | 93 | S. Creek |
| Moore, Israel | 103 | S. Creek |
| Mosely, Thomas D. | 270 | S. Creek |
| Mays, James | 220 | Cumberland River |
| Mosely, William | | B. Creek |
| Puffer, Samuel | | |
| Pitman, Henry M. | 225 | Barton's Creek |
| Ray, Samuel | 14 | |
| Ray, Elisha | 14 | |

1831

| | | |
|---|---|---|
| Ray, Joseph | 50 acres S. Creek | |
| Ray, Simpson | 130 S. Creek | |
| Ross, Allen | 221 S. Creek | |
| Ray, William | | |
| Roach, Alexander | 170 B. Creek | |
| Rider, Reuben | 2 S. Creek | |
| Ray, John | 62 S. Creek | |
| Rieff, Catharine | 200 S. Creek | |
| Ray, Alsey | 101 S. Creek | |
| Ross, John | 210 S. Creek | |
| Ray, Willis | 125 S. Creek | |
| Ray, Benjamin | 6 | |
| Sanders, Richard | 212 | |
| Sanders, Joseph P. | | |
| Smith, William | 140 | |
| Stewart, Cyrus | 160 | |
| Sanders, Nathaniel | | |
| Taylor, Hugh | | |
| Tipton, James | 145 | |
| Tipton, William | | |
| Turner, Samuel | | |
| Tipton, Rus B. heirs | 122 Spencer's Creek | |
| Turner, John G. | | |
| Tipton, Jonathan | | |
| Turner, John | | |
| Tatum, Dabney | 121 Cumberland River | |
| Taylor, Robert | 64 Cumberland River | |
| Vaughan, Thomas (Va) | | |
| Vaughan, Thomas | 60 Spencer's Creek | |
| Vaughan, Turner | | |
| Vaughan, Mary T. | 156 Spencer's Creek | |
| Vaughan, Melcijah | | |
| Vaughan, Edmund | | |
| Walker, James D. | 282 | |
| Whitson, John | 50 Spencer's Creek | |
| Webb, John | | |
| Wright, Anderson | 50 Spencer's Creek | |
| Wright, Isaac | 140 Spencer's Creek | |
| Wood, Josiah | 151 | |
| Wood, John | | |
| Wood, Thomas | | |
| Wynne, Joseph D. | 154 | |
| Willis, Thomas | | |
| Wilkinson, William | | |
| Whitson, Abram heirs | 100 Spencer's Creek | |
| Wright, John | | |
| Wood, Isham | | |
| Young, Robert | | |

## CAPTAIN P. ANDERSON'S COMPANY

| | | |
|---|---|---|
| Archer, Jacob | 114 acres Spring Creek | |
| Alexander, George | 50 Spring Creek | |
| Alexander, John | | |
| Archer, Hezekiah | 23 Spring Creek | 1831 |

| Name | Acres | Location |
|---|---|---|
| Anderson, Francis | 40 acres | |
| Anderson, Paulden | 67 | |
| Byrns, Brantley | 156 | Barton's Creek |
| Bone, Enos | 90 | Spring Creek |
| Bundy, John | 140 | Spring Creek |
| Bundy, David | | |
| Bundy, James | | |
| Bundy, Nathan | | |
| Clifton, L. | 140 | |
| Carruth, James T. | | |
| Carruth, William R. | 50 | Spring Creek |
| Carruth, Samuel C. | | |
| Carruth, James | 135 | Spring Creek |
| Clark, Pryor | | |
| Chamberlain, Thomas, Jr. | 125 | Spring Creek |
| Coe, John | | |
| Carruth, Walter | 290 | Spring Creek |
| Clifton, Hannah | 130 | |
| Donnell, Robert | 238 | |
| Dew, Nancy | 240 | |
| Graves, Joseph | | |
| Guthrie, Thomas | 160 | S. Creek |
| Harris, Thomas | | |
| Hearn, Stephen L. | | |
| Hearn, Ebenezer | | |
| Hearn, Milbry | 208 | S. Creek |
| Harrison, Elizabeth | 106 | S. Creek |
| Hartsfield, Solomon | 260 | S. Creek |
| Hancock, Martin | 220 | Barton's Creek |
| Hancock, Samuel | | |
| Hancock, Hope | | |
| Hearn, William | | |
| Hearn, Thomas | 169 | |
| Hancock, Simon | 280 | Barton's Creek |
| Hancock, Green | | |
| Harris, Edward | 120 | Spring Creek |
| Harris, Charles | | |
| Henry, Alexander | | |
| Johnson, Jeremiah | 150 | Spring Creek |
| Jones, James | | |
| Johnson, Robert | 235 | Barton's Creek |
| Jones, John | 209 | Spring Creek |
| Jones, John, Jr. | | |
| Jones, Elijah | | |
| Johnson, Littleberry | 26 | Spring Creek |
| Lindsley, Phillip | 2360 | Spring Creek |
| Lester, Daniel | | |
| Lester, Henry | 21 | Spring Creek |
| Lane, W. | 73 | |
| Lash, Hamman | 160 | |
| McCown, Sampson | | |
| Moore, George D. | | |
| Morris, William P. | 48 | |
| Morris, Isham | 132 | |
| Martin, James M. | 363 | |

1831

| | | |
|---|---|---|
| Morris, Allison | | |
| Moxley, Joseph | 196 | Spring Creek |
| Nickens, James | 100 | Spring Creek |
| Nickens, Archibald | | |
| Newby, John | 162 | |
| Pemberton, Josiah | | |
| Richardson, Willis | | |
| Scott, James P. | | |
| Smith, H. | 200 | Spring Creek |
| Seat, Lebum | | |
| Smith, Josiah, Sr. | 120 | |
| Smith, Josiah, Jr. | | |
| Stembridge, Mary | 100 | |
| Stembridge, William | | |
| Sims, Matthew | 139 | |
| Tally, James | | |
| Walch, James | 50 | Spring Creek |
| Walch, Norman | | |
| Wynne, William | | |
| Willard, Alligood | 31 | |
| Woolard, Allison | | |
| Willard, Alfred | | |
| Whorton, Joseph | 912 | |
| Yates, John B. | 110 | |

## CAPTAIN ALLGOOD'S COMPANY

| | | | |
|---|---|---|---|
| Allen, Wiley | | | |
| Allgood, William | 556 | Cumberland River | |
| Allgood, Joel | | | |
| Bell, Joseph G. | 42 | Cumberland River | |
| Browning, Thomas P. | | | |
| Bowers, Green C. | | | |
| Browning, James | 100 | D Branch | |
| Bell, John | 50 | C Branch | |
| Brady, George | 154 | C Branch | |
| Calhoun, James | 88 | D Branch | |
| Corley, Austin | 63 | Cumberland River | |
| Corley, William | 150 | Cumberland River | |
| Corley, Nathan | 52 | Cumberland River | |
| Duncan, George F. | 175 | C Branch | |
| Dillard, William | 50 | C Branch | |
| Dillard, Allen | 50 | C Branch | |
| Dill, Jacob | 212½ | Cumberland River | |
| Douglass, Ennis | 72 | Cumberland River | |
| Eastland, Nicholas | 200 | R Creek | |
| Furlong, James | | | |
| Furlong, Martin | 100 | D Branch | |
| Gold, Pleasant | | | |
| Gold, Thomas | | | |
| Goodwin, James B. | | | |
| Grubbs, Polly | 18 | Cumberland River | |
| Holder, Benjamin S. | 151 | Cumberland River | |
| Harris, Sneed | 76 | Cumberland River | |
| Harrison, Edmund R. | 147 | R Creek | 1831 |

| | | |
|---|---|---|
| Hay, William | 1604 acres | C Branch |
| Hooks, Clinton | | |
| Jones, Elijah | 130 | |
| Jackson, Coleman, Sr. | 91 | Cumberland River |
| Jackson, Coleman, Jr. | | |
| Jackson, Robert | | |
| Jackson, Burwell | | |
| Jackson, Warren | | |
| Jackson, Jesse | | |
| Lyon, Richard | | |
| Lyon, Thomas | | |
| Lowe, Green B. | 564 | Cumberland River |
| Lowe, Easton | 184 | Cumberland River |
| Martin, Pleasant | | |
| McDonald, Randolph | 94 | Cumberland River |
| McDonald, Elias | 112 | Cumberland River |
| McDonald, Andrew J. | 177 | Cumberland River |
| Martin, George | 250 | C Branch |
| Motsinger, Jefferson | | C Branch |
| Palmer, John W. | 31 | |
| Powell, William | | |
| Pinkston, Moses | 49 | Cumberland River |
| Shaw, Alsey | 78 | D Creek |
| Standifer, William | 78 | |
| Seay, Beverly W. | 50 | C Branch |
| Swann, Andrew | 234 | C Branch |
| Swann, James | | |
| Shaw, Jeremiah | 93 | D Branch |
| Shaw, Solomon | | |
| Terry, Elijah | 108 | Cumberland River |
| Taylor, Mary | | |
| Terry, Peter G. | | |
| White, George | 136 | C Branch |
| Wheeler, Edward B. | 200 | C Branch |
| Whitehead, James | | |
| Woodcock, Mary | 80 | |
| Woodcock, Henry | | |
| White, Samuel | 55 | C Branch |
| Williams, John | 74 | C Branch |
| Woodward, Hezekiah | 180 | D Branch |
| Woodcock, Jesse | 124 | C Branch |
| Williams, George | 50 | C Branch |
| Ward, Henry | 180 | D Branch |

CAPTAIN ALLEN'S COMPANY

| | | |
|---|---|---|
| Anderson, John | | |
| Allen, James | | |
| Allen, Mary | 110 acres | Round Lick |
| Borum, John | 145 | Cedar Creek |
| Belcher, Sutton E. | | Round Lick |
| Borum, Richard | 612 | C Creek |
| Borum, James | | |
| Bell, Amzi | | |
| Bell, John | 640 | C Creek |

1831

| | | |
|---|---|---|
| Bartlett, William | | |
| Bradley, Samuel B. | 50 | C Creek |
| Bell, Jefferson | 60 | |
| Baker, William | 23 | |
| Boyd, John | 100 | C Creek |
| Borum, John, Jr. | | |
| Borum, William | | |
| Bell, Robert | | |
| Bradley, Jonas | 352 | C Creek |
| Bradley, Everett | | |
| Bradley, John | | |
| Bradley, David | 200 | C Creek |
| Carter, William W. | 100 | C Creek |
| Chappell, Thomas | | |
| Chary, James | | |
| Calhoun, Thomas | 225 | C Creek |
| Davis, John L. | 100 | C Creek |
| Donnell, George | 60 | |
| Davis, James | 138 | C Creek |
| Davis, William H. | | |
| Debow, Archy | 300 | C Creek |
| Ellis, Moses | 415 | C Creek |
| Evans, William | | |
| Ellis, Nathan heirs | 92½ | C Creek |
| Eason, Ira E. | | |
| Ellis, James | 15 | C Creek |
| Ferrell, William W. | 130 | C Creek |
| Foster, Robert | 95 | C Creek |
| Franklin, George | 120 | Round Lick |
| Green, Anderson | 100 | Round Lick |
| Graves, Rice | 100 | Cedar Creek |
| Grainger, Garland | 120 | Cedar Creek |
| Harris, Eli | 125 | Round Lick |
| Heron, Frederick | | |
| Harris, McGee | 160 | Cedar Creek |
| Hamilton, Thomas | 250 | Round Lick |
| Hatcher, William | | |
| Hobbs, Esther | 30 | Cedar Creek |
| Harlan, Samuel | | |
| Harris, Fergus S. | 286 | Cedar Creek |
| Harris, John heirs | 110 | Cedar Creek |
| Harris, Catherine | | |
| Harlan, Thomas | | Cedar Creek |
| Johnson, John | 95 | Round Lick |
| Johnson, Robertson | 320 | Cedar Creek |
| Johnson, Daniel | 172 | Cedar Creek |
| Johnson, William | 500 | Round Lick |
| Jones, Michael | 47 | Cedar Creek |
| Johnson, Zealous | 40 | Cedar Creek |
| Johnson, James | 220 | Cedar Creek |
| Kious, Henry heirs | 100 | Round Lick |
| Lyon, Merriot | | |
| Lyon, John | 224 | Cedar Creek |
| McSpadden, William | 147 | Cedar Creek |
| Martin, Pugh | 72 | Round Lick | 1831 |

| Name | Acres | Location |
|---|---|---|
| McMurray, David | 385 acres | Cedar Creek |
| McMurray, James B. | | |
| Martin, Thomas | | |
| McSpadden, Thomas C. | 109 | |
| Martin, John | 177 | Cedar Creek |
| Martin, David | | |
| Mooningham, Elijah | | |
| Mallory, Hugh R. | | |
| Owen, Wadkin | 37 | Round Lick |
| Owen, John | 100 | Round Lick |
| Organ, Woodford | | |
| Owen, William | 150 | Round Lick |
| Owen, Richard | | |
| Philips, Henry | 74 | Cedar Creek |
| Pilkinton, Henry B. | | |
| Payne, Thomas E. | 95 | |
| Provine, John | 192 | Cedar Creek |
| Provine, Samuel F. | | |
| (     ), Robert | 50 | Cedar Creek |
| Provine, Alexander | 206 | Cedar Creek |
| Provine, William A. | | |
| Pemberton, Jesse | | |
| Roan, Hannah | 200 | Cedar Creek |
| Richardson, Loyd | | |
| Rutherford, Griffith W. | 305 | Cedar Creek |
| Scoby, David | 50 | Round Lick |
| Sherrill, Hugh | 100 | Round Lick |
| Swindle, Joel | 100 | Cumberland River |
| Sweatt, George   heirs | 174 | Round Lick |
| Stephens, James | | |
| Stephens, Sanders | | |
| Simmons, John | | |
| Stephenson, Robert | | |
| Swinny, William | 40 | C Creek |
| Sneed, Hamilton | | |
| Sneed, Grief | | |
| Smith, Benjamin B. | | |
| Scoby, James | 400 | Round Lick |
| Scoby, John B. | 100 | Round Lick |
| Sanders, Reuben | | |
| Sullivan, Lee | 280 | Cedar Creek |
| Steel, William | 278½ | Cedar Creek |
| Tomlinson, Allen | 60 | Cedar Creek |
| Trout, John | | |
| Trout, Joseph | 156 | Cedar Creek |
| Tomlinson, Ervin | 50 | Cedar Creek |
| Tomlinson, William | 87 | Cedar Creek |
| Vaughan, David | | |
| Vaughan, Abraham | 126 | |
| White, John W. | 100 | Round Lick |
| Walker, William | 50 | Cedar Creek |
| Warren, Boothe | | |
| Wier, James J. | 112½ | |
| Weir, James, Sr. | 466 | Cedar Creek |
| Watkins, David | | |

1831

| | | |
|---|---|---|
| Waters, Shely | 170 acres | Round Lick |
| Wilson, William | 80 | Cumberland River |
| Young, David | 247 | Cedar Creek |

### CAPTAIN GREEN'S COMPANY

| | |
|---|---|
| Andrews, Asa | 126 acres |
| Andrews, William | 134 |
| Andrews, Bowlin | |
| Abernatha, Mark | 60 |
| Buchanan, William | 1000 |
| Bryan, Mary | 374 |
| Belcher, David | |
| Belcher, Alexander | |
| Bass, Sion | 110 |
| Cox, Henry | 175 |
| Cox, James | |
| Cox, William | |
| Carter, Bernard | 114 |
| Cartwright, Elizabeth | 200 |
| Carter, F. | 114 |
| Crutchfield, James | 255 |
| Carland, Patsy | 143 |
| Donnell, Levi | 154 |
| Donnell, Allen | |
| Edwards, John | 154 |
| Foster, John | 88 |
| Forbis, Wilie | 100 |
| Forbis, Arthur | 83 |
| Forbis, Elizabeth | 100 |
| Green, William | 39 |
| Green, John | 160 |
| Green, John, Jr. | |
| Gibbs, Thomas | |
| Harley, John | 50 |
| Henderson, Michael | |
| Hearn, James W. | 130 |
| Hearn, N. C. | |
| Hearn, Pernal | |
| Hearn, Ebenezer | 300 |
| Hearn, Wilson | 186 |
| Hankins, Arthur | |
| Hankins, William | |
| Hankins, John | |
| Holland, William W. | |
| Johnson, Phillip | 130 |
| Morris, Peterson | |
| McBride, Daniel | 90 |
| Motheral, James | 280 |
| Maholland, William | 138 |
| New William | 308 |
| Nettles, John A. | 110 |
| New, Nelson | 30 |
| Palmer, John | 160 |
| Palmer, John, Sr. | |

1831

| | |
|---|---|
| Palmer, John, Sr. | |
| Rowton, William | |
| Sims, Caswell S. | |
| Sims, Chesley | 100 |
| Spears, Lewis B. | 50 |
| Tippitt, John | 230 |
| Thomas, Robert | 70 |
| Turner, Elizabeth | 120 |
| Turner, Thomas | 142 |
| Turner, James | 600 |
| Vaughan, Thomas | |
| Whitworth, James | |
| Williford, William H. | 12 |
| Williford, James C. | 73 |
| Williford, George | |

## CAPTAIN LAWRENCE'S COMPANY

| | | |
|---|---|---|
| Alsup, William | 280 acres | Fall Creek |
| Alsup, Samuel J. | | |
| Alsup, Allen | | |
| Alsup, Richard | 382 | Hurricane Creek |
| Adams, James | 98 | Fall Creek |
| Alsup, Joseph | 283 | |
| Alsup, Asap | | |
| Ashley, James | 75 | Hurricane Creek |
| Barker, Richard | | |
| Burke, Thomas | 123 | Hurricane Creek |
| Burke, Fielding | 100 | Fall Creek |
| Burke, Lewis | | |
| Bond, Solomon | | Fall Creek |
| Baskins, Robert M. | 250 | Hurricane Creek |
| Collins, Crafford | | |
| Cluck, William | 100 | Fall Creek |
| Cluck, Henry | 100 | Fall Creek |
| Collins, Elisha | | Hurricane Creek |
| Cluck, Henry, Sr. | 70 | Fall Creek |
| Cullen, M. A. | | |
| Fane, William | | |
| Gray, James | 396 | |
| Gowin, William | | |
| Hatcher, Martin R. | 200 | |
| Haugus, John | 217 | |
| Haugus, Simon | | |
| Holland, Edward | 81 | |
| Harris, Isham | 70 | |
| Jones, John | | |
| Jackson, Larkin | 140 | Fall Creek |
| Jackson, Thomas | | |
| Johnson, Charles | 20 | |
| Lawrence, John | 57 | Hurricane Creek |
| Loving, John | 10 | Fall Creek |
| Lannum, Susan | 50 | |
| McHenry, Jesse | 102 | Hurricane Creek |
| Nelson, William | | |

183

| | | |
|---|---|---|
| Nelson, Garrett | | |
| Randle, Richard J. | 50 | Hurricane Creek |
| Robinson, Meredith | 100 | Fall Creek |
| Reynolds, Thomas | | |
| Ricketts, John L. | | |
| Robertson, Andrew | 62 | Hurricane Creek |
| Roberts, (Luke) | | |
| Richardson, Martin | 95 | Fall Creek |
| Stewart, William | | |
| Sanders, Richard | | |
| Thomas, Jacob | 150 | Fall Creek |
| Woolen, Joshua | 118 | Hurricane Creek |
| Woolen, Edward heirs | 50 | Hurricane Creek |
| Woolen, Moses | 50 | |
| Wood, James | | |
| Wrice, David | 81 | |
| Winters, John | | |
| Zachery, Allen | 50 | Hurricane Creek |

## CAPTAIN JARMAN'S COMPANY

| | | | |
|---|---|---|---|
| Allison, John L. | 30 acres | | |
| Allison, Isaiah | 31 | | |
| Allison, Samuel | 60 | | |
| Abernatha, Charles | | | |
| Ausburn, Thomas | | | |
| Arbuckle, William | | | |
| Bretherton, Henry | | | |
| Bailey, James S. | | | |
| Bretherton, John | | | |
| Barker, William | 106 | | |
| Barnet, William | | | |
| Burke, Arnold | 200 | | |
| Clayton, Benjamin | | | |
| Cain, George | 150 | | |
| Clopton, Walter, Sr. | 204 | Fall Creek | |
| Clopton, Jesse | 149 | | |
| Clopton, William | 125 | | |
| Clopton, John | | | |
| Clopton, Walter, Jr. | 293 | Fall Creek | |
| Cocke, John | 100 | Fall Creek | |
| Cason, Jeremiah | | | |
| Calahan, M. P. | | | |
| Doak, Nelson | | | |
| Dance, John E. | 390 | Fall Creek | |
| Duffer, Edward | | | |
| Duffer, Thomas | | | |
| Fouch, John | 25 | Fall Creek | |
| Florida, Patrick | 83 | | |
| Fouch, Thomas | | | |
| Godfrey, James | 185 | B. Creek | |
| Hannah, Wilson | 174 | Fall Creek | |
| Hooper, G. L. | | | |
| Hight, A. M. | 86 | | |
| Harris, Allen | 215 | Fall Creek | 1831 |

| Name | Acres | Creek |
|---|---|---|
| Huddleston, Anthony | 310 acres | Fall Creek |
| Harris, John R. | | |
| Hight, Joseph W. | | |
| Hight, John T. | | |
| Harris, Jonathan | | |
| Hutchins, William | 677 | |
| Harris, Thomas R. | | |
| Harris, Arthur | 300 | |
| Jones, William | | |
| ( ), Josiah | | |
| Jones, David | | |
| Jones, Henry | | |
| Jones, Robert | | |
| Jenkins, Nathan | 180 | Fall Creek |
| Jenkins, Turner | | |
| Jarman, Robert | 500 | Brady Creek |
| Jarman, Shadrach | | |
| Lasater, Elizabeth | 100 | |
| Lasater, Jacob B. | 90 | |
| Lasater, Hardy | 40 | Fall Creek |
| Lasater, S. H. | 75 | B. Creek |
| Lewis, Edgecomb | | |
| Luster, Presley | 100 | B. Creek |
| Medley, John | 94 | Fall Creek |
| McMurray, John M. | | |
| Matthews, James | | |
| Martin, Jacob | 100 | Fall Creek |
| Martin, Daniel | | |
| Matthews, Matthew | 103 | Bradley's Creek |
| Mathis, Samuel | 25 | Bradley's Creek |
| Mather, Henry | | |
| Mathis, Isaac | | |
| Mount, Richard | 215 | Fall Creek |
| McMinn, Newton | | |
| Persy, Williamson | | |
| Persey, Sherwood | 80 | Fall Creek |
| Puckett, P. R. | | |
| Puckett, Washington | | |
| Prior, John | | |
| Puckett, Isham | | |
| Patterson, Burrell | | Fall Creek |
| Patterson, William | | |
| Persey, Francis W. | | |
| Puckett, Isham | 142 | Fall Creek |
| Puckett, William | 93 | Fall Creek |
| Putman, Isham | 62 | B. Creek |
| Powell, Allen | | |
| Puckett, Frances | 320 | |
| Persy, Boswell | 160 | Fall Creek |
| Quarles, John (Va) | | |
| Quarles, Elizabeth | 473 | B. Creek |
| Sellars, Lard | 228 | |
| Sellars, D. H. | 66 | Fall Creek |
| Smith, William | 80 | Fall Creek |
| Trigg, William | | |

1831

| | | |
|---|---|---|
| Tubb, John | 132 acres | B. Creek |
| Trigg, John | 120 | Fall Creek |
| Trigg, Mary A. | 152 | Fall Creek |
| Trigg, Daniel | 118 | Fall Creek |
| Trigg, Haden | 118 | Fall Creek |
| Trigg, Alanson | 110 | Fall Creek |
| Trigg, Stephen | 103 | Fall Creek |
| Trigg, Abraham | 197 | Fall Creek |
| Trigg, Nancy | 121 | Fall Creek |
| Trigg, Samuel | 207 | Fall Creek |
| Upchurch, Abner | | |
| Winston, Isaac, Sr. | 248 | |
| Winston, Ann | | |
| Williams, William | 225 | |
| Williams & Cain | | |
| Word, William | 470 | Fall Creek |
| Woodard, Baker | 131 | Fall Creek |
| Williams, Elbert | 40 | Fall Creek |
| Wood, A. C. | | B. Creek |
| Winston, John | 160 | B. Creek |
| Williams, Thomas | | |
| Williams, Mahala | 100 | B. Creek |
| Wortham, W. H. | 100 | B. Creek |

## CAPTAIN HUGHLEY'S COMPANY

| | | |
|---|---|---|
| Atherly, Jonathan | 375 acres | Cedar Lick |
| Anderson, Whitmell | | |
| Ames, Thomas | | |
| Blackburn, ( as, Jr. | | |
| Bilbro, William | 250 | Cedar Lick |
| Blackburn, Sally | 50 | Stoner's Creek |
| Barton, Nelly | 196 | Stoner's Creek |
| Baird, Andrew | 686 | Stoner's Creek |
| Booth, Samuel | 260 | Sugg's Creek |
| Baird, David | 200 | Stoner's Creek |
| Binkley, Henry J. | 85 | Sugg's Creek |
| Bridges, John A. | | |
| Carter, Jack | | |
| Cawthon, John R. | | |
| Curd, Thomas | 20 | Cedar Creek |
| Curd, Elizabeth | 131 | Cedar Lick |
| Cawthon, Thomas F. | | |
| Cawthon, John R. | 417 | Stoner's Creek |
| Cawthon, Thomas H. | 120 | Stoner's Creek |
| Clay, Sydney | | |
| Clay, Wadkins | 100 | Sugg's Creek |
| Curd, Price | 250 | Cedar Lick |
| Cowan, William | 192¼ | Cedar Lick |
| Curd, James | 30 | Cedar Lick |
| Chappell, William | 64 | Stoner's Creek |
| Carver, Isaac | | |
| Chandler, Green | 33 | Cedar Lick |
| Donaldson, William heirs | 200 | Cumberland River |
| Drennan, Jonathan | 22 | Sugg's Creek | 1831 |

| Name | Acres | Location |
|---|---|---|
| Donaldson, Robert, Jr. | 445 acres | Cedar Lick |
| Donaldson, Ebenezer | | |
| Donaldson, James | 120 | Cedar Lick |
| Elliott, Robert M. | | |
| Graves, John B. | | |
| Graves, Benjamin | 170 | Stoner's Creek |
| Graves, John G. | 200 | Stoner's Creek |
| Graves, Benjamin F. | 68 | Sugg's Creek |
| Gains, Anthony | 55 | Cedar Lick |
| Guill, Thomas | | |
| Gains, Gideon | 91 | Sugg's Creek |
| Hornsby, John | | |
| Hardy, William | 608 | Sugg's Creek |
| Hughley, Charles | 147 | Sugg's Creek |
| Hughley, Henry | | |
| Hughley, Abram | 208 | Stoner's Creek |
| Hughley, William | | |
| Hubbard, Mariot | | |
| Hooser, Valentine | 160 | Cedar Lick |
| Hamilton, William | 880 | Sugg's Creek |
| Hughley, George | 55 | Cedar Lick |
| Hamilton, Alexander | | |
| Hamilton, Joseph | 200 | Cedar Lick |
| Irwin, John heirs | 1029 | Round Lick |
| Rial, James | | |
| Allen, James | | |
| Jones, Winford | 80 | Sugg's Creek |
| Lane, David | | |
| Lane, Willard | 50 | Stoner's Creek |
| Ligon, James H. | 100 | Cedar Lick |
| Lane, William J. | 86 | Stoner's Creek |
| Lane, Willard | 50 | Stoner's Creek |
| Lane, Armstead | 150 | Stoner's Creek |
| Lane, William F. | | |
| Ligon, John H. | 236 | Sugg's Creek |
| Lindsay, Lewis | | |
| Ligon, Henry | 218 | Sugg's Creek |
| Lumpkin, Obediah | 182 | |
| Martin, John | | |
| McGregor, Flowers | 979 | Cedar Lick |
| McGregor, John | 640 | Cedar Lick |
| (Moody), William | | |
| Matlock, George | 200 | Stoner's Creek |
| McDerman, Briant | 138 | Sugg's Creek |
| Moss, John | 255 | |
| Mosely, Littleton | 45 | Cedar Lick |
| McGregor, William | 275 | Cedar Lick |
| Puckett, John | | |
| Puckett, Charles, Jr. | | |
| Patterson, Isaac | | |
| Rutland, Rutherford | 320 | Stoner's Creek |
| Rutland, Milbry | 324 | |
| Rice, Thomas | | |
| Shepherd, Samuel | 67 | Stoner's Creek |
| Shepherd, John | | |

1831

| | | |
|---|---|---|
| Shepherd, James | | |
| Swingley, Jonas | 45 | Cedar Lick |
| Shaw, John | 165 | Cedar Lick |
| Sullivan, Joab | | |
| (     ), Clement | 100 | Pond Lick |
| Stone, William N. | 50 | Cedar Lick |
| Shepherd, William | 181 | Sugg's Creek |
| Sands, William heirs | 170 | Cedar Lick |
| Smith, Malcom | 100 | Cedar Lick |
| Stewart, Eline | | |
| Shepherd, Samuel | 120 | Sugg's Creek |
| Spickard, John | 100 | Sugg's Creek |
| Sullivan, Azel | 184 | |
| Thompson, William | | |
| Thomason, William | 221 | Cedar Lick |
| Thaxton, Nathaniel | | |
| Tilman, Jacob | | |
| Willis, Edward | 169 | Cedar Lick |
| Walker, Polly | 47 | Cedar Lick |
| Walker, Thomas P. | | |
| minor heir of William Walker | 30 | Stoner's Creek |
| Walker, Samuel | 120 | Stoner's Creek |
| Young, William | | |

## CAPTAIN GWYNN'S COMPANY

| | | |
|---|---|---|
| Avery, George | 120 acres | Sugg's Creek |
| Barefoot, Noah | | |
| Bridges, Joel | | |
| Barr, Joseph | | |
| Baker, John E. | 554 | Sugg's Creek |
| Brown, Samuel | 95 | Sugg's Creek |
| Brown, Robert | | |
| Barr, William G., Jr. | 75 | Sugg's Creek |
| Bond, Robert | 113 | Hurricane Creek |
| Blankenship, Allen | 130 | Sugg's Creek |
| Baird, John | 40 | Sugg's Creek |
| Barbee, Thomas | 40 | Hurricane Creek |
| Baird, John | 85 | Hurricane Creek |
| Bell, James heirs | 150 | Hurricane Creek |
| Bell, Robert | 260 | Hurricane Creek |
| Baird, Hiram | | |
| Bridges, Alexander | | |
| Brown, James M. | 125 | Sugg's Creek |
| Barr, William G. | 200 | Sugg's Creek |
| Chambers, Thomas | 170 | Pond Lick |
| Carter, Gideon | | |
| Currey, Abner B. | 70 | Sugg's Creek |
| Currey, John | 50 | Sugg's Creek |
| Clemmons, Allen | 100 | Pond Lick |
| Clemmons, Alfred | 100 | Pond Lick |
| Clemmons, John | 390 | Pond Lick |
| Cathron, John H. | | |
| Chandler, Jordan | 85 | Pond Lick |
| Chandler, Sarah | 100 | Cedar Lick |
| Chandler, William | | |

1831

| Name | Acres | Location |
|---|---|---|
| Crutchfield, James | | |
| Chandler, Andrew | 175 | Pond Lick |
| Currey, Ezekiel | 44 | Sugg's Creek |
| Dobson, Benjamin | 260 | Sugg's Creek |
| Dobson, William R. | 160 | Sugg's Creek |
| Dobson, Hiram | 100 | Sugg's Creek |
| Drennan, John | | Sinkhole Spring |
| Drennan, James | 125 | Sugg's Creek |
| Drennan, Thomas | 400 | Sugg's Creek |
| Davis, Nathaniel | 146 | Sugg's Creek |
| Devault, Henry | | Hurricane Creek |
| Eskew, Russell | 175 | Sinkhole Spring |
| Eskew, Alexander | 209 | Sugg's Creek |
| Eddins, John | 116 | Sugg's Creek |
| Eskew, John | 100 | Sugg's Creek |
| Eskew, Wilie | | Hurricane Creek |
| Fields, Brice | 71 | Hurricane Creek |
| Gwynn, Andrew | 100 | Sugg's Creek |
| Grinage, William | | |
| Gibson, Isaac | 90 | Pond Lick |
| Gleason, Thomas | 8 | Sugg's Creek |
| Goodman, Claiborne | 200 | Sugg's Creek |
| Gwynn, Robert | 130 | Sugg's Creek |
| Gibson, Samuel | 122 | Hurricane Creek |
| Gwynn, Ransom | 185 | Sugg's Creek |
| Harrell, Lea | 271 | |
| Harris, William G. | | |
| Hooker, Benjamin | 100 | Pond Lick |
| Hooker, Benjamin, Jr. | 145 | Pond Lick |
| Hamilton, George | 800 | Sugg's Creek |
| Haralson, Ephraim | | |
| Hooker, Joshua | 260 | Sugg's Creek |
| Hooker, Matt | 79 | Stoner's Creek |
| Hobson, Nicholas | 100 | Sugg's Creek |
| Hooker, Jonathan | 250 | Pond Lick |
| Hughley, Enoch | 213 | Hurricane Creek |
| Hobson, Benjamin | 95 | Cedar Lick |
| Johnson, William A. | | |
| Jones, Thomas | 50 | Sugg's Creek |
| Kirkpatrick, Thomas | 705 | Sugg's Creek |
| Leath, Peter | 200 | Hurricane Creek |
| Leath, Marcus | 96 | Hurricane Creek |
| Leath, William E. | 100 | Hurricane Creek |
| Lane, Augustus | 60 | Hurricane Creek |
| Loyd, James | | |
| Lindsey, Tailor | 277 | Sugg's Creek |
| Logue, Carnes | 350 | Sugg's Creek |
| Murray, William | 150 | Cedar Lick |
| Mitchell, John | | Pond Lick |
| Moss, Dandridge | 100 | Sugg's Creek |
| Moss, John | 50 | Sugg's Creek |
| Myers, Peter | | |
| McDerman, Wilie | 75 | Pond Lick |
| Miles, Thomas | 100 | Hurricane Creek |
| Miles, Thomas, Jr. | 260 | Hurricane Creek |

1831

| | | |
|---|---|---|
| Miles, Patterson | 349 acres | Hurricane Creek |
| Morris, Benjamin | 77 | Hurricane Creek |
| McFarland, Winny | 266 | Sugg's Creek |
| Nichols, Benjamin | 20 | Pond Lick |
| Partlow, Thomas | 200 | Sugg's Creek |
| Posey, Alexander | 100 | Pond Lick |
| Posey, Alason | 62 | Sugg's Creek |
| Puckett, Ship A. | 200 | Sugg's Creek |
| Rice, Nathaniel | 65 | Sugg's Creek |
| Rice, Benjamin | 144 | Pond Lick |
| Rutland, Joseph | | |
| Rutland, Abednego | 85 | Sugg's Creek |
| Russell, William | 125 | Cedar Lick |
| Ramsey, Richard W. | | |
| Rice, John | 70 | Sugg's Creek |
| Rice, William | 420 | Sugg's Creek |
| Rice, James | | |
| Roach, John | 140 | Sugg's Creek |
| Roach, John, Jr. | 217 | Sugg's Creek |
| Richmond, Joseph | | |
| Stringfellow, James | | |
| Sherrill, Ute heirs | 40 | Pond Lick |
| Sherrill, Archibald | 214 | Pond Lick |
| Swanner, John | 100 | Pond Lick |
| Sullivan, Holland | 149 | Sugg's Creek |
| Smith, Robert heirs | 220 | Sinkhole Spring |
| Smith, Jesse | | |
| Thornton, Seth | 100 | Pond Lick |
| Telford, Thomas | 104 | Sugg's Creek |
| Telford, Hugh, Jr. | | |
| Telford, Hugh | 311 | Sugg's Creek |
| Telford, Samuel | | |
| Telford, Robertson | 73 | Sugg's Creek |
| Townswell, Ozwell | 640 | Sugg's Creek |
| Telford, John | 150 | Sugg's Creek |
| Underwood, Elisha | | |
| Underwood, Perry heirs | 116 | Hurricane Creek |
| Vier, Thomas | | |
| Ward, Andrew | | |
| Whitaker, Mark | 65 | Pond Lick |
| Wynne, Ridley B. | 200 | Hurricane Creek |
| Woodrum, Jacob | 640 | Pond Lick |
| Woodrum, William | | |
| Welch, Thomas | | |
| Welch, John | | Sugg's Creek |
| Wood, Reuben | 220 | Sugg's Creek |
| Yandle, James | 165 | Stone's River |
| Yandle, William | | |

## CAPTAIN HILL'S COMPANY

| | | | |
|---|---|---|---|
| Avery, John | 100 | Barton's Creek | |
| Allen, Absolom | | | |
| Arrington, James | 100 | Sp Creek | |
| Blackwell, Charles | | | |
| Bradley, Thomas | 957 | | 1831 |

| Name | Acres | Location |
|---|---|---|
| Bradley, Charles | 400 acres | Sp Creek |
| Briant, David | 50 | |
| Burnett, John | | |
| Cloah, Elijah | 130 | Cumberland River |
| Cowger, Adam | 140 | Barton's Creek |
| Cox, James | 65 | Spring Creek |
| Cowger, John | 233 | Spring Creek |
| Carr, Dabney | | |
| Carr, John | 150 | Cumberland River |
| Corum, Eli | | |
| Compton, Allen J. | | |
| Crocker, Jesse | 50 | Spring Creek |
| Coppage, John | | |
| Compton, John, Sr. | 111 | Spring Creek |
| Compton, William heirs | 32 | Barton's Creek |
| Compton, John, Jr. | | |
| Carr, Richardson | 108 | |
| Chandler, John | 75 | |
| Davis, Isham | 295 | Barton's Creek |
| Davis, Hezekiah | | |
| Davis, Zachariah | 200 | Barton's Creek |
| Dill, John | | |
| Davis, William | 100 | |
| Dill, William | | |
| Estes, Bartlett | | |
| Estes, Samuel E. | | |
| Ferguson, John | 230 | Spring Creek |
| Gilbert, Ebenezer | 175 | Cumberland River |
| Glenn, Thompson | | |
| Hasley, John | | |
| Hasley, Talbot | 60 | |
| Harpole, Sampson | 64 | |
| Harpole, Adam, Sr. | 193 | Spring Creek |
| Halbrooks, William | | |
| Hunter, Isaac | 200 | Cedar Creek |
| Harpole, George | 166 | Spring Creek |
| Horn, William | | |
| Hughes, Robert | 100 | Spring Creek |
| Hill, Braxton | 58 | Spring Creek |
| Hobson, Henry | 197 | Barton's Creek |
| Holt, Jesse | | |
| Hunter, Jacob | | |
| Hobson, Benjamin H. | 150 | Spring Creek |
| Holman, Thomas P. | | |
| Jackson, William H. | 200 | Spring Creek |
| Jewell, Barnet | | |
| Jarrett, Francis | | |
| Jewell, William | | |
| Jewell, Joshua | | |
| Jones, Thomas | 16 | Barton's Creek |
| Jarrett, John | 141 | D & S Creeks |
| Jarrell, Hiram | | |
| Kennedy, William | | |
| Kindred, Thomas | 56 | Cumberland River |
| King, George | 50 | Spring Creek |

1831

| | | |
|---|---|---|
| Moser, Daniel | 160 acres | Barton's Creek |
| Moss, Thomas B. | 200 | Barton's Creek |
| Mosely, John | | |
| Miles, William | | |
| McDaniel, James | 274 | Cumberland River |
| McDaniel, Nancy | 88 | Cumberland River |
| Mansfield, Granville | 100 | Cumberland River |
| Mabry, David D. | | |
| Martin, William L. | 220 | Spring Creek |
| Measles, Wiley | | |
| Moss, William | 229 | |
| for Matthew Carr's heirs | 134 | |
| for James C. Moss heirs | 30 | |
| Martin, James | 55 | |
| Melton, Benjamin | | |
| Melton, Thomas | 150 | |
| Melton, John | | |
| Nowlin, Bird | | |
| Peace, William H. | 564 | Barton's Creek |
| for Walker Kizias | 50 | Cedar Lick |
| Paine, John | | |
| Proctor, Edmund | 180 | Spring Creek |
| for Hill's heirs | 132 | |
| Rochel, William | | |
| Robb, John | 316 | Spring Creek |
| Robb, Jesse | | |
| Sypert, Robert | 245 | Barton's Creek |
| Shepherd, Thomas C. | | |
| ( lock, Dudley | 40 | Spring Creek |
| Swann, John | 184 | Cedar Creek |
| Summerhill, William | | |
| Sutton, Nicy | 130 | Spring Creek |
| Sypert, Thomas | 40 | |
| Taylor, James | 125 | |
| Tucker, Green | 202 | Spring Creek |
| Travillian, Edward | 200 | Cumberland River |
| Tallow, Benjamin | 19 | Barton's Creek |
| Tallow, Peterson | 70 | Barton's Creek |
| for Compton's heirs | 64 | |
| Walker, Radford | 57 | Spring Creek |
| Walker, Noah | | |
| Walker, William | | |
| Walker, Millner | 286 | Barton's Creek |
| Walker, Delila | 500 | Barton's Creek |
| Wright, Berry | 90 | Cumberland River |
| Wright, James | 107 | Barton's Creek |
| Walker, Henry heirs by H. Hobson | 300 | Barton's Creek |
| Walker, William heirs by R. Walker | 230 | |
| Walker, Elizabeth | | |
| Yourie, Patrick | 100 | Spring Creek |

## CAPTAIN LAWRENCE'S COMPANY

| | | |
|---|---|---|
| Atwood, Edwin | 40 acres | H. Creek |
| Barbee, William H. | | |
| Belcher, Isaac | | 1831 |

| Name | Acres | Location |
|---|---|---|
| Belcher, James | | |
| Blythe, Alexander | | |
| Booker, William L. | 50 | |
| Burke, Samuel | | H. Creek |
| Campbell, Hugh | | H. Creek |
| Compton, Matthew | 70 | |
| Davidson, James | | H P Creek |
| Ellis, Radford | | |
| Grindstaff, Isaac | 187 | H. Creek |
| Hunt, Archibald | 100 | H. Creek |
| Herndon, Young L. | | S. Fork |
| Jenkins, Joseph | | |
| Jackson, David | | |
| King, Joseph | | P. Creek |
| Lawrence, William | 433 | H. Creek |
| Lawrence, Turner M. | 220 | H. Creek |
| Lawrence, William, Sr. | 214 | H. Creek |
| Lawrence, Joseph B. | 213 | H. Creek |
| Mallory, William | 64 | P. Creek |
| Mullinax, Zadock | 198 | S. Fork |
| Mullinax, John | | |
| McMillin, John | 70 | S. Fork |
| Neal, Isaac | | |
| Neal, Elizabeth | 250 | H. Creek |
| Neal, Claiborne W. | 100 | H. Creek |
| Neal, Madison | | |
| Neal, Charles | | |
| Neal, William | 435 | |
| Neal, Pallis | 439 | |
| Oakley, William | 189 | S. Fork |
| Philips, George | 20 | |
| Smith, Daniel | 203 | |
| Tally, Haley | 122 | H. Creek |
| Tally, Archibald | | |
| Turner, James | 75 | |
| Turner, Jeremiah | 765 | H. Creek |
| Tally, Payton | | |
| Vantrease, Jacob | 267 | |
| Vantrease, John | | |
| Vantrease, William | | |
| Wheeler, Nathan | 34 | H. Creek |
| Woody, James | | |
| Wood, James | 131½ | H. Creek |
| Wooden, Fielden | 64 | H. Creek |
| Wooden, John | | |
| Young, Joseph D. | 50 | S. Fork |
| Young, Sarah | 60 | S. Fork |

## CAPTAIN LARSON'S COMPANY

| Name | Acres | Location | |
|---|---|---|---|
| Atkinson, James | 90 acres | Cedar Creek | |
| Bell, Nathaniel | | | |
| Babb, Bennett | 400 | S & B Creeks | |
| Blaze, George | 109 | Cedar Lick | |
| Baxter, John | | | |
| Baxter, George | 157 | Cedar Lick | 1831 |

| Name | Acres | Location |
|---|---|---|
| Bowden, Bennett H. | 52 acres | Barton's Creek |
| Cole, Sarah | 123 | Cedar Lick |
| Cook, Thomas | 186 | Spencer's Creek |
| Cooper, John heirs | 109 | Spencer's Creek |
| Debnum, Robert B. | | |
| Duke, John | 109 | Spencer's Creek |
| Duke, William | 98 | Cedar Lick |
| Duke, Uriah | | |
| Donaldson, Humphrey | 200 | Cedar Lick |
| Denton, Edward | 200 | Cedar Lick |
| Denton, James | | |
| Estes, Thomas | 70 | Cear Lick |
| Eddins, William, Sr. | 250 | Barton's Creek |
| Eddins, William, Jr. | | |
| Eatherly, John | 213 | |
| Ferguson, Lemuel | | Spencer's Creek |
| Guthrie, Daniel J. | 29 | Barton's Creek |
| Gholdston, John | 340 | Barton's Creek |
| Gholdston, John A. | | |
| Hicks, Thomas | 77 | Barton's Creek |
| Irby, Carter | 92 | Cedar Lick |
| Jarrott, Devereaux | 200 | Barton's Creek |
| Jackson, Asa | | |
| Jolly, Isham | 114 | Barton's Creek |
| King, John W. | | |
| McFarland, John | 259 | Cedar Lick |
| McFarland, James | 800 | |
| Moore, Warren | 105 | |
| McWherter, James | | |
| McWherter, George A. | 44 | Cedar Lick |
| Maddox, Richard | 120 | Barton's Creek |
| McWherter, Samuel C. | 64 | |
| Proctor, Green | | |
| Proctor, David | 50 | S C |
| Paine, Jesse | 217 | Cedar Lick |
| Powell, John | 400 | Barton's Creek |
| Payton, John W. | 250 | B. Creek |
| Rotramel, Frederick | | |
| Rotramel, Henry | | |
| Robertson, Higdon | 320 | |
| Robertson, Lewis | | |
| Rencher, Henry | | |
| Rhodes, Elisha | | |
| Smith, James | 184 | S. Creek |
| Sherrill, Newman | 145 | B. Creek |
| Simmons, Joseph | | |
| Tarver, Silas | 125 | Cedar Lick |
| Tarver, Benjamin | 196 | Spencer's Creek |
| Tucker, Benjamin | 154 | Cedar Lick |
| Tucker, John W. | | |
| Vivrett, Micajah | | |
| Vivrett, Henry | 98 | |
| Wynne, Albert H. | 218 | Cedar Lick |
| Winford, William W. | | |
| Winford, Benjamin heirs | 400 | B. C. |

1831

| | |
|---|---|
| White, Edward | 200 acres  S C |
| Winford, Alexander S. | 190  B C |
| Winter, Wilburn R. | |
| Winter, Ambrose V.  heirs | 210 |
| Webber, James | |
| White, William | 582  S C |
| Wynne, Alanson G. | |
| Wadkins, Joel | 70 |
| Wynne, John R. | 1204  B & S Creeks |

## CAPTAIN HAMILTON'S COMPANY

| | |
|---|---|
| Aston, Alexander | 144 acres  Cedar Creek |
| Aston, Joseph | |
| Aston, James | |
| Beasley, Josiah | 160 |
| Beasley, Benny B. | |
| Bonner, Thomas L. | 94 |
| Bonner, John S. | |
| Bodine, Thomas | 90 |
| Bodine, Westen | |
| Bonner, Williamson | 50 |
| Bonner, Benjamin F. | 62 |
| Barksdale, Francis | |
| Brown, Henry | 43  Cumberland River |
| Bonner, John | 150  Cumberland River |
| Carruth, Walter | |
| Carruth, Eli S. | |
| Carruth, Alexander | 140  Cedar Creek |
| Carruth, Alexander, Jr. | 210 |
| Carruth, William S. | 100  Cedar Creek |
| Chambers, John | 100 |
| Chambers, Lewis | 260  Cumberland River |
| Chambers, Alexander  heirs | 140 |
| Chambers, Nicholas | |
| Crutchfield, Henry | 80 |
| Campbell, Harrison | |
| Carruth, Joseph | 90  Cumberland River |
| Dwyer, Lewis H. | |
| Eason, Eli E. | 56 |
| Ferguson, Robert | |
| Freeman, Daniel | |
| Figures, Mary | 150  Cedar Creek |
| Figures, Batt | 250  Cedar Creek |
| Fobbs, Alfred M. | |
| Glenn, Giles H. | Cedar Creek |
| Glenn, Martha C. | 246  Cumberland River |
| Glenn, Benjamin | |
| Glenn, John | |
| Glenn, William | |
| Grooms, John | |
| Hamilton, Thomas J. | |
| Hughes, Tarlton | 106  Cumberland River |
| Harris, Richard | |
| Jackson, Mark | 180  Cumberland River |
| Johnson, Samuel | |

1832

| | | |
|---|---|---|
| Jackson, John M. | 152 acres | Cumberland River |
| Jopling, Elihu | 100 | Cedar Creek |
| Jackson, Henry | | |
| Jackson, Daniel | | |
| Locke, Thomas | 130 | Cumberland River |
| Locke, Charles | 70 | C. Creek |
| Locke, James W. | 110 | Cumberland River |
| Locke, Frances | 100 | Cumberland River |
| Lyon, James | | |
| Lyon, Volney | | |
| Lyon, Richard | 150 | Cumberland River |
| McDonald, Stephen | 107 | |
| Moser, Adam | 440 | Cumberland River |
| Mitchell, Everett | | |
| Martin, Matt | | |
| Motsinger, Elijah | | |
| Mitchell, Taswell | 180 | C. Creek |
| Newsom, A. B. | 200 | Cedar Creek |
| New, James | | |
| New, William O. | | |
| New, William | 300 | Cedar Creek |
| Petway, William | 96 | Cumberland River |
| Patterson, Hugh | 60 | Cumberland River |
| Pearson, William | | |
| Pearson, Howell | | |
| Ray, Martin B. | | |
| Ramsey, Richard B. | | |
| Ramsey, Thomas R. | | |
| Sims, Edmund | | |
| Sims, Christopher | | |
| Sims, Robert | | |
| Tarpley, Sterling | 500 | |
| Tarpley, Steth | | |
| Thompson, Swann | | |
| Thompson, Henry | | |
| Tarpley, John | | |
| Underwood, Joel | | |
| Underwood, Milton | | |
| Vaughan, James | | |
| Warren, Benjamin | 230 | |
| Walton, James | | |
| Woodall, Henry H. | | |

## CAPTAIN SMITH'S COMPANY

| | | | |
|---|---|---|---|
| Baird, John | 366 acres | Cumberland River | |
| Baird, William heirs | 56 | Cumberland River | |
| Birthwright, Williamson | 209¼ | Drake's Lick | |
| Baker, Joseph | | | |
| Ballentine, Coster F. | 130 | Cedar Lick | |
| Lindsley, Baird | | | |
| Cooley, Henry | 66 | Cumberland River | |
| Crabtree, Lorenzo D. | 25 | Drake's Lick | |
| Carroll, John | 400 | Cumberland River | |
| Chandler, James L. | | | |
| Carter, Nathaniel G. | 198 | Cumberland River | 1831 |

| | | |
|---|---|---|
| Crabtree, Jacob | | |
| Davis, Samuel | 250 | Cedar Lick |
| Eatherly, Isaac | 227 | Stoner's Creek |
| Eatherly, John R. | | |
| Grundy, Felix | 300 | |
| Goodman, John | | |
| Hill, Thomas | | |
| Hill, Isaac P. | | |
| Hodge, William | | |
| Hyde, Richard | 400 | Cedar Lick |
| Hooper, William | | |
| Johnson, William | 170 | Cumberland River |
| Johnson, Isham | 115 | Drake's Lick |
| Jones, Wood | 215 | |
| Lyle, Jesse | | |
| McCorkle, Miles | 200 | Stoner's Creek |
| Moore, Whitfield | 100 | Drake's Lick |
| Medlin, Gray | | |
| McClain, Alfred | 320 | Cedar Lick |
| McClain, Alexander F. | 71 | Cumberland River |
| McClain, Josiah S. | 170 | Cedar Lick |
| McClain, Mary P. | | Cedar Lick |
| McClain, Martha D. | 116 | Cedar Lick |
| Foster, Isabella Ann | 100 | Spring Creek |
| Hartwell, Mabry | | |
| Mays, Craddock H. | | |
| Mayson, Ramsey L. | 200 | Cedar Lick |
| Neighbours, John | | |
| Norris, Samuel | 111 | Cumberland River |
| Nooner, John H. | | |
| Neighbours, Thomas | | |
| Puckett, John | | |
| Puckett, Charles | 80 | Stoner's Creek |
| Perry, Albert | | |
| Roland, Isaac | 100 | Cumberland River |
| Roland, James | | |
| Robertson, Hugh | 93 | Stoner's Creek |
| Steele, George | | |
| Stevenson, Isaac T. | 106 | Cedar Lick |
| Sanderson, Wade | 214 | Cumberland River |
| Swift, Clevias W. | | |
| Smith, George | 350 | Cumberland River |
| Sayle, William P. | | |
| Smith, Hiram | | |
| Sims, L. L. heirs | 120 | Cumberland River |
| Smith, Harry (Va) | 100 | Cumberland River |
| Sanders, James | 600 | near Drake's Lick |
| Sanders, Lance | 300 | near Wood's Ferry |
| Thomas, David | | |
| Taylor, John D. | | |
| Thrift, A. D. | 106 | Cumberland River |
| Taylor, Solomon | | |
| Taylor, Howard | | |
| Taylor, Caleb | 150 | Drake's Lick |
| Taylor, Isaiah P. | | |

1831

| | | |
|---|---|---|
| Taylor, John | 138 acres | Cedar Lick |
| Trigg, A. heirs | 640 | Spring Creek |
| Vick, Samuel | | |
| Wright, Ellis G. | | |
| Williams, Jeremiah | | |
| Williams, Allen | | |
| Williams, Nathaniel | | |
| Watson, Thomas | 272 | Cumberland River |
| Willis, William | 269 | Drake's Lick |
| Williams, Thomas | | |
| Watson, Joseph | 400 | Cumberland River |
| York, Edmund | | |
| Yeargin, James | | |

## CAPTAIN WILSON PATTERSON'S COMPANY

| | | |
|---|---|---|
| Alexander, N. G. | 40 acres | Round Lick Three Forks |
| Bass, Etheldred | 186 | Round Lick |
| Bass, Ezekiel, Jr. | 33 | Round Lick |
| Barclay, B. P. | | |
| Bass, Archimack | 120 | Round Lick |
| Bass, John for Goody's heirs | 324 | Round Lick |
| | 26 | Hickman's Creek |
| Bridges' heirs | 36 | Round Lick |
| Bass, Ezekiel, Sr. | 390 | Round Lick |
| Bass, Warren | | |
| Berry, Nathaniel | | |
| Banfield, George | | |
| Cartwright, Richard | 117 | Round Lick |
| Campbell, E. G. | | |
| Cobb, Christopher | | |
| Cartwright, John | 157 | Cedar Creek |
| Campbell, William | 160 | Round LIck |
| Campbell, Hugh L. | | |
| Campbell, Archibald | 150 | Round Lick |
| Compton, Alexander J. | | |
| Compton, Charles | | |
| Compton, Rebecca | 30 | Round Lick |
| Carlock, Eben | | |
| Duke, L. C. | | |
| Garner, Wilie | | |
| Garner, John | | Round Lick |
| Garner, Jeremiah | 34 | Round Lick |
| Grindstaff, David | | |
| Eaton, Joseph | | |
| Hearn, George | 555 | |
| Hancock, Nancy | 108 | |
| Hearn, Matthew | 144 | Round Lick |
| Hinson, Lazarus | | |
| Hearn, Jacob | 220 | Round Lick |
| Hearn, Thomas | | |
| Hudson, William | 31 | |
| Jones, William F. | 154 | |
| Jacobs, Edward G. | 39 | Round Lick |
| Long, Robert | | |
| Massie, A. A. | 125 | Round LIck    1831 |

| | | |
|---|---|---|
| Maxwell, William, Sr. | 138 acres | Round Lick |
| Maxwell, Sutton M. | | |
| Morgan, William | | |
| Neal, George | 90 | Round Lick |
| Neal, Ashley | 173 | Round Lick |
| Nettles, William A. | 228 | Round Lick |
| Nettles, heirs | 8 | Round Lick |
| Nooner, Nathan | | |
| Oakley, John | | |
| Patton, Jonathan | 89½ | Round Lick |
| Patterson, William | 240 | Round Lick |
| Patton, Thomas | 80 | Round Lick |
| Patton, Joseph | 140 | Round Lick |
| Patterson, Lemuel | 68 | Round Lick |
| Philips, William | 270 | Round Lick |
| Pemberton, John | 51 | Round Lick |
| Philips, Josiah | 84 | Round Lick |
| Patton, Samuel | 178 | Round Lick |
| Philips, John | 260 | Round Lick |
| Philips, Benjamin | 160 | Round Lick |
| Philips, David | 118 | Round Lick |
| Philips, Joseph | 101 | Round Lick |
| Philips, Benjamin, Jr. | | |
| Patterson, L. F. | 105 | |
| Patterson, Julian | 180 | Round Lick |
| Patterson, Esther | 60 | Round Lick |
| Rudder, Edwin | | |
| Rudder, Benjamin | 360 | Round Lick |
| Rudder, Harris | 43 | Round Lick |
| Reed, Robert | 82 | Round Lick |
| Smith, Jacob | 48 | Round Lick |
| Smith, Daniel | 110 | Round Lick |
| Shanks, William | 100 | Round Lick |
| Sanders, Simeon | | |
| Smith, Nicholas | 175 | Round Lick |
| Shoars, Phillip | 75 | Round Lick |
| Simpson, George | | |
| Thompson, E. A. | 456 | Round Lick |
| Tracy, Thomas | | |
| Taylor, John | | |
| Vaught, Elijah | 466 | Round Lick |
| Vowell, W. A. | 40 | |
| Williams, A. S. | 47 | Round Lick |
| Womack, Elijah for | 30 | Round Lick |
| McKinnis' heirs | 30 | Round Lick |
| Womack, Rachel | 160 | Round Lick |
| Waters, William | 125 | Round Lick |
| Wood, Jesse | | |
| Waters, Wilson T. | 170 | Round Lick |

## CAPTAIN MAJOR'S COMPANY

| | | |
|---|---|---|
| Alexander, William S. | 116 acres | |
| Alexander, John | 150 | |
| Alexander, Isabella | 75 | |

1831

| | | |
|---|---|---|
| Braden, Charles | 500 acres | |
| Booker, Samuel | 160 | |
| Booker, John | 65 | |
| Bond, Lewis | 150 | |
| Bond, William | | |
| Boothe, Mary | 82 | |
| Bingham, Thomas | 106 | |
| Bingham, John | | |
| Bradshaw, Amzi | 85 | |
| Bingham, Thomas W. | | |
| Cunningham, Moses | 155 | |
| Cocke, Valentine | | |
| Cunningham, John | 83 | |
| Cunningham, James | 67 | |
| Comer, Samuel | | |
| Comer, Reuben P. | 79 | |
| Cannon, James heirs | 166 | |
| Craper, James | 100 | |
| Craper, Azra | 117 | |
| Cox, Robert | | |
| Donnell, Adnah | 245 | |
| Doak, Martha | 150 | |
| Davis, Terrell | | |
| Drollender, William | | |
| Donnell, George | 574 | |
| Donnell, James | 250 | |
| Davis, Elizabeth | 168 | |
| Davis, Thomas | | |
| Davis, Robert | | |
| Donnell, Josiah | 211 | |
| Doak, John F. | 180 | |
| Donnell, William P. | 194 | |
| Davidson, Wilson | | |
| Donnell, Robert | 105 | |
| Donnell, Martha | 63 | |
| Donnell, John | 120 | |
| Donnell, William S. | 214 | |
| Donnell, William C. | 330 | |
| Donnell, Jane | 161 | |
| Doak, Alanson F. | 80 | |
| Foster, John D. | 285 | Spring Creek |
| Foster, John W. | | |
| Foster, Alfred H. | | |
| Foster, Alexander | 300 | Spring Creek |
| Foster, James | 250 | Spring Creek |
| Foster, Emsley D. | | |
| Foster, Albert | 100 | Spring Creek |
| Graves, Bachelor | | |
| Graves, Lorenzo | | |
| Graves, Asa | | |
| Hearn, Purnell | 250 | Spring Creek |
| Hancock, John heirs | 100 | Spring Creek |
| Hudson, Obediah | 193 | |
| Hearn, Stephen H. | 472 | Spring Creek |
| Holbert, Joel B. | 50 | Round Lick     1831 |

| | | |
|---|---|---|
| Hudson, Paschal | | |
| Hancock, Westly | 60 | Round Lick |
| Jackson, Jesse | 83 | Cumberland River |
| Jones, Isham | | |
| Jones, Richard | | |
| Jones, Edward | 79 | |
| Jopling, Robert heirs | 90 | Spring Creek |
| Jenning, Samuel | | |
| Langley, John | | |
| Lindsay, Josiah B. | 153 | |
| Lea, Samuel | | |
| Lea, David | | |
| Lea, Hiram | | |
| Long, Alexander M. | | |
| Lea, Benjamin | 55 | Spring Creek |
| Massey, Eli | 15 | Spring Creek |
| Martin, Lindsey | 125 | |
| Major, John, Sr. | 465 | |
| Marrs, Martin | 240 | |
| Moser, Henry | 188 | |
| Marrs, William | 75 | |
| Marrs, Mary | 200 | |
| Moore, David B. | | |
| Marrs, Alexander | 170 | |
| Morrison, Hugh | 50 | |
| Maddox, Notley | 300 | |
| Maddox, William | | |
| Major, John Capt. | 100 | |
| Massey, Lewis | | |
| Nickens, Calvin | | |
| Patterson, David | | |
| Powell, Abraham | 150 | Spring Creek |
| Powell, James | | |
| Powell, Wilie | | |
| Oliver, James | | |
| Quesenberry, John | 150 | Hurricane Creek |
| Ragsdale, Asa | 150 | Spring Creek |
| Ragsdale, Alfred | 15 | Sinking Creek |
| Scott, William heirs | 74 | Spring Creek |
| Smith, John | 110 | Spring Creek |
| Scott, Samuel heirs | 60 | |
| Sparks, Nathan | 208 | Spring Creek |
| Smith, John C. | | |
| Smith, Thomas L. | | |
| Smith, David | | |
| Shovel, Ephraim | 160 | |
| Smart, John | 145 | |
| Spears, Sarah | 50 | Spring Creek |
| Thorn, John H. | | |
| Thorn, David K. | | |
| Trice, Edward | 76 | |
| Thompson, Moses | 414 | Spring Creek |
| Thompson, William A. | 100 | |
| Thompson, Moses H. | 36 | |
| Thorn, William | 150 | |

1831

| | | | |
|---|---|---|---|
| Vowell, William A. | | | |
| Vowell, James L. | 320 | | |
| Williams, Nathaniel | 130 | | |
| Waddle, John | | | |
| Wilie, Mary Ann | 90 | Spring Creek | |
| Young, John | | | |

## CAPTAIN ODUM'S COMPANY

| | | | |
|---|---|---|---|
| Arnold, John | | | |
| Alexander, Ezekiel | | Sander's Fork | |
| Alexander, Abner | 87 | | |
| Arnold, heirs | 148 | Sander's Fork | |
| Arnold, Nancy | 73 | Sander's Fork | |
| Alexander, Aswin | | | |
| Bryson, Joseph, Jr. | | Sander's Fork | |
| Bryson, John, Sr. | 45 | Sander's Fork | |
| Bryson, John heirs | | | |
| Bogle, George | 340 | Sander's Fork | |
| Bogle, Joseph H. | | | |
| Bryson, Joseph, Sr. | 45 | Sander's Fork | |
| Bryson, Samuel | | | |
| Bogle, Sarah | | | |
| Bogle, Joseph heirs | 100 | Sander's Fork | |
| Bryson, Samuel, Sr. | 100 | Sander's Fork | |
| Bogle, Thomas heirs | 100 | Sander's Fork | |
| Byrn, James | 247 | Lick Creek | |
| Bumpass, Robert | 650 | Barnett's Creek | |
| Bell, Elisha | 63 | Luck's Creek | |
| Cooper, Christopher | 257 | Sander's Fork | |
| Cooper, Sam | 100 | Luck's Creek | |
| Cooper, Frances | | Sander's Fork | |
| Cooper, Abraham | | Sander's Fork | |
| Cooper, Benjamin B. | | Sander's Fork | |
| Davenport, Edmund | 40 | Sander's Fork | |
| Davenport, Reuben | 27 | Sander's Fork | |
| Davenport, Warren | 50 | Sander's Fork | |
| Davenport, Abraham | 20 | Sander's Fork | |
| Davenport, Hardy heirs | 20 | Sander's Fork | Joseeph Bryson, extr. |
| Davenport, Wiley | | Sander's Fork | |
| Francis, Armstead | 270 | Sander's Fork | |
| Francis, Epaphroditus | | | |
| Gunn, Ann | 220 | Sander's Fork | |
| Gibson, William | | | |
| Higgins, William | 50 | Hurricane Creek | |
| Higgins, John, Sr. | 100 | Hurricane Creek | |
| Howard, Mary | 179 | Sander's Fork | |
| Harris, Elijah | | Luck's Creek | |
| Ingram, Martin | | | |
| Jones, Erasmus, Sr. | 226 | Hurricane Creek | |
| Jones, Erasmus, Jr. | | | |
| Jones, Aaron | | | |
| Jones, Michael | 16 | | |
| Kennedy, William B. | 116 | | |
| Landson, Hugh | 130 | Hurricane Creek | 1831 |

| | | |
|---|---|---|
| Leech, Thomas | 120 acres | Leech's Creek |
| Leech, John heirs | 70 | Leech's Creek |
| Leech, James | 70 | Barnett's Creek |
| Moore, Abner | 410 | Sander's Fork |
| Morrison, Andrew | | |
| Milligan, David | | |
| Marshall, Robert | 380 | Sander's Fork |
| Montgomery, Elizabeth | 179 | Sander's Fork |
| Montgomery, Alexander | 157½ | Sander's Fork |
| Montgomery, James | 157½ | Sander's Fork |
| McKee, Daniel | 75 | Lick Creek |
| Marshall, Carson | 175 | Lick Creek |
| Milligan, James | 24 | Hurricane Creek |
| McMinn, Zedediah | 237 | Barnett's Creek |
| McMinn, Jehu | 244 | Lick Creek |
| Owen, Nelson | | Hurricane Creek |
| Odum, James, Sr. | 290 | Sander's Fork |
| Odum, Samuel | 32 | Sander's Fork |
| Odum, James S. | 340 | Sander's Fork |
| Odum, William C. | | |
| Odum, Benjamin F. | | |
| Owen, Josiah | 243 | Lick Creek |
| Owen, Jesse | 88 | Hurricane Creek |
| Patterson, John | 263 | Lick Creek |
| Patterson, Ezekiel | 60 | Lick Creek |
| Rackley, John | | Sander's Fork |
| Reed, Hali | | Sander's Fork |
| Reed, James | 5 | Sander's Fork |
| Reed, Levi | | |
| Richardson, Brice | | |
| Stanley, John | | Hurricane Creek |
| Somers, Anthony | 275 | Sander's Fork |
| Somers, Matthew | 470 | Sander's Fork |
| Somers, James | 233 | Sander's Fork |
| Somers, John W. | 90 | Sander's Fork |
| Somers, Reddin | | |
| Sauls, Henry | | |
| Shelton, William | 218 | Leech's Creek |
| Thomas, James | 163 | Barnett's Creek |
| Thomas, Jacob heirs | 147 | Barnett's Creek |
| Thomas, John G. | | |
| Witherspoon, Alexander heirs | 56 | Sander's Fork |
| Witherspoon, Enos | | |
| Wilson, Charles | 25 | Lick Creek |
| Willard, John | 20 | Hurricane Creek |
| Wall, Merrett | | |

CAPTAIN YOUNG'S COMPANY

| | |
|---|---|
| Arnold, William | 70 acres |
| Arnold, John | 113 |
| Alison, Elizabeth | 160 |
| Adams, Parker | 62½ |
| Baxter, John | 78 |
| Briant, John | 100 |
| Browning, Guilford | |

1831

| | | |
|---|---|---|
| Briant, Richard | 123 acres | |
| Belt, Dodson | 104 | |
| Cloyd, James | 127 | |
| Coffee, James D. | | |
| Garmany, Margaret | 132 | |
| Goodman, Edmund | 183 | |
| Grier, Samuel | | |
| Grier, James | 416 | |
| Grier, Ezekiel C. | | |
| Green, James | | |
| Gum, Sarah | 63 | |
| Holland, Alexander G. | 300 | |
| Hicks, John | | |
| Harris, Braxton | 400 | |
| Hammons, Samuel H. | | |
| Johns, William | | |
| Jones, William F. | | |
| Jewell, William | 65 | |
| Johnson, Dennis K. | | |
| Lasater, Frederick | | |
| Lasater, Abraham | | |
| Landson, Susannah | 300 | |
| Lackey, Sealy | 50 | |
| Landson, Robert | | |
| Martin, George W. | 330 | |
| Morrison, Robert | 70 | |
| Morrison, Joseph | | |
| Puckett, Coleman | 87 | |
| Pennebaker, Samuel W. | 613 | |
| Quarles, James | 170 | |
| Rhodes, Clayton | 318 | |
| Reynolds, John | 50 | |
| Sims, Matthias | 100 | |
| Sims, Thomas | 80 | |
| Sims, James T. | 100 | |
| Sublett, William L. | 61 | |
| Sharp, Joseph | 501 | |
| Sharp, Ezekiel A. | | |
| Stroud, John | | |
| Stroud, Archibald | 150 | |
| Smith, William P. | 37 | |
| Stevens, Elisha C. | | |
| Smith, George K. | 150 | |
| Thomas, Jacob H. | 300 | |
| Thomas, John F. | 32 | |
| Witty, Ezekiel C. | 120 | |
| Weatherly, Wright M. | 70 | |
| Weatherly, Abner | | |
| Young, Charles | 240 | |

## CAPTAIN CARLOCK'S COMPANY

| | | | |
|---|---|---|---|
| Bone, James | 172 | Fall Creek | |
| Bone, Ednah | | | |
| Bone, Margaret | 263 | Fall Creek | |
| Bone, James | 140 | Fall Creek | 1831 |

| | | |
|---|---|---|
| Bone, John | | |
| Bone, John | 110 | Fall Creek |
| Bone, James C. | 130 | Fall Creek |
| Bone, Henry F. | 125 | Fall Creek |
| Belt, Jeremiah | 100 | Fall Creek |
| Blankenship, Daniel | | |
| Barnett, Isaac | | |
| Bond, James | 270 | Hurricane Creek |
| Bonfield, John | 140 | Fall Creek |
| Cummings, William | 330 | |
| Copeland, Samuel | 125 | Fall Creek |
| Crook, William | | |
| Comer, John | | Fall Creek |
| Carlock, Epenetus | 70 | Spring Creek |
| Clements, Samuel  heirs | 143 | Hurricane Creek |
| Cason, Joseph | 520 | Fall Creek |
| Carpenter, Conrod | 327 | Fall Creek |
| Cox, Garrett | 278 | Fall Creek |
| Donnell, David  guard for William P. Foster | 185 40 | Fall Creek Spring Creek |
| Donnell, John | 130 | Fall Creek |
| Donnell, Adnah | | |
| Donnell, John | 104 | Spring Creek |
| Edwards, Green B. | | |
| Edwards, Sterling | | |
| Edwards, Sally | 125 | Hurricane Creek |
| Goodwin, Allen H. | | |
| Gilliam, Ann | 150 | Fall Creek |
| Gilliam, William | | |
| Gilliam, Edmund | 150 | Fall Creek |
| Goard, William | 50 | Fall Creek |
| Gunn, John | | |
| Hudson, Richard | 50 | Fall Creek |
| Hurd, John A. | | |
| Henderson, Preston | 35 | Hurricane Creek |
| Howard, Bradford | 225 | Fall Creek |
| Hackney, Seth | | |
| Hazelwood, John | | |
| Jones, David, Sr. | 60 | Fall Creek |
| Jones, Samuel | | |
| Lanier, William | | |
| Merritt, William B. | 371 | Spring Creek |
| Merritt, Thomas J. | 215 | Spring Creek |
| Merritt, John W. | 185 | Fall Creek |
| Martin, Amos | | |
| Mayson, James | | |
| Merritt, James P. | 242¼ | Fall Creek |
| Moore, R. R. | | |
| Moore, John | | |
| McMinn, Elihu | 200 | Fall Creek |
| Norvell, James | | |
| Pursell, Hiram | | |
| Patterson, Newsom | | |
| Porterfield, Samuel C. | | |
| O'Neal, Asa | 40 | Fall Creek |

1831

| | | |
|---|---|---|
| O'Neal, William P. | | |
| Quarles, Milton | 200 | Fall Creek |
| Quesenberry, James | 100 | Hurricane Creek |
| Rhea, William | | |
| Rhea, Archibald | 67 | Fall Creek |
| Rhea, Robert | | |
| Smith, Charles | 150 | Spring Creek |
| Sherrill, Abel | 125 | Fall Creek |
| Smith, William | 500 | Fall Creek |
| Simpson, Robert | 100 | Fall Creek |
| Short, Thomas | | |
| Sellars, Alvis | 75 | Fall Creek |
| Sellars, Alfred | 51 | Fall Creek |
| Simmons, Alexander | | |
| Smith, George | 234 | Fall Creek |
| Sanders, Jordan heirs | 400 | Fall Creek |
| Smith, John | 150 | Fall Creeks |
| Simpson, Hannah | | |
| Teague, William | 200 | Hurricane Creek |
| Teague, Joshua | | . |
| Weatherly, William | | |
| Weatherly, Denny | | |
| Ware, Dudley | 80 | Fall Creek |
| Word, John | 170 | Fall Creek |
| Wallace, Cary | 280 | |
| Word, Henry B. | 40 | Fall Creek |
| Williams, Julius H. | 106 | |
| Womack, Robert | 52 | Fall Creek |
| Williams, Washington | 123 | Fall Creek |
| Williams, Williamson | 194 | |
| Williams, Thomas | | |

## CAPTAIN GORE'S COMPANY

| | | |
|---|---|---|
| Askins, Franklin | | |
| Askins, Addison | | |
| Barber, Josephus | 160 acres | Round Lick |
| Bartlett, B. F. | | |
| Barber, John | | |
| Barbee, Mary | | |
| Biles, Jane | 100 | |
| Barbee, Thomas | | |
| Branch, Thomas | 104 | |
| Boyd, William | 198 | |
| Barbee, Daniel | 175 | |
| Boon, John | | |
| Baker, John | | |
| Branch, Fanny | 193 | |
| Branch, Andrew J. | 81 | |
| Branch, Robert C. | 20 | |
| Branch, James H. | 93 | |
| Barbee, Joseph, Jr. | | |
| Baker, Jeremiah | 81 | |
| Baird, David | 135 | |
| Brown, Thomas | | |
| Biles, M. H. | | |

1831

| | |
|---|---|
| Bomer, Thomas | |
| Compton, William | 157 |
| Compton, Margaret | 130 |
| Compton, Elizabeth | |
| Cartwright, Matthew T. | 36 |
| Cox, Thomas | |
| Christie, Thornton | |
| Caplinger, John | 45 |
| Clark, George Esqr. | 310 |
| Corder, Benjamin | |
| Chapman, Thomas | |
| Conrod, John | |
| Donnell, Leo | |
| Doss, Samuel | |
| Dearing, Alben | 164 |
| Dowly, William | |
| Dowly, Robert | 221 |
| Davis, Solomon | 139 |
| Echols, Joseph | |
| Edge, Elam | 84 |
| Faust, Elizabeth | 100 |
| Gore, Joseph | |
| Grindstaff, John | 100 |
| George, John | 100 |
| Holmes, James | 220 |
| Heflin, Joab | |
| Hailey | 137 |
| Johnson, Margaret | 200 |
| Kelly, Dennis heirs | 100 |
| Kooliss, William | |
| Lawrence, John, Jr. | 156 |
| Lawrence, John, Sr. | 220 |
| Marks, James | 106 |
| Manning, Robert | |
| Moore, Thomas | |
| Moore, James | 85 |
| Marks, John | 50 |
| Midgett, Richard | |
| Nunn, Nicholas | |
| New, William | 110 |
| Newby, Roland | |
| Newby, Whaley | 100 |
| Odum, Britain | 70 |
| Philips, Thomas | 135 |
| Pritchett, George heirs | 75 |
| Pritchett, Catharine | 32 |
| Rains, John | |
| Rodgers, John | |
| Searcy, Hiram | |
| Spring, Aaron | |
| Sanders, Joseph | |
| Smith, John | |
| Steele, Miner | |
| Taylor, J. B. | 75 |
| Taylor, John | 300 |
| | 100 |

183

| | | |
|---|---|---|
| Taylor, Joshua | 140 acres | |
| Taylor, J. B. | | |
| Taylor, Fanny | 60 | |
| Taylor, Robert | 36 | |
| Taylor, John L. | 110 | |
| Tracy, Evan | 150 | |
| Thornton, Henry | 50 | |
| Womack, Richard | 170 | |
| Waters, Shelah, Sr. | 414 | |
| Waters, William | 100 | |
| Young, James | 125 | |

## CAPTAIN ADAMS' COMPANY

| | | |
|---|---|---|
| Alexander, Isaac | | |
| Adamson, Simon | 314 acres | P. Creek |
| Adams, John | 226 | Smith's Fork |
| Adamson, Weales | 67 | Smith's Fork |
| Brashers, John | 50 | Smith's Fork |
| Brogan, Armstead | 105 | P. Creek |
| Chumley, Dennis | | |
| Chumley, Daniel | 41 | Smith's Fork |
| Candler, John | | |
| Chumley, Richard | | |
| Candler, Winston | | Smith's Fork |
| Chumley, William | 90 | Smith's Fork |
| Coleman, Theophilus | | |
| Dunn, William | | |
| Edge, Edward | 50 | Smith's Fork |
| Fuston, James G. | 180 | P. Creek |
| Fite, Joseph | 247 | P. Creek |
| Fite, Leonard | 200 | P. Creek |
| George, Charles | | |
| George, James, Jr. | | |
| Gatlin, Joseph | 55 | P. Creek |
| George, James, Sr. | 142 | P. Creek |
| Goth( ), Robert | | |
| Hutcherson, Bailey | | Smith's Fork |
| Hathaway, Elijah | | |
| Hass, Henry | | |
| (Henry), Isaac | 50 | |
| Hughes, John | | |
| Hathaway, John | | |
| Hass, John | 160 | Smith's Fork |
| Hays, Nathaniel | 84 | P. Creek |
| Hays, James | | |
| Hays, Pleasant | | |
| Jennings, Joel | 120 | Smith's Fork |
| Jones, Thomas | 26 | Smith's Fork |
| Johnson, Hardy | | |
| Kelly, Nathaniel, Sr. | 44 | Smith's Fork |
| Kelly, Nathaniel, Jr. | | |
| Moore, Lemuel | 100 | P. Creek |
| McKee, Robert | | |
| Neighbours, William | 75 | Payton's Creek |
| Oliver, William | 150 | Payton's Creek | 1831 |

Parson, Elijah O.
Pugh, George R., Jr.
Pugh, Isaiah
Perriman, James
Rutledge, Daniel L.
Robinson, Edward
Robinson, James          230  Payton's Creek
Rich, Obadiah
Rogers, Robert
Robinson, Stephen
Sharp, Benjamin
Sadler, Jane             120  Smith's Fork
Sadler, William
Smith, Harris
Turner, Jonathan         120  P. Creek
Underwood, Joseph
Wilson, Allen
Williamson, Robert
Williams, Thomas J.      610  P. Creek
Wilson, William
Webb, Woodson
Williamson, Zachariah     50  P. Creek
Williamson, Thomas
Williams, Burnett             P. Creek

### CAPTAIN JOHN R. WILSON'S COMPANY

Alford, Ludwich B.       75 acres  Sugg's Creek
Alford, Wilie            247  Sugg's Creek
Alexander, George        316  Stoner's Creek
Ahart, Moses             144  Sugg's Creek
Ahart, Nimrod
Ahart, Joseph
Alexander, Benjamin      142
Breedlove, Aylette
Brooks, Moses T.          10  Stoner's Creek
Bernard, Horatio
Cloud, Joseph             74  Stoner's Creek
Crudup, John
Cowgill, John             10  Stoner's Creek
Cannon, John N.
Caldwell, John
Cloyd, David              72  Stoner's Creek
Cloyd, Newton
Cannon, Samuel           135  Stoner's Creek
Cloyd, John              142  Stoner's Creek
Cloyd, Alexander          94  Stoner's Creek
Cloyd, Ezekiel           220  Stoner's Creek
Davis, John              385  Stoner's Creek
Drollender, Mary         200  Stoner's Creek
Evans, Anderson
Drennan, William
Green, Samuel                 Stoner's Creek
Gleaves, Absolum         130  Stoner's Creek
Green, John
Guill, Josiah            120  Sugg's Creek        1831

| | | |
|---|---|---|
| Guill, Barnett | | |
| Hays, Hugh | 422 | Stoner's Creek |
| Hager, Jonathan | 61 | Stoner's Creek |
| Hewet, John | | |
| Hays, William J. | 88 | Sugg's Creek |
| Hays, Jane | 45 | Stoner's Creek |
| Hays, Elizabeth | 68 | Sugg's Creek |
| Hays, James | 68 | Sugg's Creek |
| Hays, Preston | 63 | Stoner's Creek |
| Hughley, Samuel | 223 | Sugg's Creek |
| Hamilton, Thomas | 152 | Sugg's Creek |
| Harrison, Answorth | | |
| Humphreys, Henry | | |
| Hessey, John | 432 | Sugg's Creek |
| Heralson, Zary | 110 | Sugg's Creek |
| Hamilton, Joseph | 200 | |
| Hamilton, Robertson T. | | |
| Hamilton, James C. | | |
| Jenkins, William | 100 | Sugg's Creek |
| Jackson, Obadiah, Jr. | | |
| Jackson, Obadiah, Sr. | 158 | |
| Jackson, Abraham | | |
| Jenkins, Tarber T. | | |
| Jenkins, John | | |
| Jackson, William | | |
| Jackson, Josiah | 152 | Stoner's Creek |
| Ligon, Josiah | 38 | Sugg's Creek |
| Lane, Tyre | 75 | Sugg's Creek |
| Lantern, Thomas | | |
| Lantern, Henry | | |
| Lea, Cloe | | |
| Lantern, Joseph | 60 | Sugg's Creek |
| Moore, Joseph | | |
| McCully, David | | |
| Melvin, John | | |
| McCully, John | 70 | |
| Martin, Rebecca | 75 | Sugg's Creek |
| Murray, John | | |
| Murray, Jeremiah | | |
| O'Briant, William | | |
| O'Briant, Cheatam | | |
| Pride, Shelton | 200 | |
| Parham, Mary | 80 | |
| Radford, Edward | | |
| Rutland, Henry | | |
| Rutland, Isaac | 263 | Sugg's Creek |
| Smith, Mary R. | 76 | Stoner's Creek |
| Sharp, James G. | 130 | Stoner's Creek |
| Stewart, Joseph | 132 | Stoner's Creek |
| Seaborn, Isaac R. | 225 | Stoner's Creek |
| Seaborn, John H. | | |
| Seaborn, Christopher | | |
| Sullivan, Jesse, Jr. | | |
| Sperry, Thomas | 260 | Sugg's Creek |
| Sperry, Samuel | | |

1831

| | | |
|---|---|---|
| Searcy, Reuben | 380 acres | Cedar Lick |
| Searcy, William | | |
| Thompson, James | 225 | Stoner's Creek |
| Thompson, Elizabeth | 200 | Stoner's Creek |
| Thompson, John heirs | 112 | |
| Thompson, Margaret | | |
| Tate, Robert L. | 212 | Stoner's Creek |
| Tate, John W. | | |
| Tate, Zachariah | 128 | Stoner's Creek |
| Thompson, Ausborne | 130 | Stoner's Creek |
| Thompson, William | 147 | Cedar Lick |
| Tate, Richard B. | 77 | Stoner's Creek |
| Williamson, George | 360 | Stoner's Creek |
| Williamson, William | 532 | Stoner's Creek |
| Williamson, Margaret | | |
| Williamson, Joseph | | |
| Wright, Thomas | 230 | Stoner's Creek |
| Wright, Charles, Sr. | 75 | Stoner's Creek |
| Wood, Archer | 184 | Stoner's Creek |
| Wright, Joseph | 200 | Sugg's Creek |
| Wright, Samuel, Sr. | 103 | |
| Wright, Samuel, Jr. | 52 | Sugg's Creek |
| Wright, Samuel | | |
| Wright, Jonathan | 28 | Sugg's Creek |
| Wilson, John R. | 150 | Cedar Lick |
| Williamson, John A. | | |
| Wright, Solomon D. | | |
| Williamson, Margaret, Jr. | | |
| Wilkinson, Meredith | 120 | Stoner's Creek |
| Wright, Lewis | 36 | Sugg's Creek |
| Wright, Charles, Jr. | | |
| Williamson, Nancy | | |
| Wilson, James | 108 | |
| Williamson, Thomas | 215 | |

## CAPTAIN CAPLINGER'S COMPANY

| | |
|---|---|
| Anderson, William | |
| Bailey, Jonathan | 390 |
| Bell, Risen | |
| Bell, George | |
| Bell, Benjamin T. | |
| Bell, Benjamin | |
| Bone, Henry P. | 170 |
| Bradley, John, Sr. | 156 |
| Bradley, Bernard | |
| Bradshaw, John | 36 |
| Cutrell, Midget | |
| Caplinger, Solomon | 200 |
| Cartwright, Samuel | 130 |
| Caplinger, William | |
| Chastain, Elisha | 166 |
| Chick, Ambler | |
| Cutrell, Joseph | 60 |
| Coe, Isaiah | 100 |
| Cartwright, Hezekiah | 240 |

1831

| Name | Acres |
|---|---|
| Dice, William | 35 acres |
| Dudley, Woodson | 45 |
| Davidson, William | 180 |
| Davidson, Francis | 116 |
| Duff, Robert | |
| Dotson, William | |
| Enoch, Davis | 113 |
| Davis, E. Washington Phelps, guard. | |
| Echols, David | |
| Edwards, James | 331 |
| Fisher, Phillip | 211 |
| Grisham, R. W. heirs | 307 |
| Goodall, William | 125 |
| Goodall, Hardin | 124 |
| Goodall, Franky | 100 |
| Gill, William B. | 103 |
| Grissom, Joseph | |
| Goodall, John T. | 100 |
| Huffman, Robert | 153 |
| Huffman, Leonard | |
| Huffman, Archibald | |
| Huffman, Burrell | |
| Harrison, William | 50 |
| Hobbs, Campbell | 89 |
| Henry, Charles | 88 |
| Herndon, John | |
| Henry, Esacour | |
| Jones, Elizabeth | 136 |
| Lindsay, Elizabeth | 150 |
| Lannum, Thomas | 40 |
| Murphy, Aaron | 85 |
| Motsinger, Joshua | |
| McBride, Daniel | |
| Manning, Lewis | |
| Manning, Katharine | 60 |
| Manning, John | 60 |
| Marks, Thomas | 125 |
| Mayo, Stephen | |
| Marks, James | |
| Midgett, George C. | |
| Palmer, William | 150 |
| Pride, Frances | |
| Philips, Alfred | 200 |
| Philips, William | 77 |
| Philips, Bailey | 74 |
| Reese, Thomas B. | 240 |
| Reese, William | |
| Rather, Elizabeth | |
| Seay, John | 100 |
| Spring, John, Jr. | 120 |
| Spring, Moses | 100 |
| Spring, Samuel | 200 |
| Spring, Abner | 190 |
| Spring, John, Sr. | 40 |
| Swann, George | 90 |

1831

| | | |
|---|---|---|
| Swann, John the 3rd | 177 acres | |
| Swann, William, Jr. | | |
| Sweatt, William Sr. | 400 | |
| Sweatt, Edward | 400 | |
| Sweatt, Robert | | |
| Sweatt, Azariah | | |
| Sweatt, Joseph | 100 | |
| Swann, William | 100 | |
| Swann, James | 130 | |
| Swann, John | 50 | |
| Spring, Benjamin | | |
| Sadler, John W. | | |
| Turner, William | | |
| Thomas, Neal | | |
| Violett, Anderson | | |

## CAPTAIN RAGLAND'S COMPANY

| | | |
|---|---|---|
| Barton, Gabriel | 113 acres | Spring Creek |
| Brevard, Thomas | 187 | Spring Creek |
| Bradshaw, James C. | | |
| Billings, Benjamin H. | | |
| Belcher, John R. | | |
| Billings, David | 640 | |
| Cox, Anderson | 124 | |
| Clary, James | | |
| Clifton, Thomas | 150 | |
| Coe, William | 220 | |
| Dallace, Robert | 90 | Cedar Creek |
| Dallace, Morgan | | |
| Delap, Thomas | | |
| Edwards, William | 163 | Spring Creek |
| Elmore, Jesse | | |
| Ellis, Robert | | |
| George, Lucas | | |
| Hankins, Richard | 430 | |
| Hankins, John | | |
| Hankins, Matthew | 100 | Spring Creek |
| Hartsfield, William | 140 | |
| Jackson, Thomas R. | | B C |
| Jackson, Thomas | 111 | S. Creek |
| Johnson, Matthew | 100 | S. Creek |
| Jones, Wiley | | |
| Johnson, Joshua | | |
| Lumpkin, Charles | | |
| Lumpkin, James | | |
| Newman, John | | |
| Motley, B. T. | 2602 | S. Creek |
| Mabry, B. T. | 40 | C C |
| Mason, Thomas | | |
| McNelly, Enoch | 150 | |
| Organ, Enos | 107 | |
| Owens, Jeremiah | | |
| Organ, Simpson | | |
| Pemberton, William | 50 | C C |
| Pemberton, Joshua | | |

1831

| | | |
|---|---|---|
| Pemberton, John | 50 acres | |
| Powell, Scymon | | |
| Stone, Samuel | | |
| Stone, Thomas | 130 | Spring Creek |
| Shorter, B. B. | 189 | B. Creek |
| Seat, Martin | | |
| Satterfield, Reuben | 124 | |
| Tally, Henry | 85 | Spring Creek |
| Tally, Ephraim | | |
| Williams, Robert | | |
| Watkins, David | | |
| Wier, Thomas | 25 | |
| Wier, James C. | | C. Creek |
| Wood, James | 33 | |
| Wier, John | | |
| Wier, Joseph | 100 | |
| Walls, Alexander | | |

## CAPTAIN LANE'S COMPANY

| | | |
|---|---|---|
| Baird, John | 400 acres | Pond Lick |
| Baird, Hardy | 100 | Barton's Creek |
| Bennett, William K. | 73 | Cedar Lick |
| Baird, Batt | | |
| Bennett, Baxter | | |
| Baird, Clinton | 69 | Pond Lick |
| Cunningham, Joseph | | Pond Lick |
| Climer, John | 40 | Pond Lick |
| Chandler, Eddins | | |
| Crawford, Edmund | 100 | Pond Lick |
| McCartney, Lewis heirs | 233 | Barton's Creek |
| Cummings, John | 100 | Pond Lick |
| Caraway, Lovett | 81 | Cedar Lick |
| Cole, Elisha | 95 | Cedar Lick |
| Escue, Benjamin | 110 | Cedar Lick |
| Escue, Alfred | | |
| Gholdston, Elis | 50 | Cedar Lick |
| Grigg, Jesse A. | | |
| Graves, Lewis | | |
| Goodman, Albert M. | | |
| Huddleston, William W. | 50 | |
| Hill, William | 100 | Pond Lick |
| Hearn, George | | |
| Jolly, Hansell B. | | |
| Jackson, James | 100 | H. Creek |
| Lane, John | 132 | Pond Lick |
| Lannom, John | | |
| Lane, Thornton | | |
| Lane, Christopher | | |
| Lane, Armstead | | |
| Neal, Zeppiniah, Sr. | 225 | Pond Lick |
| Neal, Zeppiniah, Jr. | 42 | Pond Lick |
| Ozment, John | 100 | Pond Lick |
| Ozment, Richard, Sr. | | H. Creek |
| Ozment, David | | |
| Ozment, Richard, Jr. | | |

1831

| | | |
|---|---|---|
| Ozment, Thomas | | |
| Rice, John | 90 | Pond Lick |
| Polon, John W. | 100 | Cedar Lick |
| Rice, James | | |
| Ray, William | | |
| Ragsdale, L. M. | | |
| Robertson, Newel | 89 | Cedar Lick |
| Right, Abraham | 75 | Pond Lick |
| Richmond, Alexander | 296 | Pond Lick |
| Rogers, Brinkley M. | 260 | Pond Lick |
| Roper, James | 320 | Barton's Creek |
| Richmond, Daniel & Andrew | 476 | Pond Lick |
| Swain, William M. | 60 | Pond Lick |
| Swain, Caleb W. | | |
| Swain, James M. | | |
| Sullivan, Jesse | 150 | Pond Lick |
| Sullivan, Barnet J. | | |
| Summers, James | 500 | Pond Lick |
| Summers, George | | |
| Spinks, John | 130 | Pond Lick |
| Sheron, Joanna | 290 | Pond Lick |
| Sheron, Thomas | | |
| Stewart, John | | |
| Swingley, George | 63 | Barton's Creek |
| Sullivan, Benjamin | 50 | Pond Lick |
| Smart, Phillip | 150 | Pond Lick |
| Shannon, Henry | 50 | Barton's Creek |
| Swain, John H. | | |
| Toule, Richard | | |
| Terrill, William | 349 | |
| Young, Stacy | | |
| Young, Francis | 207 | P. Creek |
| Young, Gilbert | | |

## CAPTAIN JENNINGS' COMPANY

| | | |
|---|---|---|
| Alsup, William H. | 279 acres | Fall Creek |
| Alsup's heirs | 171 | Fall Creek |
| Beadles, Ozburn | 150 | Smith's Fork |
| Beadles, William | | |
| Bailey, Jonathan | 24½ | Smith's Fork |
| Beadles, Abram | 77 | Smith's Fork |
| Blankenship, C. | 175 | |
| Craddock, John C. | | |
| Craddock, Nancy | 170 | Smith's Fork |
| Carpenter, W. W. | | |
| Candler, John | 50 | Smith's Fork |
| Collier, Joseph | | |
| Etheridge, Silman | | |
| Edwards, Warren | | |
| Garrison, Samuel | | |
| Harris, Wallace | 60 | Smith's Fork |
| Hill, Samuel | 600 | Smith's Fork |
| Jennings, William | 225 | Smith's Fork |
| Jennings, Uriah | | |
| Jennings, Jacob | 35 | Fall Creek |
| Jennings, Robert, Jr. | 90 | Fall Creek |

```
Jennings, E. C.
Jennings, Ashel         79   Smith's Fork
King, David
King, David            100
Lester, William        144   Smith's Fork
Lester, Manson
Lester, Joshua         103   Smith's Fork
Lester, Edward
McCaffrey, James       146
Mount, William
McHany, William
Porterfield, James
Porterfield, S. H.     590
Patterson, Burwell
Patterson, Lewis       150   Smith's Fork
Smith, Shadrach        210   Fall Creek
Smith, Shadrach C.
Spradley, A. B.
Shearl, William
Smith, Sampson         310   Fall Creek
Smith, William H.       47
(  ly, Tavner           35   Smith's Fork
Tolbert, William
Wood, Benton
Ward, Hasa              42   Fall Creek
Warren, William        176   Fall Creek
Warren, Enoch
Williams, Jeptha
Williams, Argales
Williams, Edward
Williams, Moses              Smith's Fork
Webb, Anderson          40
Whitlow, Henry         310
Whitlock, Thomas                                  1831
```

The aggregate amount of the county taxes for the year 1831 on land:

```
    294,866 acres of land at 57½¢ per hundred acres   $1105.76
      2139  Free poles at 25¢ on each                   534.75
      2358  Black poles at 50¢ on each                 1179.00
       110  Town lots at 50¢ on each                     55.00
        48  Stud horses at 100¢ each                     48.00
To which add ½ of the state tax on land                2922.49
Black poles and town lots                               725.50
22 retail stores at $5.00 omitted above is              110.90
```

## CAPTAIN HOLMAN'S COMPANY 1832

| | |
|---|---|
| Allcorn, Prudence | 250 acres |
| Allcorn, James | 640 |
| Allcorn & Johnson | |
| Anderson, S. | |
| Allcorn, John heirs | 224 |
| Allen, Mary | |
| Ashworth, Jasper R. | 375 |
| Brown, Samuel | |
| Bettes, Alfred | |
| Bonner, Thomas E. | |
| Bullard, George H. | 200 |
| Bone, A. M. | |
| Booker, David | |
| Burton, Robert M. | 684 |
| Brown, Jorden | |
| Chambliss, Henry | |
| Chapman, Benjamin | 100 |
| Connor, William | |
| Candler, Henry | |
| Chapman, Silas | |
| Carr, Elisha G. | 270 |
| Chandler, Kellis E. | 100 |
| Chandler, Robert | 100 |
| Cox, William | 60 |
| Cummings, George D. | 100 |
| Cox, John | 2 |
| Crutchfield, Henry | 80 |
| Clifton, William | 80 |
| Canady, William | |
| Clark, Joseph | |
| Conyers, Andrew | |
| Caruthers, Robert L. | 176 |
| Cummings, Charles | 100 |
| Cage, Thankful | 200 |
| Carruth, J. C. | 2 |
| Crutcher, Foster G. | |
| Cook, A. | 87 |
| Dew, Arthur | 120 |
| Dearing, Lewis | |
| Dew, Davis | |
| Dew, Matthew | |
| Douglass, Burchett | 498 |
| Dew, Nancy | 12 |
| Dew, Jack H. | |
| Dwire, John | |
| Douglass, Norval | 234 |
| Douglass, Henry L. | |
| Dew, Elizabeth | |
| Davidson, John | |
| E ), Adam | |
| Echols, Joseph | |
| Edwards, Thomas | |
| Finley, O. G. | 512 |

| | |
|---|---|
| Fuliton, Robert | 30 acres |
| Fuliton, Nathan | 7 |
| Frazer, James | 167 |
| Foster, Elizabeth, Sr. | 100 |
| Freeman, Joseph | |
| Forbes, Arthur | 83 |
| Gibson, Jesse | 50 |
| Garrison, Person | 130 |
| Golloday, Isaac | |
| Gillespie, David | |
| Gillespie & Mabry | |
| Harrison, Seth | 100 |
| Holman, John B. | 140 |
| Holman, Robert M. | 100 |
| Hibbitts, David C. | 230 |
| Hoggatt, James W. | 87 |
| Hunt, Britain B. | |
| Hill, John | |
| Hegerty, Patrick | |
| Hearn, Samuel | |
| Hearn, Edward | |
| Hegerty, Dennis | |
| Harrison, Joshua | |
| Ingram, John | |
| Irvin, James M. | |
| Irby, John | 100 |
| Johnson, Joseph | |
| Jones, John | |
| Johnson, James H. | 140 |
| Johnson, Henry H. | |
| Joall, John B. | |
| (    ), William | |
| Johnson, Rollen H. | |
| Killinsworth, James | |
| Lytle, W. F. | |
| Loyd, Lemuel | 107 |
| Loyd, Jarratt | 122 |
| Ligon, Robert | 117 |
| (    ), Levi. | |
| Michaels, James | 175 |
| McClain, Josiah S. | 50 |
| McClain, Martha D. | 110 |
| Mabry, George W. | 110 |
| McClain, William P. | |
| Matthews, William | |
| Miles, William | |
| (    ), William | |
| Nolin, M. | |
| Palmer, John | |
| Proctor, Green | |
| Prim, William | |
| Pemberton, Joseph | |
| Roulston, James C. | 20 |
| Ray, John | |
| Rutledge, Alexander | 140 |

1832

| | |
|---|---|
| Smith, Henry F. | 20 acres |
| Stewart, E. R. | |
| Searcy, W. W. | |
| Summerhill, William | |
| Sanders, James | |
| Sypert, Lawrence | |
| Seawell, H. H. | |
| Sypert, Hardy | |
| Seay, John | |
| Spradley, James | 18 |
| Sypert, A. | |
| Sypert, William L. | |
| Trout, Adam | |
| Tapp, John S. | 187 |
| Tapp, John | |
| Trayler, Edward D. | 60 |
| Thompson, Thomas J. | |
| Tolliver, Zachariah | |
| Trigg, Lancen heirs | 640 |
| Sherroll, Andrew | |
| Vick, Allen W. | |
| Wheer, William | |
| Wilson, Joseph L. | 173 |
| Wilson, W. | |
| Woolard, John | |
| Woodrill, H. H. | |
| Wall, Bird | 140 |
| White, W. L. | |
| White, E. A. | |
| White, John | |
| Yerger & Golloday | |

## CAPTAIN TREWETT'S COMPANY

| | | |
|---|---|---|
| Billingsley, John | | |
| Bagwell, Lunceford | 75 | |
| Bland, Arthur | | |
| Clemmons, Etheldred | 119 | |
| Clemmons, Jeptha | | |
| Caraway, Moses | 179 | |
| Caraway, Merritt | 20 | |
| Caraway, Willice | | |
| Comer, James | | |
| Caraway, John | | |
| Connor, William | 103 | Barton's Creek |
| Covington, George W. | | |
| Clanton, Edmund | | |
| Casselman, Benjamin heirs | 260 | |
| Casselman, Jacob | 29½ | |
| Brewer, Morris | 143 | |
| Freeman, Obediah | 117 | |
| Green, Isham | | |
| Green, Thomas B. | | |
| Green, Thomas | | |
| Guthrie, James B. | 132 | |

1832

| | |
|---|---|
| Grissom, John | 89 acres |
| Golsom, Charles M. | |
| Hickman, Snoden | 124½ |
| Harrison, Thweatt heirs | 120 |
| Hallum, Robert | 47 |
| Hallum, Andrew | 62 |
| Hallum, Gilpin | 76 |
| Hail, Jamima | |
| Hickman, John | 160 |
| Hickman, William | |
| Hickman, Snoden | |
| Holloway, Ezekiel | |
| Hancock, L. | |
| Hancock, Melinda | 23 |
| Holloway, Levi | |
| Hancock, Dawson | 500 |
| Hancock, Henry M. | 158 |
| Hickman, L. | 79 |
| Hickman, Right | |
| Hancock, Nelson | 96 |
| Hancock, Lesley | |
| H ), Jesse | |
| Hancock, Lee | 170 |
| Hartsfield, William for Anderson, P. heirs | 75 |
| Harris, Alfred B. | 80 |
| Hallum, P. & R. | 33 |
| Hawks, John | |
| Hancock, Green | |
| Justice, John | |
| Johnson, Robert | 218 |
| Justice, Lemuel | 170 |
| Link, James A. | |
| Ozment, James | |
| Moore, Jesse | |
| Moore, James | |
| Pentecost, Thomas | |
| Pool, Giles B. | |
| Richmond, James | 861 |
| Read, Elum | |
| Read, William | |
| Ranels, John N. | |
| Read, Henry | |
| Reed, Robert | |
| Read, Federick | |
| Reed, Robert D. | |
| Rogers, Henry | |
| Shannon, Robert | 300 |
| Shannon, Robert, Jr. | 130 |
| Shannon, John A. | |
| Shannon, Henry | 300 |
| Seth, Steed | |
| Skean, John | 160 |
| Shorter, Berry B. | 128 |
| Tribling, William | |

1832

| | |
|---|---|
| Terrell, Thomas | |
| Truett, Elige | 531 |
| Truett, Henry | |
| Tucker, Andrew | |
| Thrower, Eli | |
| Wade, Charles | |
| Vivrett, William | 90 |
| Wade, Allen W. | 60 |
| Wade, Robert | |
| Wade, T. H. | |
| Wall, Bird heirs | 205 |
| Wall, Benjamin | 100 |
| Wall, Adam | |
| Wall, Bird | 200 |

## CAPTAIN ANDERSON'S COMPANY

| | |
|---|---|
| Anderson, Samuel | |
| Anderson, John | |
| Anderson, James heirs | 178 acres |
| Barrett, William | 120 |
| Bond, William | 30 |
| Bernett, Thomas | 150 |
| Bacchus, Minchey | 50 |
| Bennett, John | 110 |
| Bernett, Jacob | 25 |
| Bond, John | 44 |
| Beard, William | 690 |
| Bond, David | 200 |
| Baird, James | |
| Baird, Len | |
| Bond, Samuel | |
| Bond, Seldon | 163 |
| Clemmons, Samuel T. | 40 |
| Clemmons, James | 178 |
| Callis, Richard heirs | 40 |
| Edwards, Crawford | |
| Edwards, Henry | |
| Edwards, John | 20 |
| Edwards, Eli | |
| Edwards, Edward | |
| Edwards, Eaton | |
| Edward, ( tock | 190 |
| Edwards, John | 50 |
| Edwards, Henry | 488 |
| Edwards, Hugh | |
| Edwards, John | 62 |
| Edwards, Green D. | 100 |
| Donnell, Samuel | 195 |
| Fields, Richard | 30 |
| Fields, John | |
| Guest, John | |
| Gipson, John | 80 |
| Gipson, Aron | 25 |
| Grissom, Elijah | |

1832

| | |
|---|---|
| Grissom, Stephen | |
| Grissom, Asa | |
| Howell, Joseph | |
| Huddleston, G. A. | 50 |
| Hudson, William | 50 |
| Hackney, Seth | |
| Hail, Thomas | 30 |
| Harris, Isham | 57 |
| Hancock, Wesley | 60 |
| Hancock, John | 100 |
| Howard, William | 80 |
| Jackson, James | 100 |
| Merritt, Lewis | 198 |
| Merritt, Silas | |
| Merritt, Sherwood | |
| Merritt, S. | |
| Merritt, Obediah | 5 |
| Milton, Jacob | |
| Martin, Lindsay | 125 |
| Morris, William | 25 |
| Milton, Joseph | |
| Merritt, Mark | |
| Ozment, Samuel | 20 |
| Ozment, Jonathan heirs | 178 |
| Ozment, Sarah | 89 |
| Phipps, William | 656 |
| Patterson, Peter | |
| Parton, Henry | |
| Quesenberry, Daniel | 15 |
| Quesenberry, James | 150 |
| Reynolds, Zebby | |
| Rogers, Tobias | |
| Rogers, Samuel | |
| Ragsdale, G. | |
| Spain, John | |
| Townsend, Richard | |
| Spain, Labon | 200 |
| Sanderson, John | |
| Warren, Seloma | 30 |
| Warren, William | |
| Warren, Sina | 100 |

## CAPTAIN LASH'S COMPANY

| | | |
|---|---|---|
| Archer, Jacob | 114 | |
| Anderson, Richard | 120 | |
| Alexander, George | | |
| Alexander, John | | |
| Anderson, Francis | 36 | |
| Burns, Brantley | 156 | |
| Bundy, John | 149 | |
| Bundy, David | | |
| Bundy, Nathan | | |
| Bone, Enos | 80 | |
| Coe, John | | |
| Carruth, James | 120 | 1832 |

| | |
|---|---|
| Carruth, Walter | 270 acres |
| Cates, John | 30 |
| Carruth, James T. | |
| Clifton, Lovett | 102 |
| Clifton, Jesse heirs | 40 |
| Chamberland, Charles | 65 |
| Clark, Parson | |
| Carlin, Patsy | 142 |
| Clifton, Hannah | 150 |
| Clifton, Thomas | 165 |
| Clifton, Benjamin heirs | 90 |
| Donnell, Robert | 235 |
| Donnell, Thomas | 200 |
| Guthrie, Daniel | 160 |
| Graves, Joel | |
| Hearn, William | |
| Hearn, Stephen L. | |
| Hartsfield, Solomon | 266 |
| Hearn, Ebenezer | |
| Harrison, Elizabeth | 100 |
| Hancock, Martin | 180 |
| Harris, Charles | |
| Holbert, Joel B. | 50 |
| Hancock, Lemuel | 35 |
| Hart, William | 45 |
| Hearn, Milbry | 208 |
| Harrington, Song Bird | |
| Harris, Thomas | |
| Ingram, James | |
| Harris, Edward | 130 |
| Ingram, Thomas | |
| Ingram, Allen | |
| Johnson, Jemima | |
| Johnson, Robert | 267 |
| Jones, John | 240 |
| Jones, Allen | 64 |
| Jones, Allen | 60 |
| Jackson, Jesse | 83 |
| Johnson, Jordan | |
| Jones, James | |
| Lindsley, Philip | 256 |
| Lester, Henry D. | 27 |
| Lester, L. | |
| Lash, John C. | |
| Lash, Harman | |
| Loyd, Anderson | 47 |
| Lane, Woodson | 42 |
| Morris, Isham | 360 |
| Moore, George D. | |
| Moxley, Josiah | 194 |
| Martin, James | 250 |
| Nickens, James | 100 |
| N ), John | 130 |
| Pemberton, Joel | |
| Richardson, Willis | 183 |

| Name | Acres |
|---|---|
| Smith, Hary | 200 acres |
| Scott, James P. | 65 |
| Smith, Josiah, Jr. | |
| Smith, Josiah, Sr. | 120 |
| Smith, James | |
| Smith, John Y. | 105 |
| Sims, Matthew | 140 |
| Stembridge, William | 100 |
| Scott, Labon | |
| Tally, James | |
| Tally, Coleman | |
| Thomas, Robert | 70 |
| Wynne, William | |
| West, James | 54 |
| Woolard, Alfred | |
| Woolard, Godfrey | 31 |
| Wynne, John | |

### CAPTAIN ALLGOOD'S COMPANY

| Name | Acres |
|---|---|
| Allgood, Joel | |
| Allgood, William | 556 |
| Allen, Willis | 60 |
| Bell, John | 50 |
| Bell, Joseph G. | |
| Browning, Thomas D. | 42 |
| Bowers, William | |
| Bowers, Green | |
| Bradley, George | 134 |
| Corley, Austin | 63 |
| Corley, Nathan | 52 |
| Calhoun, James | 80 |
| Caplinger, William | 100 |
| Calhoun, James | 91 |
| Duncan, George A. | 175 |
| Dillard, Allen R. | 55 |
| Douglass, Ennis | 72 |
| Dillard, William M. | 50 |
| Furlong, James M. | |
| Furlong, Martin | 100 |
| Goodwin, James | |
| Gold, Pleasant | |
| Grubbs, William | 18 |
| Hay, William | 1604 |
| Harris, Sneed | 70 |
| Harrison, Edward R. | 134 |
| Holder, Benjamin L. | 187½ |
| Harrison, Samuel | 14 |
| Jopling, Thomas | 504 |
| Jackson, Coleman | |
| Jones, Elijah | 130 |
| Jackson, Robert | |
| Jackson, Coleman | 91 |
| Jackson, Bennett | |
| Jackson, Warren | |
| Ligon, Thomas | |

1832

| | |
|---|---|
| Lyons, Richard | |
| Lowe, Easton P. | 186 |
| Lowe, Green B. | 560 |
| M    ), George W. | |
| Martin, Pleasant M. | |
| Moser, Henry | 45 |
| McDonald, Elias | 112 |
| McDonald, Andrew J. | 255 |
| McMeans, John | 76 |
| Mooningham, William | |
| Moore, Alston | 50 |
| Palmer, John W. | |
| Roland, Robert | 75 |
| Shaw, Alsea | 78 |
| Shaw, Jesse | |
| Shaw, Jeremiah | 95 |
| Shaw, James | |
| Shaw, Solomon R. | |
| Seay, Beverly | |
| Terry, Elijah | 108 |
| Terry, Jeremiah | |
| White, George | 136 |
| Whitehead, William | |
| Whitehead, James | |
| Woodcock, Mary | 80 |
| White, Samuel | 55 |
| Wheeler, Edward B. | 200 |
| Warren, Boothe | |
| Woodward, Hezekiah | 95 |
| Woodcock, Jesse | 124 |

## CAPTAIN ALLEN'S COMPANY

| | |
|---|---|
| Allen, Wyley | |
| Allen, William | |
| Allen, Mary | 110 acres |
| Allen, James A. | |
| Belcher, Sutton E. | 165 |
| Braley, David   heirs | 200 |
| Borum, William | |
| Bradley, Samuel | 50 |
| Bradley, Morris | |
| Bradley, James | 350 |
| Bell, Samuel | |
| Belcher, Pleasant | |
| Borum, John | 165 |
| Belcher, Isaac | 100 |
| Belcher, John | |
| Bell, John | 140 |
| Butcher, Charles | |
| Bell, Jefferson | 60 |
| Baker, William | 30 |
| Boyd, John | 100 |
| Borum, Richard | 612 |
| Bell, Robert | |
| Belcher, John | |

1832

| | | |
|---|---|---|
| Barton, Gabriel | | |
| Bradley, John | | |
| Calhoon, Thomas | 225 | |
| Carter, William W. | 100 | |
| Calhoon, Samuel | 500 | |
| Chappell, Thomas B. | | |
| Calhoon, Martin | 200 | |
| C   ), Henry  heirs | 93 | |
| Craper, Thomas | | |
| Clary, John | | |
| Debow, Archibald | 300 | |
| Davis, James | 130 | |
| Donnell, George | 60 | |
| Davis, John | 100 | |
| Ellis, James | 15 | |
| Ellis, Moses | 465 | |
| Ellis, Nathan  heirs | 92 | |
| Evans, William | | |
| Eastland, Nicholas W. | 52 | |
| Fulks, A. M. | | |
| Foster, Robert | 95 | |
| Franklin, George | 170 | |
| Graves, Rice | 100 | |
| Green, Anderson | 220 | |
| Hamilton, Thomas | 250 | |
| Harris, Meger | 160 | |
| Hall, Julius M. | | |
| Harris, F. Y. | 301 | |
| Hatcher, William | 40 | |
| Harris, William | | |
| H   ), William | | |
| Hobbs, Hetty | 30 | |
| Hamlett, William | | |
| H   ), Thomas | 130 | |
| Harris, Eli | 215 | |
| Howell, Pettes | | |
| Johnson, John | 85 | |
| Johnson, James | 220 | |
| Johnson, Daniel | 274 | |
| Irby, Joseph | 130 | |
| Johnson, Zealous | 140 | |
| Jones, Michael E. | 47½ | |
| Johnson, Davidson | | |
| Johnson, William | 500 | |
| Johnson, Samuel | 108 | |
| King, Richard | 48 | |
| Langford, Robert | | |
| Ligon, Joseph | 72 | |
| Langford, Thomas | | |
| Martin, Thomas | | |
| Martin, Pugh | | |
| Martin, Noel | 47 | |
| Martin, John | 178 | |
| Martin, David | | |
| McSpadden, Thomas | 109 | 1832 |

| | |
|---|---|
| McNeal, Enoch   heirs | 150 acres |
| McMurray, David | 385 |
| Moore, William | 66 |
| Mooningham, Thomas | |
| McMurray, James | |
| Moore, R. L. | 44 |
| McSpadden, William | |
| Owen, John | 100 |
| Owen, Richard | 160 |
| Owen, William | |
| Owen, Mary | |
| Owen, Wadkins | |
| Purvine, Allen | 206 |
| Paine, Thomas | 95 |
| Paine, William | |
| Purvine, M. | |
| Pemberton, Jesse | |
| Pemberton, James | |
| Purvine, William | 100 |
| Paine, George | |
| Pully, Robert | 54 |
| Provine, John | 190 |
| Roane, Harris | 200 |
| Richardson, Loid | |
| Scoby, David | 50 |
| Sherrill, Hugh | 100 |
| S    ), Robert | |
| Seay, Edward S. | |
| Sneed, Hamilton | |
| Steele, William | 378 |
| Swany, William | 40 |
| Swindle, Joseph | |
| Swindle, Joel | 100 |
| Swindle, William H. | |
| Stevens, James | |
| Swindle, John | |
| Simmons, John | |
| Tomlinson, Allen | 65 |
| Taylor, John M. | 15 |
| White, John W. | 100 |
| Weir, James | 489 |
| Wilson, William | 80 |
| Weir, Thomas | 23 |
| Wadkins, Reece | 36½ |
| Young, David, Jr. | |
| Young, David | 240 |

## CAPTAIN LANNOM'S COMPANY

| | |
|---|---|
| Alsup, Richard | 302 acres |
| Adams, James | |
| Alsup, William | 288 |
| Alsup, Nathan | |
| Alsup, Samuel J. | 100 |
| Alsup, Joseph | 285 |
| Alsup, Asap | 150 |

1833

| Name | Amount |
|---|---|
| Bowers, Bartlett | |
| Baskin, Robert | 250 |
| Burke, Thomas | 122 |
| Burke & Alexander | 160 |
| Barker, Richard | 50 |
| Burke, Lewis | 50 |
| Cluck, Henry, Sr. | 60 |
| Cluck, William | 100 |
| Cluck, Henry, Jr. | 100 |
| Collins, Elisa | 100 |
| Collins, Crawford | |
| Collins, Jesse | |
| Dodd, Simon | |
| Drennan, Hiram A. | |
| Doherty, Samuel B. | 50 |
| Doherty, William | |
| Goodwin, William | |
| Griffin, Thomas | |
| Gray, James | 250 |
| Grimes, William | |
| Howard, Hiram | |
| Holland, Edward | 82 |
| Hedgpeth, Silas | |
| Hodge, John | 240 |
| Johnson, Charles | 30 |
| Jackson, Larkin | 144 |
| Jackson, Thomas | |
| Jarman, John | 136 |
| Lockhart, Elias | |
| Jarman, Susan | |
| King, William | |
| Morgan, Astin | |
| McCulloch, William | 110 |
| McCulloch, Nathan | |
| McHenry, Jesse | 102 |
| Mason, James | |
| Nooner, George | 100 |
| Nelson, Jarrett | |
| Nelson, William | |
| Oliver, James | |
| Oliver, Edward | |
| Oliver, Alexander | |
| Pague, John | |
| Parham, James H. | |
| Poe, James | |
| Ricketts, John L. | |
| Rice, David | 80 |
| Robertson, Meredith | |
| Richardson, Martin B. | 95 |
| Reynolds, Thomas | |
| Ragsdale, Sarah | 50 |
| Ragsdale, Richard | |
| Roberts, McKee | 100 |
| Sanders, Richard | |
| Stewart, William | |

1832

| | |
|---|---|
| Smith, Matthew | |
| Thomas, Jacob | 150 |
| Vaughter, Ludwich | 60 |
| Wright, John | |
| Woolen, Joshua | 118 |
| Woolen, Moses | 50 |
| Woolen, Luvina | 50 |
| Zachery, Allen | 50 |
| Zachery, Hartwell | 76 |
| Burke, Fielden | 100 |
| Fields, Richard | 120 |

## CAPTAIN HILL'S COMPANY

| | |
|---|---|
| Harrington, James | 100 acres |
| Avery, John W. | 100 |
| Allen, Absolum | |
| Brevard, John | |
| Bryant, David | 50 |
| Bryant, William | |
| Butt, John | 50 |
| Butt, Hazel | |
| Bradley, Charles | 400 |
| Booker, Lemuel | 295 |
| Cherry, Daniel | 400 |
| Bunby, William | |
| Bradley, Thomas | 557 |
| Brooks, John | |
| Burnett, John | 100 |
| Broom, William | |
| Buckley, Patrick | |
| Carr, Richardson | 108 |
| Compton, John, Sr. | 111 |
| Compton, Nancy | 16 |
| Compton, John | 16 |
| Cowger, John | 233 |
| Crutcher, Jesse | 50 |
| Coppage, John | |
| Compton, Vinson | 10 |
| Clay, John | |
| Carr, Dabney | |
| Carr, John | 75 |
| Corum, Eli | |
| Cowger, Adam | 130 |
| Clay, Elijah | 130 |
| Carr, Martha | 144 |
| Compton, Allen | |
| Cherry, Willie | 700 |
| Corley, Robert | |
| Davis, Zachariah | 116 |
| Davis, Isham | 250 |
| Dorch, Richard | |
| Davis, William | |
| Davis, William | 100 |
| Davis, Hezekiah | |

1832

| Name | Amount |
|---|---|
| Dill, John | |
| Douglass, Ila | 250 |
| Dillard, Allen | 150 |
| Estes, Bartlett | |
| Edwards, Mariah | |
| Furguson, Barbary | 230 |
| Furguson, Samuel | |
| Gilbert, Ebenezer | 175 |
| Gilbert, John | |
| Hicks, Alfred | |
| Hobson, Henry Esqr. | 357 |
| Hail, Thomas | |
| Harris, Edward | |
| Holderfield, Jacob | |
| Harris, Richard | |
| Harpeth, George | 166 |
| Hobson, Benjamin H. | 150 |
| Hobson, Henry  Ad of H. Walker | 180 |
| Horsley, Tolbert | 60 |
| Halbrooks, William | |
| Huner, Isaac | 200 |
| Harpole, Sampson | 40 |
| Hill, Braxton | 58 |
| Hunter, Jacob | 50 |
| Hughes, Robert | 100 |
| Hughes, Simpson | |
| Jackson, William H. | |
| Hibbitts, David C. | 200 |
| Jarrett, John | 140 |
| Jarrett, Frances | 8 |
| Jarrell, William | |
| Jarrell, Joshua | |
| Jones, Thomas | 32 |
| Kindred, Thomas | 56 |
| Kindred, John | |
| Lavender, William | |
| McDaniel, James | 274 |
| McDaniel, Nancy | 88 |
| Moss, Thomas | 209 |
| Moss, William | 242 |
| Moss, James C. | 30 |
| Mansfield, Granville | 100 |
| Mabry, Benjamin F. | 135 |
| Moser, Daniel | 160 |
| Moser, Alfred | |
| Murphy, Nicholas | |
| Moore, William | 112 |
| McNichols, Alexander | |
| Miles, William | |
| Martin, James  for Jesse Eason heirs | 58 |
| Milton, John | |
| Martin, William S. | 220 |
| Mabry, David D. | |

1832

| | |
|---|---|
| Measles, Ulelis | |
| Milton, Thomas | 150 |
| Mosely, John | |
| McNichols, Daniel | |
| Nowland, Byrd | |
| Proctor, Edward | 180 |
| Peace, William H. | 566 |
| Proctor, E. Guard for the heirs of John Hill | 132 |
| Robb, John, Sr. | 616 |
| Robb, John, Jr. | |
| Robb, William | |
| Ring, M. | |
| Rochell, James | |
| Scurlock, Dudley | 40 |
| Swinny, John | 184 |
| Sutton, Tolliver | |
| Shepherd, Thomas | |
| Sypert, Robert | 244 |
| Sypert, Thomas | 240 |
| Travillian, Edward | 207 |
| Taylor, James | 120 |
| Tucker, Green | 202 |
| Taller, Bird | 22 |
| Taller, Poleman | 114 |
| Williams, William | |
| Wright, James | 107 |
| Wright, Berry | 90 |
| Walker, William | |
| Wynne, Manerva | 220 |
| Walker, Radford | 186 |
| Walker, Millander | 286 |
| Walker, Delila | 500 |
| Walton, Harris | 340 |
| Yourie, Patrick | 100 |
| Walker, Noah | |
| Walker, Kesiah | 54 |
| Walker, William heirs | 200 |

## CAPTAIN HAMILTON'S COMPANY

| | |
|---|---|
| Aston, Alexander | 144 acres |
| Aston, Joseph | |
| Borum, Henry | 43 |
| Bonner, John | 150 |
| Bonner, John S. | |
| Bonner, Benjamin F. | 82 |
| Bodin, Westen | |
| Bodin, Penelope | 100 |
| Beasley, Benny B. | |
| Beasley, G. | |
| Beasley, Joseph | |
| Bonner, Thomas S. | 100 |
| Chambers, John | 100 |
| Carruth, Alexander | 150 |

| | |
|---|---|
| Carruth, Walter | |
| Cunningham, M. | |
| Carruth, Eli | 100 |
| Chambers, Lewis | 261 |
| Chambers, Alexander heirs | 144 |
| Chambers, Nicholas | |
| Carruth, Alexander | 191 |
| Clary, James | |
| Carruth, William S. | 100 |
| Dillard, Earnest | |
| Dyer, Lewis H. | |
| Eason, Eli E. | 57½ |
| Exum, William | |
| Freeman, Dorrell | |
| Figures, Batt | 462 |
| Figures, Mary | |
| Forkum, Earnest P. | 100 |
| Grimes, John | |
| Glenn, Thompson | |
| Glenn, Giles H. | |
| Glenn, Marthus | 248 |
| Glenn, B. | |
| Glenn, John | |
| Harris, Richard | |
| Hunter, Wright | 130 |
| Hughes, Salton | 106 |
| Harris, Charles | |
| Hamilton, S. J. | |
| Jackson, Sarah | 100 |
| Johnson, Rody | |
| Jackson, Josiah | |
| Jackson, Donnell | |
| Jackson, Henry | 86 |
| Jackson, John M. | 152 |
| Johnson, James C. | |
| Joplin, Elisha | 100 |
| Jackson, Dolly | |
| Keeling, George | 160 |
| Lack, Frances | 100 |
| Ligon, Richard | 150 |
| Ligon, Valentine | |
| Ligon, James S. | |
| Locke, James W. | 110 |
| Locke, Charles | 70 |
| Lyon, Merritt | |
| Locke, Thomas | 130 |
| Lyon, John | 227 |
| Lyon, James | |
| Luplin, William | 200 |
| Motsinger, Elijah | |
| McDaniel, Stephen | 107 |
| Moser, Adam | 333½ |
| Malom, Hugh R. | |
| New, William | 300 |
| New, William O. | |
| Newsom, A. B. | |

1832

| | |
|---|---|
| New, James | |
| Petway, William | 96 |
| Person, William | |
| Ramsay, Richard B. | |
| Ramsay, Thomas K. | |
| Rutherford, Griffith W. | 305 |
| Sims, Edward | |
| Sims, Christopher | |
| Stephens, Sanders | |
| Stephens, S. B. | 50 |
| Thompson, Henry | |
| Tarpley, Sterling | 500 |
| Tomlinson, William | 87 |
| Tarpley, John | |
| Thompson, Swan | |
| Tarpley, Steth T. | |
| Underwood, Milton | |
| Underwood, Joel | |
| Vaughan, Abram | 126 |
| Warren, Luce | 25 |
| Walton, James | 43 |
| Warren, Benjamin | 278 |
| Woodall, George W. | |

## CAPTAIN MAJOR'S COMPANY

| | |
|---|---|
| Andrews, William M. | 134 acres |
| Alexander, William L. | 129 |
| Alexander, Isabella | 75 |
| Bingham, John A. | |
| Bingham, Thomas | 106 |
| Butt, Mary | 58 |
| Bond, Lewis | 136 |
| Bond, William | 23 |
| Braden, Charles | 450 |
| Bingham, Thomas W. | |
| Comer, Reuben | 77 |
| Coker, Valentine | |
| Comer, Samuel R. | |
| Carlock, Eber | |
| Cunningham, John | 83 |
| Cunningham, James | 67 |
| Cropper, Ebenezer | 118 |
| Choplin, Robert heirs | 75 |
| Doak, Manson F. | 80 |
| Doak, Mar ) | 160 |
| Donnell, William | |
| Donnell, George | 556 |
| Davis, Terrell | |
| Donnell, ( ) | 162½ |
| Donnell, Mary | 245½ |
| Donnell, Robert | 105 |
| Donnell, Martha | 63 |
| Davis, Thomas | |
| Davis, Elizabeth | 168 |
| Donnell, William L. | 286 |

1832

| | |
|---|---|
| Donnell, John | 120 acres |
| Davis, Robert | |
| Donnell, Josiah | 211 |
| Donnell, William | |
| Donnell, James | 224 |
| Donnell, William P. | 105 |
| Donnell, Calvin | 91 |
| Duke, Littleton | 39 |
| Doak, John F. | 388 |
| Ealey, Josiah | 22 |
| Foster, John D. | 285 |
| Foster, Alexander | 356 |
| Foster, James | 250 |
| Foster, Albert | 100 |
| Foster, Alfred H. | |
| Foster, John W. | |
| Graves, Asa | |
| Graves, Bachelor | |
| Graves, Luvenia | |
| Hearn, Stephen H. | 250 |
| Hudson, Obediah | 193 |
| Hudson, Paskel P. | |
| Jones, Edward | 132 |
| Jones, Isham | 50 |
| Jones, Richard | 75 |
| Lee, Benjamin   heirs | 55 |
| Lee, David | |
| Lee, Samuel | |
| Lindsay, Josiah B. | 150 |
| Morrison, Hugh | 125 |
| Morrison, William | |
| Martin, M. | 240 |
| Morris, Mary | 200 |
| Morris, William | 95 |
| Maxwell, John | |
| Massie, Garrett | |
| Moose, David B. | |
| Major, John | 465 |
| Major, John A. | 100 |
| Major, Eli | 155 |
| Maddox, Notley | 220 |
| Maddox, William | 55 |
| Maddox, Charles B. | 75 |
| Morris, Alexander | 170 |
| Moser, Henry | 188 |
| Morrison, Levi | 85 |
| Morse, R. B. | 104 |
| Powell, James | 126 |
| Ragsdale, Asa | 150 |
| Ragsdale, Alfred | |
| Serrell, Ephraim | 160 |
| Smith, S. G. | 83 |
| Smith, David | |
| Smith, John | 83 |
| Skean, James | |

1832

| | |
|---|---|
| Shannon, James H. | |
| Sparks, Nathan | 208 |
| Sorter, John | 161 |
| Trice, Edward | 76 |
| Thompson, Moses | 412 |
| Thompson, Moses, Jr. | 38 |
| Thompson, William D. | 100 |
| Thorn, John H. | |
| Thorn, James | |
| Thorn, William | |
| Vowell, William A. | |
| Vowell, Jesse H. | |
| Williams, Samuel | 130 |
| Williams, John | |
| Williams, Thomas R. | |
| Wadle, John | |
| Young, John | |

## CAPTAIN GREEN'S COMPANY

| | |
|---|---|
| Andrews, Asa | 124 acres |
| Andrews, Robin | |
| Andrews, Ebenezer | |
| Aleratha, Mark | 60 |
| Belcher, Alexander | |
| Brown, Thomas | |
| Benthal, Samuel | 121 |
| Belcher, Charles B. | |
| Bass, Sion | 110 |
| Buchanan, William | 700 |
| Berge, Peterson | 83 |
| Bass, Cader | |
| Bennett, William T. | 40 |
| Bundy, James | |
| Cox, Henry L. | 26 |
| Cox, James | |
| Carter, B. | 114 |
| Crenshaw, David | |
| Crutchfield, Samuel | 312 |
| Cox, William | |
| Crutchfield, Henry | |
| Carlin, Spencer | 66 |
| Carter, Federick | 114 |
| Cox, Anderson | 130 |
| Chavis, Daniel | 10 |
| Caplan, Martha | 140 |
| Cropper, James | 100 |
| Calin, Isham | |
| Cox, Robert | 18 |
| Connell, William | 49 |
| Donnell, Levi | 190 |
| Foster, John S. | 50 |
| Forbes, Thomas W. | 112 |
| Forbes, Elizabeth | 100 |
| Green, John, Sr. | 175 |

1832

| | |
|---|---|
| Hankins, William | 50 acres |
| Hankins, John | |
| Hankins, Arthur | |
| Hearn, James | 150 |
| Hearn, William C. | |
| Hearn, Pernal | |
| Hoxley, John | |
| Hall, B. B. | |
| Hearn, Wilson | 186 |
| Hearn, Alexander | 300 |
| Johnson, Philip | 130 |
| Jones, Elija | |
| McBride, Daniel | 80 |
| Motheral, James | 280 |
| Morris, Patterson | |
| Michaels, Alexander | |
| Morris, Alenson | |
| Maholland, John | |
| Maholland, William | |
| Nettles, John | 170 |
| New, William | 368 |
| Nelson, heirs | 30 |
| Palmer, Thomas K. | 40 |
| Powell, Abraham | 78 |
| Routon, William | |
| Routon, Richard | 130 |
| Rains, John | |
| Smith, John | 145 |
| Sims, Caswell | 100 |
| Shanks, William | 1 |
| Spears, Lewis | 50 |
| Sims, Chesley | 100 |
| Turner, William | 124 |
| Turner, James | 541 |
| Turner, N. G. | |
| Tippitt, John C. | 230 |
| Turner, Thomas | 463 |
| Taylor, John | |
| Vaughan, Thomas | 67 |
| Williford, William, Jr. | 12 |
| Williford, George A. | |
| Winford, Alexander | |

## CAPTAIN GORE'S COMPANY

| | |
|---|---|
| A    ), Thompson | |
| B    ), David | 195 |
| Baker, Joseph, Jr. | |
| Barber, Mary | 130 |
| Booker, B. | 35 |
| Barbee, Eliza | 35 |
| Barbee, Joseph | 160 |
| Barbee, Daniel | 230 |
| Barbee, Elias | |
| Barbee, William | 40 |

1832

| Name | Acres |
|---|---|
| B    ), William | 197 acres |
| Boon, John | |
| Barbee, N. | |
| Britain, Joseph | |
| Bails, Jane | 100 |
| Barbee, James | 40 |
| Barker, John | 85 |
| Branch, Fanny | 193 |
| Branch, A. G. | 81 |
| Branch, R. C. | 20 |
| Branch, H. I. | 93 |
| Bartlett, F. B. | |
| Clark, George | 310 |
| Cartwright, Martha T. | |
| Cartwright, Elijah | 200 |
| Compton, William | 150 |
| Compton, Margrett | 135 |
| Collins, John | |
| Cox, Thomas | |
| Corder, Benjamin | |
| Carrod, John | |
| Chapman, Thomas | |
| Cartwright, Hericha | |
| Colwick, William | |
| Dearing, Albin | 164 |
| D    ), Presley | 104 |
| D    ), Samuel | |
| Dotson, L. | 300 |
| Donnell, Levi | |
| Doughtry, Robert | 221 |
| Doughtry, Lorenzo | |
| Day, G. | 186 |
| E    ), Eda | |
| Edwards, John | 171 |
| Faust, Elizabeth | 100 |
| Francis, Corban | |
| George, John | 100 |
| Grindstaff, John | 100 |
| Haley, James | 137 |
| Hoffer, Jacob | |
| Harris, James | 250 |
| Johnson, Margrett | 200 |
| Kelly, Dennis  heirs | 100 |
| Lawrence, John | 147 |
| Moore, Thomas | |
| Moore, James | 85 |
| Midgett, Richard | |
| Marks, John | 50 |
| Newby, Wholey | 100 |
| New, Nicholas | |
| New, William | 114 |
| Odum, Britain | 72 |
| Oclay, John | |
| Pritchett, Catherine | 32½ |
| Philips, Thomas | 175 |

1832

| | |
|---|---|
| Pritchett, Elizabeth | 75 acres |
| Partin, Randolph | |
| Smith, D. | 211½ |
| Taylor, John | 300 |
| Trace, Evans | 130 |
| Taylor, John | 114 |
| Taylor, Robert | 36 |
| Taylor, Joshua | 32 |
| Taylor, Isaac | |
| Taylor, Henry | |
| Taylor, James B. | 78 |
| Taylor, Fanny | 60 |

## CAPTAIN RAGLAND'S COMPANY

| | |
|---|---|
| Billings, David | |
| Billings, Benjamin | |
| Bl ), A. | |
| Bradley, Everett | |
| Bradshaw, James C. | 119 |
| Coe, William | 225 |
| Dellas, Morgan | |
| Dellas, Robert | 134 |
| Donaldson, R. heirs | 140 |
| Edwards, William | 163 |
| Elamon, Jesse | |
| Ellis, Robert H. | |
| Ferrell, William W. | |
| Greer, Joseph L. | |
| George, Lucas | |
| Hankins, John | |
| Hankins, Martha | 110 |
| ( ), Samuel | |
| Hankins, Richard | 463 |
| Jackson, Thomas | 100 |
| ( ), Pleasant | |
| Johnson, Littleberry | 77 |
| Jackson, Thomas L. | |
| Johnson, Matthew | 100 |
| Johnson, Robertson | 320 |
| Johnson, Matthew | |
| Mickle, John | |
| Mason, Thomas | |
| Malloy, Benjamin | |
| Malloy, Benjamin G. | 100 |
| M ), Asa | |
| N ), John | |
| Organ, ( ) | 166 |
| ( ), J. | |
| Organ, ( ) | 109 |
| Pemberton, William | |
| Pemberton, John | |
| Powell, Seymore | |
| Ragland, Pettus | 300 |
| ) _ ( ) | 56 |
| Roane, Thomas | |

1832

| | |
|---|---|
| Satterfield, Rheuben | 124 acres |
| Stone, Newbern P. | 50 |
| Sweatt, Edward | 400 |
| Sweatt, William, Sr. | 44 |
| Sweatt, V. | |
| Seat, Martin | |
| Smith, G. D. | |
| Sherrill, Elizabeth | 150 |
| Scoby, James | 400 |
| Scoby, John | 100 |
| Sweatt, William, Jr. | |
| Tally, Henry | 85 |
| Tally, Ephraim | |
| Trout, Joseph | 134 |
| Trout, John | |
| Weir, James C. | 225 |
| Wood, James | |
| Weir, James | 100 |
| Weir, John B. | |
| Weir, James | 152 |
| Williams, Robert | |

### CAPTAIN TURNER'S COMPANY

| | |
|---|---|
| Astin, Addison | |
| Anderson, William | |
| Bell, Benjamin | |
| Bell, James | |
| Bell, Resin | |
| Bradley, John | 156 |
| Bradley, Barnett | |
| Belcher, William | |
| Bradshaw, John | 36 |
| Bailey, Jonathan | 390 |
| Bone, Henry | 143 |
| Cutrell, Joseph | 108 |
| Caplinger, Solomon | 200 |
| Chastain, Elisha | 144 |
| Cartwright, Samuel | 133 |
| Caplinger, John | 40 |
| Cutrell, Midgett | |
| C    ), Isaac | 100 |
| Caplinger, William | |
| Courtney, George | 72 |
| Click, (     ) | |
| Dice, William | 235 |
| Duff, Robert | |
| Darity, William | |
| Davidson, Frances | 116 |
| Davidson, William | 187 |
| Davis, Enoch | 106 |
| Dudley, Woodson | 45 |
| David, Echols | |
| Edwards, James | 33 |
| Fisher, Philip | 211 |

1832

| Name | Acres |
|---|---|
| Gill, William | 130 acres |
| Goodall, John T. | 116 |
| Goodall, William | 160 |
| Goodall, Harden | 126 |
| Goodall, Francis | 100 |
| Huflan, Burrell | |
| Harrison, William | 50 |
| Hufman, Genova | 173 |
| Hufman, Robert | |
| Henry, Charles | 86 |
| Hobbs, Green | |
| Hobbs, J. | 225 |
| Hearn, F. | |
| Jenkins, William H. | 89 |
| Jones, C. | 136 |
| Lindsley, E. | 150 |
| Lannom, J. | |
| Murphy, Aron | 85 |
| Motsinger, James | |
| Marks, Thomas | 125 |
| Marks, James, Jr. | |
| Midgett, George | |
| Palmer, William | 150 |
| Philips, Alfred | 246 |
| Philips, Bailey | 74 |
| Philips, William | 78 |
| Philips, Henry | 40 |
| Peace, Alexander | 240 |
| Ramsey, George | |
| Rather, Elizabeth | |
| Spring, B. | |
| Smith, Robert | |
| (     ), John | 90 |
| (     ), Moses | 100 |
| Spring, Moses | 100 |
| Swan, Philip | |
| Spring, Abner | 190 |
| Swan, John | 50 |
| Spring, Gamma | |
| Swan, William | 100 |
| Swan, James, Sr. | 130 |
| Swan, James, Jr. | |
| Swan, John | 740 |
| Spring, William | |
| Sweatt, Joseph | 100 |
| Spring, John | |
| Turner, William | |
| Swan, George | |
| Swan, William | |
| Nesbett, Adison | |
| Waters, Shely | 170 |
| Waters, William | 140 |
| (     ), John | 50 |
| Cartwright, Hezekiah | 240 |
| Grissom, Elizabeth | 200 |

1832

Grissom, Joseph
H    ), B.
Garrison, Thomas            40
Pride, Francis
Manning, Lewis
Manning, Catherine          60
Manning, John               60                    1832

## NAME INDEX

Abanatha, Mark 22
Abernatha, Charles 25,77
Abernatha, Mark 75
Acles, Joseph 54
Adams, Captain 101
Adams, Greenberry 7
Adams, James 7,23,76,120
Adams, James W. 30
Adams, John 47,101
Adams, Parker 43,96
Adams, William 7,60
Adams, William, Jr. 67
Adamson, Simon 47,101
Adamson, Weales 101
Adamson, William, Sr. 67
Adkins, J. 54
Adkison, Thomas 14
Afflax, John 20
Ahart, Joseph 102
Ahart, Moses 102
Ahart, Nimrod 102
Aleratha, Mark 128
Alexander, Abner 41,95
Alexander, Aswin 95
Alexander, Benjamin 49,102
Alexander, Daniel 54
Alexander, Ezekiel 41,95
Alexander, George 17,49,
  69,102,115
Alexander, Gideon 20
Alexander, Isaac 47,101
Alexander, Isabella 92,126
Alexander, Israel 40
Alexander, John 17,40,69,
  92,115
Alexander, N. G. 91
Alexander, Nelson G. 38
Alexander, P. M. 61
Alexander, William L. 126
Alexander, William S. 40,
  92
Alford, Lodwich B. 49,102
Alford, Wiley 49
Alford, Wilie 102
Alison, Elizabeth 96
Allcorn, James 1,54,110
Allcorn, John 110
Allcorn, Prudence 1,54,110
Allen, Absolom 83,122
Allen, Archibald 33
Allen, Captain 20,72,118
Allen, Isaiah 7
Allen, James 20,72,80

Allen, James A. 118
Allen, Larkin 54
Allen, Mary 1,20,54,72,110,118
Allen, Wiley 71
Allen, Willas 18
Allen, William 1,118
Allen, William E. 20
Allen, William, Sr. 54
Allen, Willis 117
Allen, Wyley 118
Allgain, John 1
Allgin, John 54
Allgood, Captain 71,117
Allgood, Joel 18,71,117
Allgood, William 18,71,117
Allison, Elizabeth 43
Allison, Isaiah 77
Allison, John L. 25,77
Allison, Samuel 25,77
Almore, Solomon 25
Alsup, Allen 76
Alsup, Asap 23,76,120
Alsup, Joseph 23,76,120
Alsup, Nathan 120
Alsup, Richard 23,76,120
Alsup, Samuel 8,61
Alsup, Samuel J. 23,76,120
Alsup, William 76,120
Alsup, William H. 23,108
Ames, Elizabeth 5,14,58,66,67
Ames, Thomas 26,79
Ames, William 5,58
Anderson, Captain 114
Anderson, F. 17
Anderson, Francis 70,115
Anderson, James 11,46,63,114
Anderson, John 7,20,60,72,114
Anderson, L. C. 11
Anderson, P. 69,113
Anderson, Patrick 1
Anderson, Paulden 17,70
Anderson, Richard 5,14,115
Anderson, Richard, Jr. 67
Anderson, Richard, Sr. 67
Anderson, S. 110
Anderson, Sam C. 11
Anderson, Samuel 114
Anderson, Samuel C. 63
Anderson, Whitwell 26,79
Anderson, William 51,104,132
Andrews, Asa 22,75,128
Andrews, Bowlin 75
Andrews, Ebenezer 128

Andrews, Gray 14,66
Andrews, Pernel 22
Andrews, Robin 128
Andrews, Rowland 22
Andrews, William 40,75
Andrews, William M. 126
Anman, John H. 66
Arbuckle, William 77
Archer, Hezekiah 69
Archer, Hisekins 17
Archer, Jacob 17,69,115
Armstrong, Elijah 42
Armstrong, J. M. 61
Armstrong, James M. 8
Arnold, Butler 5
Arnold, Henry 41
Arnold, John 43,95,96
Arnold, Nancy 41,95
Arnold, Noel 43
Arnold, Thomas 5
Arnold, William 43,96
Arrington, James 30,83
Ashley, James 23,76
Ashworth, Jasper R. 1,54, 110
Askew, Franklin 46
Askew, Russell 49
Askins, Addison 99
Askins, Franklin 99
Astin, Addison 132
Aston, Alexander 35,88, 124
Aston, Daniel 1
Aston, James 88
Aston, Joseph 35,88,124
Atherly, James 12,65
Atherly, John 26
Atherly, Jonathan 26,79
Atherly, Robertson 26, 65
Atherly, Warren 12,65
Atkins, Joel 1
Atkinson, James 86
Atkinson, Joseph 33
Atkinson, Rial 5,58
Atwood, Edwin 32,85
Ausburn, Thomas 77
Aust, Elizabeth 14
Aust, Henry 14
Aust, Joseph 14,66
Aust, Thomas 14,66
Avery, George 81
Avery, John 5,83
Avery, John W. 18,122
Ayers, James 8

Ayres, James 61
Babb, Bennett 33,86
Babb, Thomas 5,58
Baccus, Minchey 11,64,114
Bacon, Edmund P. 44
Badgett, John 22
Bagwell, Lunceford 56,112
Bagwell, Lunsford 3
Bailey, James S. 25,77
Bailey, Jonathan 9,104,108,132
Bailey, Samuel 47
Bailey, Washington L. 61
Bailey, William 61
Bails, Jane 130
Baird, Andrew 26,79
Baird, Batt 107
Baird, Clinton 107
Baird, David 26,46,79,99
Baird, Hardy 107
Baird, Hardy H. 24
Baird, Hiram 24,81
Baird, James 9,11,61,64,114
Baird, John 24,37,81,89,107
Baird, Len 114
Baird, Lindsay 24
Baird, Seldon 11,64
Baird, William 11,12,64,89
Baker, Jeremiah 46,99
Baker, John 46,99
Baker, John E. 28,81
Baker, Joseph 89
Baker, Joseph, Jr. 129
Baker, William 20,73,118
Balentine, Coster F. 37,89
Balue, James 20
Bandfield, John 44
Bandy, Epson 67
Bandy, Richard 67
Banfield, George 91
Barbee, Captain 46
Barbee, Daniel 99,129
Barbee, Donnell 46
Barbee, Elias 129
Barbee, Eliza 129
Barbee, James 130
Barbee, John, Jr. 46
Barbee, John, Sr. 46
Barbee, Joseph 1,46,129
Barbee, Joseph, Jr. 99
Barbee, Mary 99
Barbee, N. 130
Barbee, Thomas 46,81,99
Barbee, William 129
Barbee, William H. 85
Barber, John 99

Barber, Josephus 99
Barber, Mary 129
Barclay, B. P. 91
Barefoot, Noah 81
Barker, John 130
Barker, Richard 24,76,121
Barker, William 25,77
Barkley, Benjamin 38
Barkley, Robert 1
Barksdale, Francis 88
Barksdale, Thomas W. 17,54
Barnet, William 77
Barnett, Isaac 25,98
Barnsfield, George 8
Barr, Joseph 28,81
Barr, Silas 28
Barr, William 28
Barr, William G. 81
Barr, William G., Jr. 81
Barr, William H. 28
Barratt, William 11
Barrett, William 64,114
Bartlett, B. F. 99
Bartlett, Benjamin F. 46
Bartlett, F. B. 130
Bartlett, William 22,73
Barton, Ann 1
Barton, Eleanor 26
Barton, Gabriel 53,106,119
Barton, John 1
Barton, Nelly 79
Baskin, Robert 121
Baskin, William 24
Baskins, Robert M. 24,76
Bass, Archibald 38
Bass, Archimack 91
Bass, Cader 22,26,65,128
Bass, Etheldred 38,91
Bass, Ezekiel 38
Bass, Ezekiel, Jr. 91
Bass, Ezekiel, Sr. 91
Bass, Harmon 65
Bass, James 65
Bass, John 38,91
Bass, Sion 13,22,65,75,128
Bass, Solomon 13,65
Bass, Warren 91
Bates, James 12
Bates, John 13
Batts, John 65
Baxter, George 34,86
Baxter, John 34,43,86,96
Bay, Andrew 14,67
Beadle, Henry 8
Beadle, Osburn 8

Beadles, Abram 108
Beadles, Ozburn 108
Beadles, William 108
Beard, William 114
Beasley, Benny B. 35,88,124
Beasley, G. 124
Beasley, Gabriel 35
Beasley, Joseph 124
Beasley, Josiah 35,88
Beckers, James 17
Beel, Nathaniel 34
Belcher, Alexander 22,75,128
Belcher, Charles B. 128
Belcher, David 75
Belcher, Isaac 22,33,85,118
Belcher, James 33,86
Belcher, John 61,118
Belcher, John R. 106
Belcher, Pleasant 22,61,118
Belcher, Richard 22
Belcher, Sutton E. 20,72,118
Belcher, Thomas 22,61
Belcher, William 132
Belcher, Woodford 61
Bell, Amzi 20,72
Bell, Benjamin 51,104,132
Bell, Benjamin T. 18,104
Bell, Elisha 95
Bell, George 104
Bell, James 24,51,81,132
Bell, Jefferson 53,73,118
Bell, John 18,20,52,71,72,117,118
Bell, Joseph G. 18,71,117
Bell, Nathaniel 86
Bell, Resin 132
Bell, Risen 104
Bell, Robert 24,73,81,118
Bell, Robert D. 20
Bell, Samuel 118
Belt, Dodson 97
Belt, Jeremiah 43,98
Belt, Polly 38
Bennett, Baxter 107
Bennett, Drury 11
Bennett, Jacob 11,114
Bennett, Jacob, Jr. 64
Bennett, James 11
Bennett, John 11,64,114
Bennett, Simpson 18
Bennett, Thomas 11,63
Bennett, William F. 22
Bennett, William K. 107
Bennett, William T. 128
Benthal, Samuel 128
Berge, Peterson 128

Bernard, Horatio 49,102
Bernett, Thomas 114
Berry, Jesse 40
Berry, Nathaniel 38,91
Bettes, Alfred 5,54,110
Bettes, James 30
Bettes, John 33,59
Bettes, Samuel 54
Bettes, William 33,58
Bilbro, William 26,79
Biles, Jane 46,99
Biles, M. H. 99
Billings, Ben H. 52
Billings, Benjamin 131
Billings, Benjamin H. 106
Billings, David 52,106, 131
Billingsley, John 3,56, 112
Bingham, John 40,93
Bingham, John A. 126
Bingham, Thomas 40,93,126
Bingham, Thomas W. 40,93, 126
Binkley, Henry J. 28,79
Birthwright, Williamson 37,89
Blackburn 79
Blackburn, John 67
Blackburn, Sally 79
Blackburn, Washington 26
Blacknell, Charles 30
Blackwell, Charles 83
Blair, William 7,60
Blair, William R. 56
Blalock, Charles, Jr. 67
Blalock, Charles, Sr. 67
Blalock, Charles W. 14
Bland, Arthur 3,56,112
Blankenship, Allen 28,81
Blankenship, C. 108
Blankenship, Daniel 98
Blankenship, Ganes 8
Blaze, George 34,86
Bloodworth, Web 14
Bloodworth, Webb 67
Blythe, Alexander 86
Blythe, Frances 48
Bodin, Penelope 124
Bodin, Westen 124
Bodine, Thomas 88
Bodine, Westen 88
Bogle, George 42
Bogle, Joseph 42,95
Bogle, Sarah 95

Bogle, Thomas 42,95
Bomer, Thomas 100
Bond, David 11,64,114
Bond, Elisha 11
Bond, James 25,40,44,98
Bond, John 11,25,114
Bond, John, Sr. 64
Bond, Lewis 93,126
Bond, Margaret 25
Bond, Robert 28,81
Bond, Samuel 11,64,114
Bond, Seldon 114
Bond, Solomon 76
Bond, William 11,40,63,93,114,126
Bone, A. M. 110
Bone, A. W. 8,61
Bone, Adnah 44
Bone, Amos 57
Bone, Amos M. 3
Bone, Auger 61
Bone, Azer 8
Bone, Ednah 97
Bone, Enos 17,70,115
Bone, Henry 132
Bone, Henry F. 44,98
Bone, Henry P. 51,104
Bone, J. P. 61
Bone, James 97
Bone, James C. 44,98
Bone, John 44,61,98
Bone, Margaret 97
Bone, Thomas 8,61
Bonfield, John 98
Bonner, Benjamin F. 88,124
Bonner, Benjamin T. 35
Bonner, John 35,88,124
Bonner, John L. 35
Bonner, John S. 88,124
Bonner, Thomas E. 1,54,110,124
Bonner, Thomas L. 35,88
Bonner, Williamson 35,88
Booker, B. 129
Booker, David 110
Booker, John 40,93
Booker, Lemuel 122
Booker, Samuel 40,93
Booker, William L. 33,86
Boon, John 46,99,130
Boothe, James 40
Boothe, John 40
Boothe, Mary 40,93
Boothe, Samuel 26,79
Borke, Thomas 23
Borum, Henry 124
Borum, James 20,72

Borum, John 20,72,118
Borum, John, Jr. 73
Borum, Jones 47
Borum, Richard 20,72,118
Borum, William 20,73,118
Boswell, William F. 8,61
Bowden, Bennett 33
Bowden, Bennett H. 87
Bowers, Bartlett 121
Bowers, Green 117
Bowers, Green C. 71
Bowers, Sopan 17
Bowers, William 117
Boyd, Charles H. 1,54
Boyd, James 61
Boyd, John 20,73,118
Boyd, William 46,99
Bradberry, James 67
Braden, Charles 40,93,126
Bradley, Barnett 51,132
Bradley, Bernard 104
Bradley, Charles 1,84,122
Bradley, David 20,73
Bradley, Everett 20,73,
  131
Bradley, George 18,117
Bradley, James 118
Bradley, John 1,73,119,
  132
Bradley, John, Jr. 51
Bradley, John, Sr. 104
Bradley, Jonas 20,73
Bradley, Morris 118
Bradley, Samuel 118
Bradley, Samuel B. 20,73
Bradley, Sarah 43
Bradley, Thomas 30,83,122
Bradshaw, Amzi 40,93
Bradshaw, James C. 52,106,
  131
Bradshaw, John 104,132
Bradshaw, Thomas 65
Bradshaw, Thomas, Jr. 65
Bradshaw, Wilson 12,65
Brady, George 71
Braley, David 118
Branch, A. G. 130
Branch, Andrew J. 99
Branch, Fanny 46,99.130
Branch, H. I. 130
Branch, Jackson 46
Branch, James 61
Branch, James H. 46,99
Branch, R. C. 130
Branch, Robert C. 46,99

Branch, Thomas 46,99
Brashears, John 7,60
Brashers, John 101
Breedlove, Aylette 102
Breedlove, Aylette B. 49
Bretherton, Henry 77
Bretherton, John 77
Brevard, John 122
Brevard, Thomas 52,106
Brewer, Morris 3,57,112
Briant, Archibald 67
Briant, David 31,84
Briant, Hiram 14,67
Briant, John 13,43,65,96
Briant, Mary O. 22
Briant, Richard 43,97
Briant, Samuel 14,67
Bridges 91
Bridges, Alexander 26,81
Bridges, Allen H. 12,65
Bridges, Brinkley 12,65
Bridges, David 26
Bridges, Joel 81
Bridges, Joel C. 26
Bridges, John A. 26,79
Bridges, Sampson 26
Britain, James H. 14,67
Britain, Joseph 130
Brittle, Milton 46
Brocherton, Henry 25
Brocherton, John 25
Brogan, Armsted 47,101
Brooks, John 122
Brooks, Moses 49
Brooks, Moses T. 102
Broom, William 122
Brown, David 67
Brown, Elizabeth 26,54
Brown, George 14,67
Brown, Henry 35,88
Brown, Jackson N. 14,67
Brown, James M. 81
Brown, John 13,65
Brown, John C. 26,49,54
Brown, John H. 14,67
Brown, Jordan 54,110
Brown, Jordan H. 1
Brown, Matthew 14,67
Brown, Poindexter 52
Brown, Richard 14,67
Brown, Robert 28,81
Brown, Samuel 1,28,81,110
Brown, Thomas 99,128
Brown, William 65
Browning, Gilford 43

Browning, Guilford 96
Browning, James 18,71
Browning, Thomas D. 117
Browning, Thomas P. 18,71
Bryan, Mary 75
Bryan, Nelson 7,60
Bryan, Richard 7
Bryant, David 122
Bryant, William 122
Bryson, James 43
Bryson, John 42,95
Bryson, John, Jr. 42
Bryson, John, Sr. 95
Bryson, Joseph 42
Bryson, Joseph, Jr. 95
Bryson, Samuel 95
Bryson, Samuel, Jr. 42
Bryson, Samuel, Sr. 42,95
Bryson, William 42
Buchanan, John 1
Buchanan, William 22,75, 128
Buck, Elias 1
Buckley, Patrick 122
Buckley, Sally 9
Bullard, George H. 54,110
Bullard, William 49
Bumpass, Garrett 61
Bumpass, Robert 9,95
Bumpass, Robert H. 8,61
Bumpass, Robert, Sr. 42
Bunby, William 122
Bunderant, Robert 14,67
Bundy, David 22,70,115
Bundy, James 22,70,128
Bundy, John 22,70,115
Bundy, Nathan 17,70,115
Burdine, Penelope 35
Burdine, Weston 35
Burge, Peterson 22
Burge, William 52
Burk, Edward 1
Burke, Arnold 24,77
Burke, Edward 54
Burke, Fielden 24
Burke, Lewis 76,121
Burke, Samuel 33,86
Burke, Thomas 76,121
Burnett, John 30,84,122
Burns, Brantley 1,115
Burton, Edmund 65
Burton, Robert M. 1,54
Butcher, Charles 118
Butt, Hazel 122
Butt, John 122

Butt, Mary 126
Byrn, James 95
Byrn, R. L. 61
Byrns, Brantley 70
Caffy, James D. 43
Cage, Claiborn C.
Cage, Thankful 110
Cain, Elisha G. 54
Cain, George 25,77
Calahan, M. P. 77
Caldwell, John 102
Calhoon, James 20
Calhoon, John 1
Calhoon, Moses P. 25
Calhoon, Samuel 20,119
Calhoon, Thomas 20,119
Calhoun, James 71,117
Calhoun, Samuel 54
Calhoun, Thomas 73
Calin, Isham 128
Callis, Richard 114
Campbell, Archibald 38,91
Campbell, David 34,54
Campbell, David, Jr. 54
Campbell, E. G. 91
Campbell, Harrison 33,88
Campbell, Hugh 33,38,86
Campbell, Hugh L. 91
Campbell, James 9
Campbell, James, Jr. 62
Campbell, James, Sr. 62
Campbell, Joseph W. 34
Campbell, Robert 15,67
Campbell, Thomas 33
Campbell, William 38
Campbell, Wilson 9,62,91
Campsey, John 1,54
Canady, William 110
Candler, Henry 110
Candler, John 7,101,108
Candler, Winsor 47
Candler, Winston 101
Caniers, Thomas 15
Cannon, James 40,93
Cannon, John A. 27
Cannon, John N. 102
Caplan, Martha 128
Caplinger, Captain 51,104
Caplinger, John 100,132
Caplinger, Solomon 51,104,132
Caplinger, William 51,104,117,13?
Caraway, John 59,112
Caraway, Lovett 107
Caraway, Merritt 4,57,112
Caraway, Moses 4,57,112

Caraway, Willice 112
Caraway, Willis 4,57
Carland, Patsy 75
Carlin, Hugh 53
Carlin, Patsy 17,116
Carlin, Spencer 128
Carlock, Captain 44,97
Carlock, Eben 91
Carlock, Eber 38,126
Carlock, Epenetus 45,98
Carmus, Thomas 67
Carpenter, Conrod 44,98
Carpenter, W. W. 108
Carr, Dabney 31,84,122
Carr, Elisha G. 110
Carr, John 31,84,122
Carr, Martha 122
Carr, Matthew 85
Carr, Richardson 31,84, 122
Carr, Walter 31
Carr, Wilson 67
Carrod, John 130
Carroll, John 37,89
Carroll, William 37
Carruth, Alexander 35, 88,124,125
Carruth, Alexander C. 35
Carruth, Alexander, Jr. 88
Carruth, Eli 125
Carruth, Eli S. 35,88
Carruth, J. C. 110
Carruth, James 17,35,70, 115
Carruth, James C. 35
Carruth, James S. 17
Carruth, James T. 70,116
Carruth, Joseph 88
Carruth, Joseph W. 35
Carruth, Samuel C. 17,70
Carruth, Walter 35,70, 88,116,125
Carruth, William R. 17,70
Carruth, William S. 35, 88,125
Carson, Henry 20
Carter, B. 128
Carter, Bernard 22,75
Carter, F. 75
Carter, Federick 128
Carter, Frederick 22
Carter, Gideon 29,81
Carter, Jacha 27
Carter, Jack 79
Carter, John T. 35

Carter, Leroy C. 17
Carter, Nathaniel G. 37,89
Carter, William W. 1,73,119
Cartmell, Nathan 15,67
Cartmell, Nathaniel 5,59
Cartwright, Benajah 22
Cartwright, Elijah 130
Cartwright, Elizabeth 75
Cartwright, Hericha 130
Cartwright, Hezekiah 46,51,104, 133
Cartwright, John 38,91
Cartwright, Matthew T. 100,130
Cartwright, Richard 38,91
Cartwright, Samuel 51,104
Caruthers, Robert L. 1,110
Carver, Isaac 27,79
Carver, William 27
Cason, James R. 9
Cason, Jeremiah 45,77
Cason, Joseph 45,98
Casselman, Benjamin 112
Casselman, Jacob 57,112
Castleman, Jacob 4
Casy, Jesse 46
Casy, John 31
Cate, Thankful 54
Cates, John 17,116
Cathcot, Midget 51
Cathron, John H. 81
Cawnthey, George 51
Cawthon, John 27
Cawthon, John H. 29
Cawthon, John R. 79
Cawthon, Lawson 27
Cawthon, Thomas F. 27,79
Cawthon, Thomas H. 79
Chamberland, Charles 116
Chamberlain, Thomas, Jr. 70
Chamberlin, Thomas 17
Chambers, Alexander 88
Chambers, John 35,88,124
Chambers, Lewis 88;125
Chambers, Nicholas 35,88,125
Chambers, Thomas 29,81
Chambliss, Henry 54,110
Chance, Alexander 4
Chandler, Andrew 28,82
Chandler, Captain 28
Chandler, E. A. 54
Chandler, Eddins 107
Chandler, Ekilles 1
Chandler, Green 27,79
Chandler, Henry 1,54
Chandler, James 37

Chandler, James L. 89
Chandler, John 31,84
Chandler, Jordan 29,81
Chandler, Josiah 29
Chandler, Kellis E. 110
Chandler, Robert 1,54,110
Chandler, Sarah 81
Chandler, Widow 29
Chandler, William 27,81
Chapman, Benjamin 1,54,110
Chapman, Silas 1,54,110
Chapman, Thomas 100,130
Chappel, Thomas B. 20
Chappell, Robert 27
Chappell, Thomas 73
Chappell, Thomas B. 119
Chappell, William 27,79
Chary, James 73
Chastain, Elisha 51,104, 132
Chaver, David 56
Chavis, Daniel 128
Cherry, Daniel 1,54,122
Cherry, Wiley 1
Cherry, William 54
Cherry, Willie 122
Chick, Ambler 104
Chick, Hamblin 51
Choplin, Robert 126
Christie, Thornton 100
Chumley, Beverly 62
Chumley, Daniel 47,101
Chumley, Dennis 101
Chumley, Denny 47
Chumley, Richard 47,101
Chumley, William 47,101
Chumney, Beverly 9
Clanton, Edmund 112
Clark, George 46,100,130
Clark, Joseph 110
Clark, Joshua 1,54
Clark, Parsons 17,116
Clark, Pryor 70
Clary, James 20,106,125
Clary, John 17,119
Clay, Archie 59
Clay, Arthur 5
Clay, Charles 67
Clay, Elijah 122
Clay, John 54,122
Clay, Sidney 27
Clay, Sydney 79
Clay, Wadkins 29,79
Clayton, Benjamin 25,77
Clayton, Pheba 15

Clayton, Phebe 67
Cledemen, Joseph G. 67
Clements, Samuel 98
Clemmons, Alfred 29,81
Clemmons, Allen 29,81
Clemmons, Elizabeth 57
Clemmons, Etheldred 4,112
Clemmons, James 11,57,114
Clemmons, Jeptha 4,57,112
Clemmons, John 28,81
Clemmons, Samuel 44
Clemmons, Samuel T. 3,114
Clemmons, William L. 29
Clendenon, Joseph 15
Click 132
Click, Matthias B. 31
Clifton, Benjamin 17,116
Clifton, Hannah 70,116
Clifton, Jesse 116
Clifton, L. 70
Clifton, Lovett 116
Clifton, Lovin 3
Clifton, Thomas 17,106,116
Clifton, William 110
Climer, John 107
Cloah, Elijah 84
Clopton, Jesse 77
Clopton, Jesse B. 25
Clopton, John 77
Clopton, Walter, Jr. 25,77
Clopton, Walter, Sr. 25,77
Clopton, William 25,77
Cloyd, Alexander 49,102
Cloyd, David 49,102
Cloyd, Ezekiel 49
Cloyd, James 97
Cloyd, James M. 43
Cloyd, John M. 49
Cloyd, Joseph 49,102
Cloyd, Newton 49,102
Cluck, Henry 76
Cluck, Henry, Jr. 24,121
Cluck, Henry, Sr. 24,76,121
Cluck, William 24,76,121
Coapland, Samuel 45
Cock, Jarrett 45
Cocke, Fleming 14
Cocke, Flemming 67
Cocke, Henry 14
Cocke, John 25,77
Cocke, L. 62
Cocke, Valentine 93
Cocke, William 14,67
Coe, Isaiah 52,104
Coe, John 17,70,115

Coe, William 53,106,131
Coffee, James D. 97
Coker, Valentine 40,126
Cole, Elisha 107
Cole, Sarah 34,87
Coleman, Linsey 9,62
Coleman, Theophilus 47,101
Coles, Isaac G. 67
Coles, John 67
Coles, Robert 15
Coles, Robert N. 67
Coles, Samuel 15,67
Coles, William T. 14,67
Colewick, William 51
Collier, Joseph 108
Collins, Crafford 76
Collins, Crawford 121
Collins, Elisa 121
Collins, Elisha 76
Collins, Jesse 121
Collins, John 130
Collins, William C. 25
Colwick, William 130
Comer, James 112
Comer, John 11,98
Comer, Reuben 126
Comer, Reuben C. 40
Comer, Reuben P. 93
Comer, Samuel 93
Comer, Samuel R. 40,126
Comer, William 4,57
Compton, Alexander J. 91
Compton, Alexander L. 38
Compton, Allen 122
Compton, Allen J. 84
Compton, Charles 38,91
Compton, Elizabeth 100
Compton, John 122
Compton, John, Jr. 91,84
Compton, John, Sr. 31,84, 122
Compton, Margaret 46,100
Compton, Margrett 130
Compton, Matthew 33,86
Compton, Nancy 31,122
Compton, Rebecca 38,91
Compton, Robert 31
Compton, Vinson 122
Compton, William 84,100,130
Connell, William 128
Conner, William 110,112
Conrod, John 100
Conyers, Andrew 59,110
Conyers, John 1
Conyers, Thomas 59

Conyers, Thomas, Sr. 5
Conyers, William 1
Cook, A. 110
Cook, Green B. 5,59
Cook, Jesse 5,59
Cook, Samuel A. 1,54
Cook, Thomas 34,87
Cook, William R. 9
Cooley, Henry 13,89
Cooper, Abraham 42,95
Cooper, Benjamin B. 42,95
Cooper, Christopher 42,43,95
Cooper, Frances 42,95
Cooper, John 87
Cooper, Margaret 15,67
Cooper, Sam 95
Copeland, Samuel 98
Coppage, Charles 5,67
Coppage, Charles, Sr. 67
Coppage, Elias 14
Coppage, James 67
Coppage, John 15,84,122
Coppage, Thomas 67
Corder, Benjamin 46,100,130
Corley, Alfred 18
Corley, Austin 19,71,117
Corley, Nathan 71,117
Corley, Nathaniel 18
Corley, Robert 122
Corley, Samuel 19
Corley, William 18,71
Corn, John A. 42
Corum, Eli 31,84,122
Corvin, James 6
Couch, Thomas 9
Courtney, George 132
Covington, George W. 112
Cowan, James 59
Cowan, William 79
Cowan, William M. 67
Cowger, Adam 31,84,122
Cowger, John 31,84,122
Cowgill, John 49,102
Cox, Anderson 53,106,128
Cox, Captain 22
Cox, Garrett 98
Cox, Henry 22,75
Cox, Henry L. 128
Cox, James 22,31,75,84,128
Cox, John 1,22,54,110
Cox, Robert 40,93,128
Cox, Thomas 100,130
Cox, William 75,110,128
Cox, William, Jr. 22
Cox, William, Sr. 22

Crabtree, Jacob 90
Crabtree, Joseph 13,65
Crabtree, L. D. 37
Crabtree, Lorenzo D. 89
Crabtree, Rebecca 37
Craddock, John 9
Craddock, John C. 108
Craddock, Nancy 108
Craddock, William C. 25
Crage, Abner J. 29
Craig, Abner J. 57
Craper, Azra 93
Craper, James 93
Craper, Thomas 119
Crawford, Edmund 107
Crenshaw, David 128
Crenshaw, Garland C. 20
Crenshaw, William 13,65
Creswell, Mary 15
Creswell, Miner 15
Criswell, Eli 67
Criswell, Minor 67
Criswell, Robert B. 65
Crocker, Jesse 31,84
Crook, William 98
Cropper, Ebenezer 126
Cropper, James 128
Cross, James 9,62
Cross, William 62
Crowder, David 62
Crudup, Elisha P. 49
Crudup, John 49,102
Crutcher, Foster G. 110
Crutcher, Jesse 122
Crutcher, Thomas, Jr. 1
Crutcher, Thomas, Sr. 1
Crutchfield, George 57
Crutchfield, George W. 4
Crutchfield, Henry 88, 110,128
Crutchfield, James 28,49, 75,82
Crutchfield, O. F. 29
Crutchfield, Samuel 22,128
Cryer, William 54
Cullen, M. A. 76
Cummings, Charles 110
Cummings, Charles W. 54
Cummings, G. W. 11
Cummings, George D. 1,54, 110
Cummings, John 107
Cummings, Sinclair 7
Cummings, William 11,98
Cunningham, James 40,93,126

Cunningham, John 40,93,126
Cunningham, Joseph 107
Cunningham, M. 125
Cunningham, Moses 38,93
Curd, Elizabeth 26,79
Curd, Elizabeth, Jr. 27
Curd, James 27,79
Curd, Price 26,79
Curd, Thomas 27,79
Curd, William 26
Curray, A. B. 28
Curray, Ezekiel 29
Curray, James 29
Curray, John 28
Currey, Abner B. 81
Currey, Ezekiel 82
Currey, John 81
Cutheral, Joseph 51
Cutrell, Joseph 104,132
Cutrell, Midget 104,132
Dallace, Morgan 106
Dallace, Thomas 106
Dance, John E. 25,77
Daniel, James 37
Daniels, Black 11
Daniels, Captain 37
Darity, William 132
Daughty, Robert 46
Davenport, Abraham 95
Davenport, Edmund 95
Davenport, Hardy 95
Davenport, Reuben 95
Davenport, Warren 95
Davenport, Wiley 95
David, Echols 132
David, Isaiah 7,60
David, Susanah 7,60
Davidson, Francis 51,105,132
Davidson, James 33,86
Davidson, John 2,54,110
Davidson, William 51,105,132
Davidson, Wilson 93
Davis 29
Davis, Archum L. 6
Davis, Arthur L. 59
Davis, Benjamin 6,59
Davis, E. 105
Davis, Elijah 2
Davis, Elizabeth 40,93,126
Davis, Enoch 51,132
Davis, Harvey 67
Davis, Henry 15
Davis, Hezekiah 31,84,122
Davis, Isham 31,84,122
Davis, Isham F. 27,65

Davis, Jack 67
Davis, James 73,119
Davis, James H. 15,67
Davis, James N. 7,60
Davis, John 2,15,27,102, 119
Davis, John H. 1
Davis, John L. 73
Davis, Josiah 127
Davis, Nathaniel 13,65,82
Davis, Robert 40,93,127
Davis, Robert C. 2
Davis, Samuel 37,90
Davis, Solomon 46,100
Davis, Terrill 40,93,126
Davis, Thomas 15,40,67,93
Davis, William 9,15,31, 59,67,84,122
Davis, William H. 73
Davis, Wilson C. 59
Davis, Zachariah 31,84, 122
Day, G. 130
Dean, James 6,59
Dearing, Alben 100,130
Dearing, Alben J. 46
Dearing, Lewis 110
Debnum, Robert B. 87
Debow, Archibald 119
Debow, Archy 73
Dedman, Robert R. 31
Dejarnette, J. M. 62
Dejornet, John 9
Delap, Thomas 106
Delapp, Thomas 53
Dellas, Morgan 131
Dellas, Robert 131
Deloach, Jerusha 37
Deloach, Samuel 37,65
Dennis, Henry 7,60
Denton, Edward 34,87
Denton, James 87
Devault, Henry 29,82
Devenport, Absolum 42
Devenport, Edmund 42
Devenport, Hardy 42
Devenport, Reuben 42
Devenport, Warren 42
Devenport, Wiley 42
Dew, Arthur 1,54,110
Dew, Davis 1,110
Dew, Elizabeth 110
Dew, Jack H. 110
Dew, John H. 1,54
Dew, Matthew 2,54,110

Dew, Nancy 6,70,110
Dice, Jacob 19
Dice, William 51,105,132
Dickens, Samuel 6,59
Dill, Jacob 71
Dill, Joel 15,67
Dill, John 31,84,123
Dill, William 84
Dillard, Allen 71,123
Dillard, Allen R. 117
Dillard, Captain 18
Dillard, Earnest 125
Dillard, Edward 19
Dillard, William 71
Dillard, William B. 19
Dillard, William M. 19,117
Dillis, Robert 53
Dillon, James 62
Dillon, Jesse 60
Dillon, John 9,62
Dillon, William 62
Dixon, Thomas 1
Doak, A. F. 40
Doak, Alanson F. 93
Doak, John F. 40,93,127
Doak, Manson F. 126
Doak, Martha 40,93
Doak, Nelson 25,77
Doak, Rufus P. 40
Dobson, Benjamin 29,82
Dobson, Hiram 82
Dobson, William R. 29,82
Dodd, James 7
Dodd, John 7
Dodd, Joseph 7
Dodd, Richard 7,60
Dodd, Simon 121
Doherty, Samuel B. 121
Doherty, William 121
Donaldson, Daniel 65
Donaldson, Ebenezar 80
Donaldson, Humphrey 87
Donaldson, James 13,80
Donaldson, R. 131
Donaldson, Robert 13,27
Donaldson, Robert, Jr. 80
Donaldson, Robert, Sr. 65
Donaldson, William 27,79
Donnell, Adnah 93,98
Donnell, Allen 75
Donnell, Calvin 127
Donnell, David 98
Donnell, David K. 45
Donnell, Edney 40
Donnell, George 20,40,73,93,119,

Donnell, James 40,93
Donnell, Jane 40,93
Donnell, John 45,98,127
Donnell, Josiah 40,93
Donnell, Leo 100
Donnell, Leo L. 46
Donnell, Levi 22,75,128,130
Donnell, Martha 40,93,126
Donnell, Mary 126
Donnell, Robert 17,40,70, 93,116,126
Donnell, Samuel 64,114
Donnell, Thomas 40,116
Donnell, William 40,126
Donnell, William C. 93
Donnell, William L. 126
Donnell, William P. 93,127
Donnell, William S. 93
Dorch, Abel 31
Dorch, Isaac 31,67
Dorch, John 31
Dorch, Richard 122
Doss, Samuel 46,100
Dotson, L. 130
Dotson, William 105
Doughtry, Lorenzo 130
Doughtry, Robert 130
Douglass, Burchett 2,54,110
Douglass, Ennes 19,71,117
Douglass, H. L. 1,54
Douglass, Henry L. 110
Douglass, Ila 123
Douglass, Norval 1,54,110
Dowell, John 38
Dowly, Robert 100
Dowly, William 100
Downey 15
Drake, Britain 13,65
Drake, William B. 15,67
Drennan, Delphy 29
Drennan, Hiram A. 121
Drennan, James 29,82
Drennan, John 82
Drennan, Jonathan 49,79
Drennan, Thomas 29,82
Drennan, William 29,49,102
Drew, Edward 25
Drollander, William S. 40
Drollender, Mary 102
Drollender, William 93
Drollinger, John 49
Dudley, Woodson 51,105,132
Duff, Robert 51,105,132

Duffer, Edward 77
Duffer, Thomas 77
Duke, Alfred 59
Duke, John 34,87
Duke, L. C. 91
Duke, Littleton 127
Duke, Sion 34,59
Duke, Uriah 34,87
Duke, William 34,87
Duncan, George A. 19,117
Duncan, George F. 71
Dunn, Elizabeth 48
Dunn, William 47,101
Dwire, John 110
Dwyer, Lewis H. 88
Dyer, Lewis H. 35,125
Eagan, Barna 68
Eagan, Barnaba 15
Eagan, Hugh 68
Eagan, Hugney 15
Eagan, James 15,68
Eagan, Jesse 15,68
Eagan, John 68
Eagan, Reace 15,68
Eagan, William 15,68
Ealey, Josiah 127
Eands, John 9
Earheart, Joseph 49
Earheart, Moses 49
Earheart, Nimrod 49
Eason, Eli E. 35,88,125
Eason, Ira E. 20,73
Eason, J. R. 63
Eason, Jesse 123
Eastland, N. W. 55
Eastland, Nicholas 71
Eastland, Nicholas W. 119
Eatherly, Isaac 37,90
Eatherly, John 87
Eatherly, John B. 37
Eatherly, John R. 90
Eaton, Joseph 91
Echols 60
Echols, David 105,132
Echols, Joel 6
Echols, Joseph 51,100,110
Echols, Turner 59
Eddings, Captain 8
Eddings, James 15
Eddings, L. 62
Eddings, O. 62
Eddings, Ozburn 9
Eddings, William 9,34,62
Eddings, William, Jr. 34

Eddins, Captain 61
Eddins, James 68
Eddins, John 82
Eddins, William, Jr. 87
Eddins, William, Sr. 87
Edge, Edward 47,161
Edge, Elam 100
Edge, Elem 46
Edney, John 29
Edwards, Crawford 11,64,114
Edwards, Eaton 11,64,114
Edwards, Edward 11,64,114
Edwards, Eli 11,64,114
Edwards, Granville 22
Edwards, Green B. 12,98
Edwards, Green D. 114
Edwards, Henry 11,114
Edwards, Henry, Sr. 64
Edwards, Hiram 45
Edwards, Hugh 11,64,114
Edwards, James 51,105,132
Edwards, John 11,22,75,114, 130
Edwards, John, Jr. 64
Edwards, John, Sr. 64
Edwards, Mariah 123
Edwards, Nicholas 15,68
Edwards, Robert 11,64
Edwards, Sally 98
Edwards, Sterling 98
Edwards, Stokes 12,64
Edwards, Thomas 2,55,110
Edwards, Warren 43,108
Edwards, William 53,106,131
Elamon, Jesse 131
Elington, Green 2
Elliott, Robert 27
Elliott, Robert M. 80
Elliott, Samuel 20
Ellis, David 46
Ellis, Hicks 20
Ellis, Isaac 13
Ellis, James 13,20,73,119
Ellis, James L. 65
Ellis, Moses 20,73,119
Ellis, Nathan 20,73,119
Ellis, Radford 38,86
Ellis, Robert 20,106
Ellis, Robert H. 131
Ellis, Thomas 13
Ellis, Thomas W. 65
Elmore, Jesse 106
Enoch, Alfred 59
Enoch, Davis 105
Enochs, Alfred 6

Escue, Alfred 107
Escue, Benjamin 107
Escue, Robert C. 65
Eskew, Alexander 82
Eskew, Robert 82
Eskew, Wilie 82
Estes, Bartlett 31,84,123
Estes, Benjamin 6,59
Estes, Benjamin H. 59
Estes, George A. 6,59
Estes, Mary 6,59
Estes, Micajah 65
Estes, Samuel 6
Estes, Samuel E. 84
Estes, Thomas 34,87
Etheridge, Matthew 45
Etheridge, Silman 108
Evans, Anderson 49,102
Evans, G. A. 54
Evans, William 20,73,119
Everett, John 13
Everly, Adam 2,54
Evrett, Joel D. 55
Evrett, John 65
Ewing, James 7,60
Exum, William 125
Falkner, Edward P. 20
Fane, William 76
Faust, Elizabeth 100,130
Ferguson, John 84
Ferguson, Lemuel 87
Ferguson, Robert 88
Ferrell, Wiley 29
Ferrell, William 20
Ferrell, William W. 73,131
Fields, Brice 82
Fields, John 64,114
Fields, Reddin 12,64
Fields, Richard 12,64,114,122
Figures, Bart 35
Figures, Batt 88,125
Figures, Mary 35,88,125
Finley, O. G. 2,55,110
Fisher, Philip 51,105,132
Fite, Joseph 47,101
Fite, Leonard 47,101
Florida, Patrick 25,77
Fobbs, Alfred M. 88
Fonce, Elizabeth 46
Forbes, Arthur 111
Forbes, Elizabeth 128
Forbes, Thomas W. 22,128
Forbis, Arthur 75
Forbis, Elizabeth 75
Forbis, Wilie 75

Ford, Paskel 29,49
Forkum, Earnest P. 125
Foster, Albert 40,93,127
Foster, Alexander 40,93,127
Foster, Alfred H. 40,93,127
Foster, Elisha 51
Foster, Elizabeth, Sr. 111
Foster, Emsley D. 22,93
Foster, Isabella A. 90
Foster, James 40,93,127
Foster, John 75
Foster, John D. 40,93,127
Foster, John S. 22,128
Foster, John W. 93,127
Foster, Robert 20,73,119
Foster, William P. 45,98
Fouch, John 25,77
Fouch, Thomas 77
Fowler, John F. 48,62
Francis, Armstead 42,95
Francis, Corban 130
Francis, E. 42
Francis, Epaphroditus 95
Francis, Mary 42
Franklin, George 20,73,119
Frazer, Alexander 68
Frazer, James 2,55,111
Frazer, Joel 68
Freeman, daniel 32,88
Freeman, Dorrell 13,65,125
Freeman, Edward 13,65
Freeman, Joseph 55,111
Freeman, Obediah 4,57,112
Fuliton, Nathan 111
Fuliton, Robert 111
Fulks, A. M. 119
Fulks, Alfred F. 35
Fulks, And J. 35
Fullerton, Robert 4
Furguson, Barbary 123
Furguson, John 31
Furguson, Robert 17
Furguson, Samuel 123
Furlong, James 71
Furlong, James M. 117
Furlong, Martin 71,117
Fuston, James G. 48,101
Fuston, Joel 7
Fuston, John 64
Fuston, Leroy 7
Fustus, Lee Roy 60
Gaddy, Elizabeth 38
Gaddy, Ezekiel 38
Gains, Anthony 26,80
Gains, Gideon 27,80

Gains, William H. 27
Gallon, Joseph 48
Gann, Daniel 68
Ganter, John 55
Garden, Obediah 15
Garmany, Margaret 43,97
Garmany, William 43
Garner, Jeremiah 38,91
Garner, John 38,91
Garner, Wiley 38
Garner, Wilie 91
Garrison, Elijah 64
Garrison, Person 2,55,111
Garrison, Samuel 108
Garrison, Samuel J. 9
Garrison, Thomas 134
Gates, James 23
Gatlin, Joseph 101
George, Charles 48,101
George, Henry 48
George, James 48
George, James, Jr. 101
George, James, Sr. 101
George, John 46,100,130
George, Lucas 106,131
Gholdston, Elis 107
Gholdston, John 34,87
Gholdston, John A. 87
Gholston, Charles 57
Gibbs, Thomas 75
Gibson, Aaron 12,64
Gibson, David 24
Gibson, Isaac 29,82
Gibson, Jeremiah 12
Gibson, Jesse 2,111
Gibson, John 2,12,64
Gibson, Samuel 82
Gibson, Thomas 29
Gibson, William 95
Gilbert, Ebenezer 31,84,123
Gilbert, John 123
Gill, William 133
Gill, William B. 51,105
Gillam, Ann 45
Gillam, Edmund 45
Gillam, William 45
Gillespie, David 55,111
Gilliam, Ann 98
Gilliam, Edmund 98
Gilliam, L. S. 62
Gilliam, William 98
Gipson, Aron 114
Gipson, John 114
Glanton, John 13,65
Gleason, Thomas 82

Gleaves, Absolum 49,102
Gleaves, John 68
Glenn, B. 125
Glenn, Ben 35
Glenn, Benjamin 88
Glenn, Daniel 15
Glenn, Giles 35
Glenn, Giles H. 88,125
Glenn, John 88,125
Glenn, Martha 36
Glenn, Martha C. 88
Glenn, Marthus 125
Glenn, Thompson 84,125
Glenn, William 35,88
Goald, Pleasant 19
Goald, Thomas 19
Goard, William 45,98
Godfrey, James 9,77
Goens, Shadrach 51
Gold, Pleasant 71,117
Gold, Thomas 73
Golden, Thomas 29
Golladay, Isaac 2,55,111
Golson, Charles M. 113
Goodall, Francis 133
Goodall, Franky 105
Goodall, Hardin 51,105, 133
Goodall, John S. 51
Goodall, John T. 105,133
Goodall, William 51,105, 133
Goodman, Alfred M. 107
Goodman, Claiborne 82
Goodman, Coleman 29
Goodman, Edmund 97
Goodman, Edward 44
Goodman, John 90
Goodman, John J. 37
Goodwin, Allen H. 24,98
Goodwin, James 117
Goodwin, James B. 71
Goodwin, Jesse A. 57
Goodwin, William 121
Goodwin, William, Jr. 24
Goody 91
Gordon, Obediah 68
Gore, Captain 99,129
Gore, Joseph 46,100
Gossett, John 7,60
Gowin, William 76
Grainger, Garland 73
Grant, William 34
Graves, Asa 40,93,127

Graves, Bachelor 40,93,127
Graves, Benjamin 27,80
Graves, Benjamin F. 80
Graves, Joel 116
Graves, John B. 27,80
Graves, John G. 27,80
Graves, Joseph 17,70
Graves, Lewis 107
Graves, Lorenso 17
Graves, Lorenzo 93
Graves, Luvenia 127
Graves, Rice 20,73,119
Gray, James 24,76,121
Gray, John 15,68
Gray, Samuel, Jr. 68
Gray, Samuel, Sr. 15,68
Gray, William 15,68
Green, Abraham 48
Green, Anderson 73,119
Green, Captain 75,128
Green, Ezekiel C. 44
Green, Isaac 15,68
Green, James 44,97
Green, John 23,49,75,102
Green, John C. 23
Green, John, Jr. 75
Green, John, Sr. 128
Green, Joshua 49
Green, Samuel 102
Green, Thomas 112
Green, Thomas B. 57,112
Green, Thomas L. 57
Green, Thomas S. 4
Green, William 23,75
Greer, Joseph L. 131
Gregory, Thomas 15,68
Grier, Ezekiel 97
Grier, James 97
Griffin, Thomas 121
Griffis, William 40
Grigg, Jesse A. 107
Grimes, Jesse 65
Grimes, John 125
Grimes, William 121
Grinage, William 82
Grindstaff, David 23,91
Grindstaff, Isaac 33,86
Grindstaff, John 46,100,130
Grisham, R. W. 105
Grissim, John 4
Grissom, Asa 57,115
Grissom, Elijah 114
Grissom, Elizabeth 133
Grissom, John 57,113

Grissom, Joseph 105,134
Grissom, Rowlin W. 51
Grissom, Stephen 12,64,115
Grooms, John 35,88
Grubbs, Polly 71
Grubbs, William 19,117
Grundy, Felix 37,90
Guest, John 12,64,114
Guill, Barnett 103
Guill, Bernett 49
Guill, John H. 62
Guill, Josiah 49,102
Guill, Thomas 80
Gum, Sarah 97
Gunn, Amey 42
Gunn, Ann 95
Gunn, John 98
Gunn, John M. 43
Gunn, Samuel 43
Gunn, Sarah 43
Guthrie, Beverly 9
Guthrie, Daniel 116
Guthrie, Daniel J. 87
Guthrie, James 34,57
Guthrie, James B. 112
Guthrie, John 34
Guthrie, Thomas 17,70
Gwynn, Andrew 29,82
Gwynn, Captain 81
Gwynn, Ransom 29,82
Gwynn, Robert 29,82
Haas, Simeon 60
Hackney, Seth 45,98,115
Hadkins, Matthew 52
Hager, Jonathan 49,103
Hail, Jamima 113
Hail, Jeremiah 31
Hail, Thomas 115,123
Hailey 100
Hailey, James 47
Halbrook, William 31,84, 123
Hale, Thomas 53
Haley, James 130
Hall, B. B. 129
Hall, Benjamin B. 23
Hall, Julius M. 119
Hallum, Andrew 113
Hallum, P. 113
Hallum, P. A. 4
Hallum, Polly 57
Hallum, R. 113
Hallum, Robert 2,57,113
Hallum, S. R. 57

Hallum, William 2
Hamilton, Alexander 80
Hamilton, Captain 88,124
Hamilton, George 29,82
Hamilton, James C. 103
Hamilton, Joseph 27,49,80,103
Hamilton, Robertson T. 103
Hamilton, S. J. 125
Hamilton, Thomas 21,49,73,103, 119
Hamilton, Thomas J. 36,88
Hamilton, William 27,80
Hamlett, William 119
Hammer, John 38
Hammons, Samuel H. 97
Hammons, Thomas 68
Hancock, Charles 7,60
Hancock, Dawson 4,57,113
Hancock, Edward 70
Hancock, Green 70,113
Hancock, Henry 57
Hancock, Henry M. 4,113
Hancock, Hope 4,70
Hancock, John 41,93,115
Hancock, L. 113
Hancock, Lee 4,113
Hancock, Lemon 57
Hancock, Lemuel 116
Hancock, Lesley 4,57,113
Hancock, Lewis 7,60
Hancock, Martin 4,70,116
Hancock, Matilda 4
Hancock, Melinda 113
Hancock, Melisha 57
Hancock, Nancy 38,91
Hancock, Nelson D. 4,57
Hancock, Richard 7,60
Hancock, Samuel 4,70
Hancock, Simon 4,80
Hancock, Verlinda 4
Hancock, Wesley 115
Hancock, Westly 41,94
Hankins, Arthur 75,129
Hankins, John 23,53,75,106,129, 131
Hankins, Martha 131
Hankins, Matthew 53,106
Hankins, Richard 53,106,131
Hankins, William 23,75,129
Hannah, Wilson 77
Haralson, Alexander 27
Haralson, Ephraim 82
Hardy, William 27,80
Hargus, John 76

Harlan, Samuel 73
Harlan, Thomas 73
Harland, John 21
Harland, Samuel 20
Harland, Thomas 21
Harley, John 75
Harpeth, George 123
Harpole, Adam 31
Harpole, Adam, Sr. 31,84
Harpole, Captain 30
Harpole, Daniel 31
Harpole, George 31,84
Harpole, Sampson 31,84, 123
Harrell, Lea 82
Harrington, James 122
Harrington, Song Bird 116
Harris, Alexander C. 2
Harris, Alfred 4
Harris, Alfred B. 113
Harris, Alfred H. 57
Harris, Allen 25,77
Harris, Arthur 25,78
Harris, Braxton 97
Harris, Catharine 21,73
Harris, Charles 70,117, 125
Harris, Edward 4,6,116, 123
Harris, Edward R. 117
Harris, Eli 20,73,119
Harris, Elijah 95
Harris, F. Y. 119
Harris, Furgus S. 2,73
Harris, Isham 12,76,115
Harris, James 130
Harris, John 2,19,73
Harris, John D. 15,68
Harris, John R. 25,78
Harris, Jonathan 78
Harris, McGee 73
Harris, Magee 20
Harris, Meger 119
Harris, Richard 36,88,123, 125
Harris, Sneed 19,71,117
Harris, Thomas 17,70,116
Harris, Thomas R. 25
Harris, Wallace 108
Harris, William 119
Harris, William F. 15,68
Harris, William G. 82
Harrison, Answorth 15,49, 65,103
Harrison, Edmund R. 71

Harrison, Elizabeth 70,116
Harrison, Joshua 2,55,111
Harrison, Samuel 117
Harrison, Samuel R. 19
Harrison, Sanders 51
Harrison, Seth 111
Harrison, Sterling 17
Harrison, Steth 2,65
Harrison, Thweat 4,57,113
Harrison, William 51,105,133
Hart, William 116
Hartsfield, Jacob 55
Hartsfield, Sion 31
Hartsfield, Solomon 70,116
Hartsfield, William 2,106,113
Hartwell, Mabry 90
Harvey, Isaac 48
Harvey, John 23
Hasley, John 84
Hasley, Talbot 84
Hass, Henry 48,101
Hass, James 48
Hass, John 48,101
Hass, Simon 48
Hatcher, Martin R. 76
Hatcher, William 20,73,119
Hathaway, Elijah 101
Hathaway, John 48,101
Haugus, Simon 76
Hawk, Matthias 6,59
Hawks, John 4,57,113
Hay, William 19,72,117
Haynes, Herbert 24
Hays, Elizabeth 49
Hays, George 62
Hays, Harman A. 15,68
Hays, Hugh 49,102
Hays, James 48,49,101,103
Hays, Jane 49,103
Hays, Nathaniel 7,48,101
Hays, Pleasant 101
Hays, Preston 49,103
Hays, Samuel 60
Hays, William J. 103
Hayworth, Micajah 15,68
Hazelwood, John 98
Hazlewood, John 45
Heard, George W. 25
Heard, John A. 25
Hearn, Alexander 129
Hearn, Ebenezar 23,70,74,116
Hearn, Edward 111
Hearn, F. 133
Hearn, George 38,91,107
Hearn, George W. 4

Hearn, Jacob 38,91
Hearn, James 129
Hearn, James W. 23
Hearn, John 2,55
Hearn, Matthew 91
Hearn, Milbry 70,116
Hearn, Milby 17
Hearn, Pernel 17,41,93,129
Hearn, Samuel 111
Hearn, Stephen 41
Hearn, Stephen H. 93,127
Hearn, Stephen L. 17,70, 116
Hearn, Thomas 17,38,70,91
Hearn, Wallace 9,70
Hearn, William 17,116
Hearn, William C. 129
Hearn, Wilson 23,75,129
Hedgpeth, Silas 24,121
Heflin, Joab 100
Hegerty, Dennis 55,111
Hegerty, P. H. 55
Hegerty, Patrick 111
Hegerty, Thomas 2
Henderson, M. D. 41
Henderson, Michael 75
Henderson, Preston 45,98
Henry, Alexander 17,70
Henry, Charles 51,105,133
Henry, Esacour 105
Henry, Isaac 101
Henry, Jeremiah 51
Henry, Philip 52
Henry, Samuel 15,68
Henson, Lasorius 38
Heralson, Zarey 49
Heralson, Zary 103
Herndon, John 105
Herndon, young L. 86
Heron, Frederick 73
Hessey, James 49
Hessey, John 49,103
Hester, Benjamin 13,65
Hester, John 65
Hewet, John 103
Hibbitts, David C. 2,55, 111,123
Hickman, John 4,57,113
Hickman, L. 113
Hickman, Lemuel 65
Hickman, Lemuel T. 4
Hickman, Right 113
Hickman, Samuel 4
Hickman, Snoden 4,113
Hickman, Snoden, Jr. 4,57

Hickman, Snoden, Sr. 57
Hickman, William 4,57,113
Hickman, William, Jr. 55
Hickman, Wright 4,57
Hicks, A. W. 55
Hicks, Alfred 6,59,123
Hicks, John 97
Hicks, Thomas 34,87
Hide, Richard 37
Higgans, John 42
Higgans, William 42
Higgason, Samuel D. 68
Higgins, John, Sr. 95
Higgins, William 95
Hight, A. M. 77
Hight, Alfred M. 25
Hight, Joab W. 25
Hight, John T. 78
Hight, Joseph W. 78
Hight, Landson 43
Hightower, Steth 65
Hill 32,85
Hill, Braxton 31,84,123
Hill, Captain 83,122
Hill, Isaac 37
Hill, Isaac P. 90
Hill, Isaac W. 13
Hill, Jeremiah H. 57
Hill, Jesse 13,65
Hill, John 2,111,124
Hill, Lewis 15
Hill, Luke 13
Hill, Mrs. 6
Hill, Samuel 9,108
Hill, Thomas 37,90
Hill, William 107
Hinson, Lazarus 91
Hitchcock, William 68
Hobbs, Campbell 105
Hobbs, Esther 73
Hobbs, Green 133
Hobbs, Hetty 119
Hobbs, J. 133
Hobbs, James 51
Hobbs, Joseph C. 51
Hobson, Benjamin 29,31,82
Hobson, Benjamin H. 84,123
Hobson, Henry 6,84,123
Hobson, Joseph 29
Hobson, Nicholas 27,82
Hodge, John 121
Hodge, William 90
Hodge, William C. 37
Hodges, Ephraim 33
Hodges, James W. 25

Hoffer, Jacob 130
Hofter, Joab 47
Hogg, John 37
Hoggatt, James W. 111
Holbert, Joel B. 38,93,115
Holder, B. S. 19
Holder, Benjamin L. 117
Holder, Benjamin S. 71
Holderfield, Jacob 2,123
Holeman, German T. 2
Holland, Alexander G. 44, 97
Holland, Edward 24,76,121
Holland, John M. 34
Holland, Levi 27
Holland, William 7
Holland, William W. 75
Hollandsworth, Isaac 7,60
Hollandsworth, Jacob 7
Hollandsworth, John 7,60
Hollandsworth, William 7, 60
Holloway, Ezekiel 4,57,113
Holloway, John 4,57
Holloway, Levi 4,57
Holloway, Richard 4,57
Holly, Alex P. 34
Holly, Joseph 34
Holly, Joseph E. 59
Holman, Captain 54,110
Holman, John B. 2,55,111
Holman, Robert 36,55
Holman, Robert M. 111
Holman, Thomas 31
Holman, Thomas P. 2,55,84
Holmes, James 100
Holms, James 47
Holt, Jesse 31,84
Hooker, Benjamin 29,82
Hooker, Benjamin, Jr. 29, 82
Hooker, John 29
Hooker, Jonathan 82
Hooker, Joshua 29,82
Hooker, Matt 82
Hooker, Matthew 49
Hooks, Clinton 72
Hooper, G. L. 77
Hooper, George 44
Hooper, John J. 37
Hooper, William 90
Hooser, Valentine 27,80
Horn, Captain 5,58
Horn, Charles 57
Horn, E. P. 6

Horn, Etheldred P. 59
Horn, Matthew 6,59
Horn, Richard 31,55
Horn, Samuel 31
Horn, Thomas 55
Horn, William 31,84
Hornsby, John 80
Horsley, John 31
Horsley, Tolbert 31,123
Horton, Ephraim 29
Horton, Lee 29
House, Joshua 60
Howard, Bradford 12,98
Howard, George 42
Howard, Hiram 24,64,121
Howard, Mary 42,95
Howard, William 115
Howell, Caleb 15,65
Howell, Edward 13,65
Howell, Joseph 13,115
Howell, Mary 13
Howell, Pettes 119
Howell, Ransom 65
Hoxley, John 129
Hubbard, Clark 9,62
Hubbard, Hiram C. 9
Hubbard, Mariot 80
Hubbard, Merritt 27
Hubbard, Peter 2,55
Hubbard, Thomas 2
Hubbard, William 9,62
Huddleston, Anthony 25,78
Huddleston, G. A. 64,115
Huddleston, George A. 12
Huddleston, William W. 107
Hudson, Obediah 40,93,127
Hudson, Paschal 94
Hudson, Paskal W. 40
Hudson, Paskel P. 127
Hudson, Richard 45,59,98
Hudson, William 12,38,91,115
Huffman, Archibald 51,105
Huffman, Burrell 51,105
Huffman, Leonard 51,105
Huffman, Robert 51,105
Huflan, Burrell 133
Hufman, Genova 133
Hufman, Robert 133
Hughes, John 48,101
Hughes, Robert 84,123
Hughes, Salton 125
Hughes, Simpson 123
Hughes, Tarlton 88
Hughley, Abram 27,80
Hughley, Captain 26,79

Hughley, Charles 27,80  
Hughley, Enoch 29,82  
Hughley, George 80  
Hughley, George W. 27  
Hughley, Henry 80  
Hughley, Samuel 49,103  
Hughley, William 27,80  
Humphrey, John 47  
Humphreys, Henry 103  
Hunt, Alfred 59  
Hunt, Alfred M. 6  
Hunt, Archibald 86  
Hunt, Benjamin 6,15,59,68  
Hunt, Britain 55  
Hunt, Britain B. 111  
Hunt, Hardy B. 6  
Hunt, James H. 6,59  
Hunt, Jesse 6,59  
Hunt, John 6,59  
Hunt, Matthew 15  
Hunt, Thomas 6,59  
Hunter, Isaac 31,84,123  
Hunter, Jacob 31,84,123  
Hunter, Nancy 31  
Hunter, William 13,65  
Hunter, Wright 36,125  
Hurt, Henry 49  
Hurt, John A. 98  
Huse, Robert 31  
Hutcherson, Bailey 48,101  
Hutcherson, William 13  
Hutchings, Stephen 25  
Hutchings, William 25  
Hutchins, William 78  
Hyde, Richard 90  
Ingram, James 55,116  
Ingram, John 111  
Ingram, Joseph 13  
Ingram, Martin 42,95  
Ingram, Samuel 13  
Ingram, Shadrach 37  
Ingram, Sidney 42  
Irby, Captain 34,87  
Irby, James 2  
Irby, John 2,111  
Irby, Joseph 31,119  
Irby, Pleasant 53  
Irvin, James 55  
Irvin, James M. 2,111  
Irwin, John 80  
Jackson, Abraham 49,103  
Jackson, Archibald 50  
Jackson, Asa 87  
Jackson, Bennett 117  
Jackson, Burwell 72  

Jackson, Coleman 117  
Jackson, Coleman, Jr. 19,72  
Jackson, Coleman, Sr. 19,72  
Jackson, Dabney 37,65  
Jackson, Daniel 36,89  
Jackson, David 33,86  
Jackson, Dolly 36,125  
Jackson, Donnell 125  
Jackson, Henry 36,89,125  
Jackson, James 24,107,115  
Jackson, Jesse 4,72,94,116  
Jackson, John M. 36,89,125  
Jackson, Josiah 49,103,125  
Jackson, Larkin 24,76,121  
Jackson, Mark 36,88  
Jackson, Obadiah, Jr. 103  
Jackson, Obadiah, Sr. 103  
Jackson, Obediah 49,50  
Jackson, Purnel 19  
Jackson, Robert 19,72,117  
Jackson, Sarah 125  
Jackson, Thomas 16,106,121,131  
Jackson, Thomas L. 131  
Jackson, Thomas R. 53,106  
Jackson, Warren 72,117  
Jackson, William 9,31,49,103  
Jackson, William H. 84,123  
Jacobs, Edward G. 38,91  
James, Buchanan 9,62  
James, Enos 42  
James, Rial 34  
Jarman, Captain 77  
Jarman, John 121  
Jarman, Robert 25,78  
Jarman, Shadrach 25,78  
Jarman, Susan 121  
Jarrell, Boswell 6,59  
Jarrell, Fountain 6,59  
Jarrell, Hiram 32,84  
Jarrell, J. 31  
Jarrell, Joshua 123  
Jarrell, Wesley 59  
Jarrell, William 32,123  
Jarrett, Francis 84,123  
Jarrett, John 84,123  
Jarrott, Devereaux 34,87  
Jarrott, Frances A. 2  
Jarrott, John 31  
Jarrott, John G. 13  
Jenkins, John 50,105  
Jenkins, Joseph 33,86  
Jenkins, Nathan 25,78  
Jenkins, Tarber T. 103  
Jenkins, Turner 25,78  
Jenkins, Wiatt 51

Jenkins, William 49,103
Jenkins, William H. 133
Jennings, Anderson 13,65
Jennings, Asel 9
Jennings, Ashel 109
Jennings, B. C. 62
Jennings, Captain 108
Jennings, Clem 65
Jennings, Clement 13
Jennings, E. C. 109
Jennings, Elijah 9
Jennings, Jacob 9,108
Jennings, Jesse 9
Jennings, Joel 101
Jennings, John 9,62
Jennings, John A. 9,62
Jennings, Jose 9
Jennings, Rial 62
Jennings, Rial C. 9
Jennings, Robert, Jr. 9, 108
Jennings, Robert, Sr. 9
Jennings, Samuel 39,94
Jennings, Uriah 9,108
Jennings, William 108
Jennings, William C. 62
Jennings, William, Jr. 9, 62
Jennings, William W. 9
Jewell, Barnet 84
Jewell, Elihu 42
Jewell, Joshua 84
Jewell, William 84,97
Joall, John B. 111
Johns, John 4,57
Johns, William 97
Johns, William M. 44
Johnson, Charles 24,76,121
Johnson, Coleman 7,60
Johnson, Daniel 21,73,119
Johnson, Davidson 119
Johnson, Dennis K. 97
Johnson, Garrett 24
Johnson, Hardy 101
Johnson, Hartwell 48
Johnson, Henry 6,34
Johnson, Henry F. 55
Johnson, Henry H. 111
Johnson, Isham 37,90
Johnson, James 9,15,21,62, 68,73,119
Johnson, James C. 36,125
Johnson, James H. 2,55,111
Johnson, Jemima 116

Johnson, Jeremiah 17,70
Johnson, Jesse W. 50
Johnson, John 2,73,119
Johnson, Jordan 53,116
Johnson, Joseph 2,55,111
Johnson, Joshua 106
Johnson, Littleberry 17,70,131
Johnson, Margaret 47,100
Johnson, Margrett 130
Johnson, Matthew 53,106,131
Johnson, Phillip 17,75,129
Johnson, Rawlings H. 55
Johnson, Robert 4,17,57,70,113, 116
Johnson, Robertson 21,73,131
Johnson, Rody 125
Johnson, Rollen H. 111
Johnson, Samuel 15,21,36,68,88, 119
Johnson, Samuel G. 68
Johnson, Samuel M. 15
Johnson, William 21,37,42,73,90, 119
Johnson, William A. 82
Johnson, William B. 15,62
Johnson, Williamson 60
Johnson, Zealous 53,73,119
Jolly, Frederick 31,68
Jolly, Hansell B. 107
Jolly, Isham 34,87
Jolly, William 6,59
Jones, Aaron 95
Jones, Allen 17,116
Jones, C. 133
Jones, David 45,78
Jones, David, Jr. 25
Jones, David, Sr. 98
Jones, Edward 41,94,127
Jones, Elija 129
Jones, Elijah 19,70,72,117
Jones, Elisha 17
Jones, Elizabeth 51,105
Jones, erasmus 43
Jones, Erasmus, Jr. 95
Jones, Erasmus, Sr. 95
Jones, Henry 78
Jones, Henry H. 2,55
Jones, Isaiah 9
Jones, Isham 41,94,127
Jones, James 17,70,116
Jones, John 17,70,76,111,116
Jones, John C. 24
Jones, John, Jr. 17,70
Jones, Josiah 62

Jones, Michael 21,43,95
Jones, Michael E. 119
Jones, Parson 17
Jones, Richard 41,94,127
Jones, Robert 78
Jones, Samuel 13,98
Jones, Thomas 6,29,44,48,
  82,84,101,123
Jones, Tolbert 43
Jones, Wiley 53,106
Jones, Willerford 27
Jones, William 25,78
Jones, William F. 38,91,
  97
Jones, Winford 80
Jones, Wood 37,90
Joplin, Elihu 32
Joplin, Elisha 125
Joplin, Thomas 19
Jopling, Elihu 89
Jopling, Robert 94
Jopling, Thomas 55,117
Jordan, Jer R. 9
Jordan, Jesse P. 62
Joyner, William 53
Justice, Ebenezer 57
Justice, John 4,57,113
Justice, Lemuel 113
Justice, Samuel 4,57
Keas 21
Keaton, Abraham 7
Keaton, Cornelius 7,60
Keaton, Larkin 42
Keaton, Mars 60
Keaton, Mary 7
Keaton, William 7,60
Keeling, George 125
Kelly, Daniel 9,62
Kelly, Dennis 9,47,62,
  100,130
Kelly, Nathaniel 48
Kelly, Nathaniel, Jr. 101
Kelly, Nathaniel, Sr. 101
Kelly, Samuel 33
Kemp, Burrell 13
Kemp, Burwell 66
Kennedy, Ann 59
Kennedy, David 2
Kennedy, Isaac 34
Kennedy, John S. 62
Kennedy, William 42,84
Kennedy, William B. 95
Killingsworth, James 2,55,
  111
Kimbrell, Benjamin 55

Kimbrell, Nicholas 13
Kindred, John 123
Kindred, Thomas 32,84,123
King, David 109
King, Dennis 9
King, Edward 41
King, George 32,84
King, John W. 34,87
King, Joseph 86
King, Richard 119
King, Robert 7,60
King, William 121
Kious, Henry 73
Kirkpatrick, Alexander 15
Kirkpatrick, Alfred 68
Kirkpatrick, Anderson 15,68
Kirkpatrick, David 15,68
Kirkpatrick, John 15
Kirkpatrick, Joseph 15,68
Kirkpatrick, Thomas 29,82
Kizias, Walker 85
Kneel, Joseph 27
Knight, David 12
Knight, James 4,57
Knight, Jesse 57
Knox, John 9,62
Kooliss, William 100
Lack, Frances 125
Lackey, Cela 44
Lackey, Sealy 97
Lain, John J. 32
Lambert, Anderson 16
Lambert, Price 68
Lambert, Warner 6
Lambeth, Warner 59
Lampkins, Charles 53
Lancaster, Levi 58
Land, Edward 50
Landson, Hugh 95
Landson, Robert 97
Landson, Susannah 97
Lane, Armstead 27,80,107
Lane, Augusta 29
Lane, Augustus 82
Lane, Christopher 107
Lane, David 27,80
Lane, Thornton 107
Lane, Tyre 50,103
Lane, W. 70
Lane, Willard 80
Lane, William 27
Lane, William F. 27,80
Lane, William J. 80
Lane, Woodson 18,116
Langford, Thomas 119

Langley, John 94
Lanier, William 98
Lannom, Captain 23,120
Lannom, J. 133
Lannom, John 24,107
Lannum, Susan 76
Lannum, Thomas 105
Lansden, Susannah 44
Lansden, Thomas D. 44
Lantern, Henry 50,103
Lantern, Joseph 50,103
Lantern, Thomas 103
Lanum, William 9
Larson, Captain 86
Lasater, Abraham 44,97
Lasater, Alexander 25
Lasater, Elizabeth 25,78
Lasater, Federick 44
Lasater, Frederick 97
Lasater, Hardy 25,78
Lasater, Jacob B. 25,78
Lasater, Jonathan 25
Lasater, S. H. 78
Lash, Captain 115
Lash, Hamman 70
Lash, Harman 18,116
Lash, John C. 116
Laughlin, L. G., Jr. 55
Laughton, L. G. 2
Lavender, William 123
Lawrence, Captain 32,76, 85
Lawrence, John 76,130
Lawrence, John, Jr. 47,100
Lawrence, John, Sr. 47,100
Lawrence, Joseph 33
Lawrence, Joseph B. 86
Lawrence, Robert 16,68
Lawrence, Turner M. 86
Lawrence, William 86
Lawrence, William, Jr. 33
Lawrence, William, Sr. 33, 86
Lea, Benjamin 94
Lea, Cloe 103
Lea, David 94
Lea, Hiram 41,94
Lea, Samuel 41,94
Leach, C. 29
Leach, George 25
Leach, James 42
Leach, John 42
Leach, Thomas 42
Leath, Peter 24,82
Leath, William E. 29,82

Lee, Benjamin 127
Lee, David 127
Lee, Samuel 127
Leech, James 96
Leech, John 96
Leech, Thomas 96
Leek, Mark 7
Leek, William 7
Leman, Henry 45
Lening, Isaac 8
Lester, Bennett 44
Lester, Captain 35
Lester, Daniel 70
Lester, Edward 109
Lester, Henry 18,70
Lester, Henry D. 116
Lester, J. L. 62
Lester, James L. 9
Lester, Joshua 9,109
Lester, L. 116
Lester, Manson 109
Lester, William 9,109
Lester, William D. 9
Lewis, Edgecomb 25,78
Lewis, James 59
Lewis, John, Sr. 7,60
Lewis, John, Jr. 7
Lewis, Thomas 7
Ligon, Henry 27,80
Ligon, James H. 27,80
Ligon, James S. 125
Ligon, John G. 37
Ligon, John H. 27,80
Ligon, John J. 66
Ligon, Joseph 2,55,119
Ligon, Josiah 50,103
Ligon, Richard 125
Ligon, Robert 111
Ligon, Thomas 117
Ligon, Valentine 125
Lindsay, Elizabeth 52,105
Lindsay, Josiah B. 94,127
Lindsay, Lewis 80
Lindsay, Philip 18
Lindsay, Taylor 29
Lindsey, Tailor 82
Lindsley, E. 133
Lindsley, Phillip 70,116
Link, James 57
Link, James A. 4,113
Little, James 13
Little, John 13
Little, William 55
Locke, Charles 36,89,125
Locke, Frances 89

Locke, James W. 89,125
Locke, Thomas 89,125
Locke, William 36
Lockhart, Elias 121
Logue, Carn 29
Logue, Carnes 82
Long, Alexander M. 23,94
Long, Robert 39,91
Lovin, John 24
Loving, John 76
Lowe, Easton 72
Lowe, Easton P. 118
Lowe, Green B. 19,72,118
Loyd, Anderson 55,116
Loyd, Andrew 34
Loyd, Charles 55
Loyd, James 27,82
Loyd, Jarratt 111
Loyd, Jarrott 18
Loyd, Lemuel 111
Loyd, Samuel 55
Lumpkin, Charles 106
Lumpkin, James 106
Lumpkin, Obediah 27,80
Lunceford, Eaton 66
Lunsford, Eaton 13
Lupkin, William 125
Luster, Presley 78
Lyle, Jesse 90
Lyon, James 36,89,125
Lyon, John 21,73,125
Lyon, Merritt 36,73,125
Lyon, Richard 19,36,72,89
Lyon, Thomas 19,72
Lyon, Valentine 36
Lyon, Volney 89
Lyon, William 21
Lyons, Richard 118
Lytle, W. F. 111
Lytle, William 2
McAdow, James 8
McAdow, James, Jr. 8,60
McAdow, James, Sr. 60
McAdow, Jehu 8,60
McAdow, William 8,60
McBride, Abraham 23
McBride, Daniel 23,75,105,129
McCaffrey, James 10,109
McCaffrey, John 10,62
McCartney, Lewis 107
McClain, Alexander F. 37,90
McClain, Alfred 37,90

McClain, John A. 37
McClain, Josiah S. 37,90,111
McClain, Martha D. 90,111
McClain, Mary P. 90
McClain, William 37
McClain, William P. 37,111
McConnell, David 2,55
McConnell, John 2
McConnell, John M. 6
McCorkle, Miles 90
McCown, Sampson 70
McCulley, David 50
McCulley, John 50
McCulloch, Nathan 121
McCulloch, William 24,121
McCullock, Benjamin 5
McCully, David 103
McCully, John 103
McDaniel, James 32,85,123
McDaniel, Stephen 125
McDaniel, William 10,62
McDerman, Briant 80
McDerman, Brien 27
McDerman, Wiley 29
McDerman, Wilie 82
McDonald, And J. 19
McDonald, Andrew J. 72,118
McDonald, Elias 19,72,118
McDonald, Randel 19
McDonald, Randolph 72
McDonald, Stephen 36,89
McDoogle, arch 8
McDougle, Archibald 60
McElyea, H. D. 62
McFarland, James 34,87
McFarland, John 34,87
McFarland, Winny 83
McGahee, Samuel 42
McGregor, Flower 27,80
McGregor, John 27,80
McGregor, William 28,80
McGrehey, Daniel 58
McHaffney, Robert 16
McHaffrey, Henry 16
McHaney, Oney 10,62
McHany, William 109
McHenry, Jesse 24,76,121
McIntire, William 10,62
McKee, Daniel 42,96
McKee, Robert 33,101
McKinney 39
McKinnis 92
McMeans, John 118
McMillin, John 86
McMinn, Elihu 45,98

McMinn, Jehu 42,96
McMinn, Newton 78
McMinn, Samuel N. 45
McMinn, Zedediah 96
McMullin, John 48
McMurray, David 21,74
McMurray, James 120
McMurray, James B. 21,74
McMurray, John M. 78
McNeal, Enoch 120
McNeely, Enoch 53
McNichols, Alexander 123
McNichols, Daniel 124
McSpadden, Thomas 21,119
McSpadden, Thomas C. 74
McSpadden, William 21,73, 120
McWherter, George A. 87
McWherter, George B. 6,59
McWherter, George F. 5,34
McWherter, George M. 34
McWherter, James 87
McWherter, Sam C. 34
McWherter, Samuel C. 87
McWherter, William 52
McWhirter, Charles 16
Mabry, B. T. 106
Mabry, Ben S. 2
Mabry, Benjamin F. 123
Mabry, David 85
Mabry, David D. 123
Mabry, G. 55
Mabry, George W. 111
Mabry, William 33
Maddox, Captain 39
Maddox, Charles B. 127
Maddox, Elijah 6
Maddox, Notley 41,94,127
Maddox, Richard 13,87
Maddox, Sims 41
Maddox, William 41,94,127
Madlin, John 13
Madlin, Littleton 13
Mahaffy, Henry 68
Mahaffy, Isaac 68
Maholland, John 23,129
Maholland, William 23,75, 129
Major, Captain 92,126
Major, Eli 127
Major, John 41,94,127
Major, John A. 127
Major, John, Sr. 94
Major, John W. 41
Mallory, Hugh R. 74

Mallory, William 86
Malloy, Benjamin 131
Malloy, Benjamin G. 131
Malom, Hugh R. 125
Manier, James D. 6
Manning, Catherine 134
Manning, John 105,134
Manning, Katherine 105
Manning, Lewis 105,134
Manning, Robert 100
Mannon, Caty 52
Mannon, John 52
Mannon, Lewis 52
Mansfield, Granville 32,85,123
Marks, James 52,100,105
Marks, James, Jr. 133
Marks, John 47,100,130
Marks, Thomas 52,105,133
Marlow, Payton 66
Marrs, Alexander 41,94
Marrs, Martin 41,94
Marrs, Mary 41,94
Marrs, William 41,94
Marshall, Carson 42,96
Marshall, Robert 42,96
Martin, Amos 26,98
Martin, Bird B. 68
Martin, Brice 13,66
Martin, Daniel 78
Martin, David 21,74,119
Martin, George 19,72
Martin, George B. 16
Martin, George W. 44,97
Martin, Jacob 24,78
Martin, James 2,10,26,62,85,123
Martin, James M. 18,70
Martin, John 27,74,80,119
Martin, John M. 21
Martin, Lindsay 12,94,115
Martin, M. 127
Martin, Matt 89
Martin, Noel 119
Martin, Pascal 13
Martin, Peyton 13
Martin, Pleasant 72
Martin, Pleasant M. 118
Martin, Pleasant, Jr. 19
Martin, Pugh 21,73,119
Martin, Rebecca 50,103
Martin, Robert 55
Martin, Robert H. 53
Martin, Thomas 21,74,119
Martin, Wesley 55
Martin, William L. 32,85
Martin, William S. 123

Mason, James 121
Mason, Ramsey L. 37
Mason, Thomas 53,106,131
Massee, Henry 19
Massey, Abram A. 39
Massey, Eli 41,94
Massey, Lewis 94
Massey, Louis 41
Massie, A. A. 91
Massie, Garrett 127
Mather, Henry 78
Mathis, Isaac 78
Mathis, Samuel 78
Matlock, George 30,80
Matthews, Alfred 60
Matthews, James 25,78
Matthews, Matt 25
Matthews, Matthew 78
Matthews, Nathaniel 60
Matthews, Samuel 25
Matthews, William E. 3,55
Matthis, Alfred 8
Matthis, Nathan 8
Maxwell, John 127
Maxwell, Milton M. 39
Maxwell, Sutton M. 92
Maxwell, William, Sr. 92
Mayo, Stephen 23,105
Mays, Craddock H. 90
Mays, Jacob 16,68
Mays, James 16
Mays, William 16,68
Mayson, James 98
Mayson, Ramsey L. 90
Measles, Ulelis 124
Measles, Wiley 85
Meazle, Wiley 3
Medley, John 78
Medlin, Gray 37,90
Medlin, Littleton 66
Medlin, Wilson 37
Medling, John 26
Melton, Benjamin 85
Melton, John 36,85
Melton, Richard 32
Melton, Thomas 12,32,85
Merritt, Fleming 10,62
Merritt, Harris 12
Merritt, James P. 45,98
Merritt, John 5
Merritt, John W. 45,98
Merritt, Lewis 12,64,115
Merritt, Mark 12,64,115
Merritt, Obediah 12,64,115

Merritt, S. 115
Merritt, Sherwood 12,64,115
Merritt, Silas 12,64,115
Merritt, Silvanus 12,64
Merritt, Thomas J. 45,98
Merritt, William B. 98
Merritt, William P. 45
Michael, John 16
Michaels, Alexander 129
Michaels, James 111
Michie, James 8,60
Mickle, John 131
Midgett, George 52,105,133
Midgett, Richard 100,130
Miles, Patterson 29,83
Miles, Thomas 82
Miles, Thomas, Jr. 24,82
Miles, Thomas, Sr. 24
Miles, William 32,85,111,123
Miligan, David 42
Miligan, James 42
Miller, Beverly 55
Miller, Beverly J. 2
Milligan, David 96
Milligan, James 96
Milton, Jacob 64,115
Milton, John 123
Milton, Joseph 64,115
Milton, Thomas 55,124
Minick, Avery 2
Mires, Peter 29
Mitchell, Elizabeth 6
Mitchell, Everett 36,89
Mitchell, Henry 6,59
Mitchell, John 29,82
Mitchell, Robert 6,59
Mitchell, Taswell 36,89
Mitchell, Thomas 36
Mitchell, Thomas R. 6,59
Mitchell, William 2
Mitchell, Zadock 6
Montgomery, Alexander 96
Montgomery, Elizabeth 42,96
Montgomery, James 42,96
Moody, James 33
Moody, William 80
Mooningham, Elijah 21,74
Mooningham, William 118
Moore, Abner 42,96
Moore, Alfred 66
Moore, Alston 118
Moore, Captain 33
Moore, David B. 94
Moore, George 39

Moore, George D. 18,70
Moore, Israel 16,68
Moore, James 33,47,58,100, 113,130
Moore, Jesse 58,113
Moore, Jesse L. 5
Moore, John 98
Moore, Joseph 104
Moore, Lemuel 48,101
Moore, Littleberry 60
Moore, R. L. 120
Moore, R. R. 98
Moore, Robert R. 45
Moore, T. C. 42
Moore, Thomas 52,100,130
Moore, Tilford 33
Moore, Warren 34,87
Moore, Whitfield 37,90
Moore, William 10,52,62, 123
Moore, David B. 127
Moore, Joseph 50
Moren, Uriah 48
Morgan, Astin 121
Morgan, William 39,92
Morris, Alenson 129
Morris, Alexander 127
Morris, Allison 71
Morris, Benjamin 83
Morris, Edward 59
Morris, Isham 18,70,116
Morris, Mary 127
Morris, Patrick 18
Morris, Patterson 18,129
Morris, Peterson 75
Morris, Richard W. 10
Morris, Thomas E. 6,59
Morris, William 115,127
Morris, William P. 70
Morrison, Andrew 42,96
Morrison, Hugh 41,94,127
Morrison, Joseph 97
Morrison, Levi 127
Morrison, Robert 44,97
Morrison, William 127
Morse, R. B. 127
Mosely, Asa 3,55
Mosely, John 32,85,124
Mosely, Littleton 28,80
Mosely, Peter 37
Mosely, Thomas 16
Mosely, Thomas D. 68
Mosely, William 32
Moser, Adam 36,89,125
Moser, Alfred 123

Moser, Daniel 32,85,123
Moser, Henry 41,94,118,127
Moser, James W. 34
Moser, Peter 36
Moss, Dandridge 28,82
Moss, James C. 32,85
Moss, John 27,29,80,82
Moss, John W. 28
Moss, Thomas 32,123
Moss, Thomas B. 85
Moss, William 32,85,123
Motheral, James 23,75,129
Motheral, Robert 16,68
Motheral, Samuel 16,68
Motley, B. T. 106
Motley, Benjamin 21
Motsinger, Elijah 36,89,125
Motsinger, James 133
Motsinger, Jefferson 19,72
Motsinger, Joshua 52,105
Mount, Alfred 45
Mount, Matthias 45
Mount, Richard 45,78
Mount, William 109
Moxley, Joseph 23,71
Moxley, Josiah 116
Muirhead, John 2,55
Mullinax, John 86
Mullinax, Zadock 33,86
Murphy, Aaron 52,105,133
Murphy, John 32
Murphy, Nicholas 123
Murphy, Robert 52
Murphy, Tilson 52
Murphy, William 36
Murray, Abraham 13
Murray, Abram 66
Murray, Jeremiah 50,103
Murray, John 13,50,66,103
Murray, William 29,82
Myers, Peter 82
Nailor, James 3
Neal, Ashley 39,92
Neal, Charles 33,86
Neal, Claborn W. 33,86
Neal, Elizabeth 33,86
Neal, George 47,92
Neal, Isaac 33,86
Neal, Madison 33,86
Neal, Pallis 33,86
Neal, William 33,86
Neal, Zeppiniah, Jr. 107
Neal, Zeppiniah, Sr. 107
Neighbours, John 37,90
Neighbours, Thomas 90

Neighbours, William 48,101
Nelson 129
Nelson, Garrett 24,77
Nelson, Jarrett 121
Nelson, William 24,76,121
Nesbett, Adison 133
Netherland, George W. 56
Nettles, Benjamin 39
Nettles, John 39,129
Nettles, John A. 75
Nettles, William 39
Nettles, William A. 92
New, James 89,126
New, Nelson 23,75
New, Nicholas 130
New, William 23,36,75,89, 99,125,129,130
New, William O. 36,89,125
Newby, John 18,71
Newby, Roland 100
Newby, Whaley 100
Newby, Wholey 130
Newman, John 3,106
Newsom, A. B. 36,89,125
Nicholas, Benjamin 30
Nicholas, Murphy 32
Nichols, Benjamin 83
Nickens, Archibald 71
Nickens, Calvin 94
Nickens, James 18,71,116
Nickens, John 41
Nickens, Mark 5
Nickens, Prescoat 18
Nipper, Ambrose 30
Nolin, M. 111
Nooner, George 121
Nooner, John 37
Nooner, John H. 90
Nooner, Nathan 39,92
Norman, Thomas 34,59
Norris, Samuel 37,90
Norval, James 45,98
Nowlin, Bird 32,85
Nowlin, Mary 55
Nowlin, Thomas 48
Nunn, Nicholas 100
Oakley, John 23,92
Oakley, William 10,86
Oaks, William 6
O'Briant, Cheatam 103
O'Briant, William 103
O'Brion, Mary 56
Oclay, John 130
Odum, Benjamin F. 96

Odum, Britain 47,100,130
Odum, Captain 41,95
Odum, James 43
Odum, James S. 43,96
Odum, James, Sr. 96
Odum, Moses 47
Odum, Samuel 43,96
Odum, William 43
Oliver, Alexander 121
Oliver, Edward 121
Oliver, James 94,121
Oliver, William 48,101
O'Neal, Asa 12,45,98
O'Neal, John 6
O'Neal, William P. 99
Oran, Thomas 8
Organ, Ennes 53
Organ, Ennis 53
Organ, Simpson 21
Organ, Woodford 21,74
Osburn, Thomas 26
Owen, Jesse 43,96
Owen, John 43,74,120
Owen, Josiah 96
Owen, Mary 120
Owen, Nelson 43,96
Owen, Richard 74,120
Owen, Wadkin 74
Owen, Wadkins 120
Owen, William 74,120
Owens, Anthony 8,61
Owens, Fountain 8,61
Owens, John 61
Owens, John F. 21
Owens, Josiah 8
Owens, Richard 21
Owens, Robert 53
Owens, Thomas 61
Owens, Watkins 21
Owens, William F. 21
Ozment, Alfred 5,58
Ozment, Armstrong 12,58
Ozment, David 107
Ozment, James 5,58
Ozment, James A. 113
Ozment, John 107
Ozment, Jonathan 12,58
Ozment, Richard, Jr. 107
Ozment, Richard, Sr. 107
Ozment, Samuel 12,58
Ozment, Sarah 12,58
Ozment, Thomas 108
Pague, John 121
Paine, George 120

Paine, Jesse 87
Paine, John 85
Paine, Thomas 120
Paine, William 120
Palmer, John 18,75,100
Palmer, John, Sr. 75,76
Palmer, John W. 19,72,118
Palmer, Thomas K. 129
Palmer, William 105,133
Pane, Henry 10
Pane, James 10
Pane, Jesse 34
Parham, James H. 121
Parham, Mary 50,103
Parham, Thomas 23
Parker, Frances 48
Parker, John K. 16
Parmer, John 23
Parrish, William 62
Parson, Elijah 48,102
Partain, Archibald 66
Partain, Henry 64
Partin, Randolph 131
Partlow, Thomas 30,83
Parton, Henry 115
Pasale, Hiram 45
Patterson, Burrell 45,78
Patterson, Burwell 26,109
Patterson, Captain 38
Patterson, David 94
Patterson, E. S. 10
Patterson, Elijah 30
Patterson, Esther 39,92
Patterson, Ezekiel 96
Patterson, Hugh 89
Patterson, Isaac 80
Patterson, John 43,96
Patterson, Julian 39,92
Patterson, L. F. 92
Patterson, Lewis 10,12,64, 109
Patterson, Newsom 10,98
Patterson, Peter 12,64,115
Patterson, S. 53
Patterson, Samuel F. 39
Patterson, William 39,78, 92
Patton, Andrew 10,63
Patton, John 10,63
Patton, John, Jr. 10
Patton, Jonathan 39,92
Patton, Joseph 39,92
Patton, Samuel 10,92
Patton, Thomas 10,92
Payne, George 59

Payne, Henry 62
Payne, James 62
Payne, Thomas E. 74
Payton, John M. 34
Payton, John W. 34,87
Peace, William H. 21,85
Peak, John 6
Pearson, Howell 89
Pearson, William 36,89
Pemberton, George 63
Pemberton, James 21,120
Pemberton, Jesse 53,74,120
Pemberton, Jesse, Jr. 21
Pemberton, Joel 116
Pemberton, John 10,39,107,131
Pemberton, John, Sr. 62
Pemberton, Joseph 111
Pemberton, Joshua 106
Pemberton, Josiah 18,71
Pemberton, Richard 10,62
Pemberton, Samuel 39
Pemberton, Thomas 62
Pemberton, William 53,106,131
Pembleton, John 52,92
Pendleton, Abraham 47
Pendleton, James 47
Pennybaker, Samuel W. 44,97
Pentecost, Thomas 113
Perkins, John 34,56
Pernel, N. L. 48
Perriman, Alexander 10
Perriman, James 48,102
Perry, Albert 37,90
Perry, Mitchell 6,59
Perry, Richardson 13
Persey, Francis W. 78
Person, William 126
Persy, Boswell 78
Persy, Sherwood 78
Persy, Williamson 78
Petty, Henry 3,56
Petway, William 36,89,126
Phelps, Washington 105
Philips, A. 52
Philips, Alfred 105,133
Philips, Alpha 23
Philips, Bailey 105,133
Philips, Barkley 21
Philips, Benjamin 92
Philips, Benjamin F. 30
Philips, Benjamin, Jr. 39,92
Philips, Benjamin, Sr. 39
Philips, David 39,92
Philips, George 10,86
Philips, Henry 21,74,133

Philips, John 39,52,92
Philips, Joseph 39,92
Philips, Josiah 92
Philips, Thomas 8,47,61, 100,130
Philips, William 39,52,92, 105,133
Phimm, Kinzie 59
Phipps, W. R. 64
Phipps, William 115
Pickett, Edward 10,62
Pickett, H. W. 62
Pickett, Isham 26
Piercy, Boswell 26
Piercy, Frances W. 26
Piercy, Sherwood 26
Piercy, Williamson 26
Pilkington, Henry B. 21,74
Piner, John O. 30
Pinkston, Moses 72
Pitman, Captain 14,66
Pitman, Henry M. 16,68
Pitman, Hutchins M. 66
Pitman, John B. 13,66
Pitmore, William 52
Pitner, Archibald 13
Pitner, Michael 13
Pitner, William 66
Poe, James 121
Polk, John 45
Polon, John W. 108
Pool, Giles B. 5,58,113
Porterfield, James 10,109
Porterfield, John 10
Porterfield, S. H. 109
Porterfield, Samuel C. 45, 98
Porterfield, Samuel H. 10
Posey, Alexander 30,83
Posey, Alison 30,83
Pound, Daniel 45
Powell, Abraham 94,129
Powell, Abram 23
Powell, Allen 26
Powell, James 94,127
Powell, John 34,87
Powell, Nathaniel 53
Powell, Scymon 107
Powell, Seamore 53,131
Powell, Wilie 94
Powell, William 19,72
Prestley, Halum 36
Prewett, Captain 56
Pride, Frances 105,134
Pride, Freeman 52
Pride, Shelton 50,103
Prim, Kinzie 6
Prim, William 32,56,111
Prior, John 78
Pritchett, Catharine 100,130
Pritchett, Elizabeth 131
Pritchett, George 47,100
Pritchett, Nathaniel 47
Proctor, David 34,87
Proctor, E. 124
Proctor, Edmund 6,32,85
Proctor, Edward 124
Proctor, Green 34,87,111
Proctor, Thomas 34
Provine, Alexander 21,74
Provine, John 21,74,120
Provine, Samuel 21,74
Provine, William A. 74
Pryor, John 26
Puckett, Charles 28,90
Puckett, Charles, Jr. 80
Puckett, Charles R. 37
Puckett, Coleman 44,97
Puckett, Francis 26,78
Puckett, Isham 26,78
Puckett, John 80,90
Puckett, P. R. 78
Puckett, Patrick 26
Puckett, Ship A. 30,83
Puckett, Washington 26,78
Puckett, William 26,78
Puffer, Samuel 16,68
Pugh, George 36,48
Pugh, George R., Jr. 102
Pugh, Isaiah 102
Pugh, Jesse 48
Pugh, Royley 48
Pullum, Bird 32
Pully, John 21
Pully, Robert 21,120
Pully, William, Jr. 21
Pully, William, Sr. 21
Pursell, Hiram 98
Pursley, William B. 21
Purvine, Allen 120
Purvine, M. 120
Purvine, William 120
Putman, Jehu 44
Quarles, Elizabeth 44,78
Quarles, James 97
Quarles, John 78
Quarles, John B. 26
Quarles, Milton 99
Quarles, Milton W. 44
Quesenberry, Daniel 64,115

Quesenberry, James 12,99, 115
Quesenberry, John 41,94
Quigley, George 37
Quinley, Owen 30
Rachley, John 96
Radford, Edward 50,103
Ragland, Captain 52,106, 131
Ragland, Pettes 53,56,131
Ragsdale, Alfred 94,127
Ragsdale, Asa 41,94,127
Ragsdale, C. 115
Ragsdale, L. M. 108
Ragsdale, Lovin 12
Ragsdale, Richard 24,121
Ragsdale, Sarah 24,121
Railey 43
Rains, John 47,100,129
Ramsay, Richard B. 126
Ramsay, Thomas K. 126
Ramsey, George 133
Ramsey, Richard 36
Ramsey, Richard B. 89
Ramsey, Richard W. 83
Ramsey, Thomas 36
Ramsey, Thomas R. 89
Randle, Richard J. 77
Randolph, Grieff 3
Randolph, Peyton 28
Ranels, John N. 113
Rather, Elizabeth 52,105, 133
Ray, Alsey 16,69
Ray, Benjamin 69
Ray, Elisha 68
Ray, John 16,30,69,111
Ray, Joseph 16,69
Ray, Martin B. 36,89
Ray, Samuel 68
Ray, Simpson 16,69
Ray, Thomas 16
Ray, William 16,69,108
Ray, Willis 16,69
Reace, Alsey 13
Read, Elum 113
Read, Federick 113
Read, Henry 113
Read, Robert 39,113
Read, Robert D. 113
Read, William 113
Reed, Elam 58
Reed, Elum 5
Reed, Hailey 43
Reed, Hali 96
Reed, Henry, Jr. 5,58
Reed, Henry, Sr. 5,58
Reed, James 43,96
Reed, Levi 43,96
Reed, Robert 5,58,92
Reed, Robert B. 5
Reed, Robert D. 58
Reed, William 5,58
Reeder, Benjamin 39
Reeder, Edwin 39
Reeder, Harris 39
Reese, Alsy 66
Reese, Thomas B. 52,105
Reese, William 105
Reeves, Burrell 8
Reeves, Burwell 61
Reeves, Peter 28
Rencher, Henry 87
Reynolds, John 44,97
Reynolds, Thomas 24,77,121
Reynolds, Zebba 12
Reynolds, Zebby 115
Rhea, Archibald 45,99
Rhea, John 8
Rhea, Robert 8,99
Rhodes, Claborn H. 44
Rhodes, Clayton 97
Rhodes, Elisha 5,87
Rhodes, Elizabeth 56,58
Rhodes, Frederick L. 3
Rhodes, William 45
Rial, James 80
Rice, Anderson C. 66
Rice, Benjamin 30,83
Rice, David 121
Rice, James 30,83,108
Rice, John 30,83,108
Rice, Nancy 30
Rice, Nathaniel 30,83
Rice, Thomas 30,80
Rice, William 30,83
Rich, Allen 8
Rich, Charles 61
Rich, Charles, Sr. 8
Rich, Curtis 61
Rich, George 61
Rich, Joel 10,63
Rich, Obadiah 102
Richardson, Brice 43,96
Richardson, Kinchen 66
Richardson, Loid 120
Richardson, Loyd 21,74
Richardson, Martin 24,77
Richardson, Martin B. 121
Richardson, Willis 71,116

Richmond, Alexander 108
Richmond, Alexander P. 5
Richmond, Andrew 108
Richmond, Daniel 108
Richmond, James 5,58,113
Richmond, Joseph 30,83
Richmond, Thomas 10,63
Ricketts, John L. 77,121
Ricketts, John S. 24
Ricketts, William G. 10
Rider, Reuben 16,69
Rieff, Catherine 69
Rieff, Henry 16
Rieff, John 16
Rieff, Torres 16
Rieff, Torris 66
Riggan, Daniel 6
Riggan, Henry 32
Riggan, Samuel N. 6
Right, Abraham 108
Right, Anderson 16
Right, Berry 32
Right, Isaac 16
Right, James 32
Right, John 16
Right, Thomas A. 13
Ring, M. 124
Roach, Alexander 16
Roach, John 83
Roach, John, Jr. 30,83
Roach, John, Sr. 30
Roane, Hannah 21,74
Roane, Harris 120
Roane, Thomas 131
Robb, Jesse 85
Robb, John 32,85
Robb, John, Jr. 32,124
Robb, John, Sr. 124
Robb, William 124
Roberts, McKee 121
Roberts, March 24
Robertson, Andrew 24,77
Robertson, Higdon 34,87
Robertson, Hugh 37,90
Robertson, Jordan 30
Robertson, Lewis 34,87
Robertson, Meredith 121
Robertson, Newel 108
Robins, Lemuel 58
Robinson, Edward 48,102
Robinson, James 48,102
Robinson, Meredith 77
Robinson, Stephen 102
Rochel, James 32
Rochel, William 85

Rochell, James 124
Rodgers, John 100
Rogers, Brinkley M. 108
Rogers, Henry 12,58,113
Rogers, Luvan 64
Rogers, Micajah 5
Rogers, Robert 48,102
Rogers, Samuel 12,64,115
Rogers, Tobias 64,115
Rogers, Tobias W. 12
Rogers, William 6
Roland, Isaac 90
Roland, James 90
Roland, Robert 118
Roper, James 108
Ross, Allen 16,69
Ross, George 6,59
Ross, Henry P. 16
Ross, John 16,69
Ross, Samuel N. 59
Rotramel, Fed F. 6
Rotramel, Frederick 87
Rotramel, Henry 34,87
Roulston, James C. 111
Routon, Richard 23,129
Routon, William 23,129
Rowen, Hughey 48
Rowen, Robert 48,63
Rowland, Benjamin 37
Rowland, Byrd 124
Rowland, Isaac 37
Rowland, James 37
Rowland, Richardson 28,66
Rowton, William 76
Rucks, James 3
Rudder, Benjamin 92
Rudder, Edwin 92
Rudder, harris 92
Rummels, John 58
Rummels, Libby 58
Russell, John 53
Russell, William 56,83
Rutherford, G. W. 21
Rutherford, Griffith W. 74,126
Rutherford, John B. 14
Rutherford, John R. 66
Rutland, Abednego 30,83
Rutland, Edward 103
Rutland, Henry 50,103
Rutland, Isaac 50,103
Rutland, Joseph 30,83
Rutland, Milbry 80
Rutland, Rutherford 28,80
Rutledge, Alexander 3,56,111
Rutledge, Daniel 48

Rutledge, Daniel L. 102
Rutledge, Elijah 6,60
Ruyle, Aaron 48
Rye, Henry 3
Sadler, Jane 10,102
Sadler, John W. 106
Sadler, William 10,102
Samford, James 22
Sanderson, Samuel 7
Sanders, George 22
Sanders, James 38,90,112
Sanders, Jordan 45,99
Sanders, Joseph 47,100
Sanders, Joseph F. 16
Sanders, Joseph P. 69
Sanders, Lance 90
Sanders, Mrs. 12
Sanders, Nathaniel 16,69
Sanders, Reuben 74
Sanders, Richard 16,24,
  69,77,121
Sanders, Simeon 92
Sanderson, John 115
Sanderson, Wade 37,90
Sandley, John 43
Sands, William 13,80
Sanes, Abraham 10
Satterfield, Reuben 53,
  107,132
Sauls, Henry 43,96
Sayle, William P. 90
Scoby, David 3,74,120
Scoby, James 21,74,132
Scoby, John 132
Scoby, John B. 21,74
Scoggins, George W. 3
Scott 39
Scott, Ann 41
Scott, Eli 63
Scott, James 41
Scott, James P. 71,117
Scott, John 12,64
Scott, Labon 117
Scott, Lander 63
Scott, Leander 10
Scott, Samuel 94
Scott, William 94
Scott, William H. 63
Scott, Wyatt 39
Scroggins, Giles H. 56
Scruggs, Gross 7,60
Scruggs, Solomon 63
Scurlock, Dudley 32,124
Scurlock, Thomas 32
Sea, Beverly 19

Seaborn, Christopher 103
Seaborn, John H. 103
Seabourn, Christopher 50
Seabourn, Isaac R. 50
Seabourn, John h. 50
Searcy, Hiram 47,100
Searcy, Mitchell 3
Searcy, Reuben 50,104
Searcy, W. W. 112
Searcy, William 3,104
Searcy, William W. 56
Seat, Lebum 71
Seat, Martin 107,132
Seawell, H. H. 112
Seawell, Hardy H. 3,56
Seawell, William 3,56
Seay, Beverly 118
Seay, Beverly W. 72
Seay, Edward S. 120
Seay, John 105,112
Seay, John, Jr. 52
Sellars, Alfred 26,99
Sellars, Alvis 26,99
Sellars, D. H. 78
Sellars, Joseph H. 26
Sellars, Lard 45,78
Serrell, Ephraim 127
Seth, Steed 113
Shane, John 28
Shanks, William 39,92,129
Shannon, Henry 58,108,113
Shannon, Henry, Sr. 5
Shannon, James 5,58
Shannon, James H. 128
Shannon, John 5,58
Shannon, John A. 113
Shannon, Robert 113
Shannon, Robert, Jr. 5,58,113
Shannon, Robert, Sr. 5,58
Sharon, Thomas 30
Sharp, Benjamin 8,102
Sharp, Ezekiel A. 97
Sharp, James 50
Sharp, James G. 103
Sharp, Joseph 97
Sharpe, Ezekiel 44
Sharpe, Joseph 44
Shaw, Alsea 118
Shaw, Alsey 19,72
Shaw, James 118
Shaw, Jeremiah 19,72,118
Shaw, Jesse 118
Shaw, John 61,80
Shaw, John L. 8
Shaw, Solomon 19,72

Shaw, Solomon R. 118
Shaw, William 19
Shearl, William 10,109
Shelton, William 43,96
Shepherd, James 81
Shepherd, James M. 28
Shepherd, John 28,80
Shepherd, Samuel 28,80,81
Shepherd, Thomas 32,124
Shepherd, Thomas C. 85
Shepherd, William 28,80
Sheron, Joanna 108
Sheron, Thomas 108
Sheron, Wood H. 34,60
Sherrill 30
Sherrill, abel 45,99
Sherrill, Archibald 30,83
Sherrill, Elizabeth 132
Sherrill, Ephraim 35,41
Sherrill, Eve 56
Sherrill, Hugh 21,74,120
Sherrill, Newman 34,87
Sherrill, Ute 83
Sherroll, Andrew 112
Shoars, Phillip 92
Shores, Jonathan 10
Shores, Philip 10
Shors, Jonathan 63
Short, Thomas 10,99
Shorter, B. B. 107
Shorter, Berry 5
Shorter, Berry B. 113
Shovel, Ephraim 94
Simmons, Alexander 12,99
Simmons, John 74,120
Simmons, John A. 22
Simmons, Joseph 35,87
Simpson, George 92
Simpson, Hannah 45,99
Simpson, Robert 99
Sims, Benjamin 44
Sims, Caswell S. 23,76, 129
Sims, Chesley 76,129
Sims, Chesty 23
Sims, Christopher 36,89, 126
Sims, Edmund 89
Sims, Edward 36,126
Sims, James 18
Sims, James T. 97
Sims, L. L. 90
Sims, Matthew 18,71,117
Sims, Matthias 44,97
Sims, Robert 36,89

Sims, Thomas 44,97
Skean, James 127
Skean, John 8,113
Skein, John 58
Skurlock, Francis 61
Skurlock, John 61
Sloan, J. N. 63
Sloan, Jer N. 10
Smart, John 94
Smart, Phillip 108
Smith, Aley 45
Smith, Benjamin 22
Smith, Benjamin B. 74
Smith, Bird 10,48,63
Smith, Captain 89
Smith, Charles 45,99
Smith, D. 131
Smith, Daniel 33,47,86,92
Smith, David 41,94,127
Smith, David B. 10,63
Smith, Elisha 56
Smith, Fanny 48
Smith, Frank 66
Smith, G. D. 132
Smith, George 10,38,44,45,63,90, 99
Smith, George K. 97
Smith, H. 71
Smith, Harris 102
Smith, Harry 90
Smith, Hector 8,61
Smith, Henry 38
Smith, Henry F. 18,56,112
Smith, Hiram 90
Smith, J. A. 63
Smith, Jacob 39,92
Smith, James 34,87,117
Smith, Jesse 83
Smith, John 14,45,47,61,66,94,99, 100,127,129
Smith, John A. 10
Smith, John C. 41,94
Smith, John T. 39
Smith, John Y. 117
Smith, Josiah, Jr. 71,117
Smith, Josiah, Sr. 18,71,117
Smith, Malcom 81
Smith, Malcomb 28
Smith, Mary 18,117
Smith, Mary R. 50,103
Smith, Matthew 122
Smith, Nicholas 39,92
Smith, Reuben 14,66
Smith, Robert 83,133
Smith, S. C. 127

Smith, Sampson 44,109
Smith, Samuel 14,45,66
Smith, Shadrach 10,109
Smith, Shadrach C. 109
Smith, Thomas L. 94
Smith, Thomas S. 41
Smith, William 16,45,
  48,69,78,99
Smith, William B. 3
Smith, William D. 38
Smith, William H. 26,44,
  109
Smith, William P. 44,97
Sneed, Abraham 8,48,61
Sneed, Grief 74
Sneed, Hamilton 74,120
Sneed, John 8,61
Sneed, John, Jr. 61
Sneed, John, Sr. 8
Sneed, William 8,61
Somers, Anthony 96
Somers, James 96
Somers, John 43
Somers, John W. 96
Somers, Matthew 96
Somers, Reddin 96
Sorter, John 128
Southworth, James 36
Spain, John 115
Spain, Labon 115
Sparks, Nathan 41,94,128
Spears, Lewis 129
Spears, Lewis B. 76
Spears, Lewis P. 23
Spears, Sarah 23,94
Spears, William 23
Sperry, Samuel 50,150
Sperry, Thomas 50,150
Spickard, John 28,81
Spinks, John 108
Spradley, A. B. 109
Spradley, James 112
Spradley, Tavner 10
Spradlin, James 56
Spring, Aaron 100
Spring, Abner 52,105,133
Spring, B. 133
Spring, Benjamin 52,106
Spring, Gamma 133
Spring, John 52,133
Spring, John, Jr. 105
Spring, John, Sr. 105
Spring, Moses 52,105,133
Spring, Samuel 105
Spring, William 133

Spurlock, Francis 8
Spurlock, John 8
Stacy, Joseph 64
Standfield, Robert 52
Standfield, Thomas 34
Standifer, William 19,72
Standley, Benjamin 18
Standley, David 18
Standley, Thomas 8
Stanfield, Thomas 60
Stanley, John 96
Stanley, Thomas 61
Steed, Seth 58
Steel, William 74
Steele, George 90
Steele, Miner 23,52,100
Steele, William 21,23,32,120
Stembridge, Mary 71
Stembridge, Matley 18
Stembridge, William 71,117
Stephens, Elisha C. 44
Stephens, James 21,74
Stephens, Littleberry 36
Stephens, S. B. 126
Stephens, Sanders 21,74,126
Stephenson, Robert 74
Stevens, Elisha 97
Stevens, James 120
Stevenson, Benjamin F. 28
Stevenson, Isaac F. 37
Stevenson, Isaac T. 90
Steward, Joseph 50
Stewart, Cyrus 16,59
Stewart, E. R. 112
Stewart, Eline 81
Stewart, John 108
Stewart, Joseph 103
Stewart, Samuel 10,63
Stewart, William 24,77,121
Stone, John 3,56
Stone, Newbern P. 132
Stone, Samuel 107
Stone, Thomas 53,107
Stone, William N. 28,80
Stoneman, Jack 48
Stoneman, John H. 61
Stringfellow, James 83
Stroud, Archibald 97
Stroud, John 97
Stroud, O. B. 63
Sublet, William S. 44
Sublett, William L. 97
Sugg, Solomon 10
Sullivan, Asel 28
Sullivan, Azel 81

Sullivan, Barnet J. 108
Sullivan, Benjamin 108
Sullivan, Edmund 28
Sullivan, Gilbert 50
Sullivan, Holland 30,83
Sullivan, Jesse 108
Sullivan, Jesse, Jr. 50, 103
Sullivan, Jesse W. 50
Sullivan, Joab 28,80
Sullivan, Joel 50
Sullivan, John 28
Sullivan, Lea, Jr. 21
Sullivan, Lea, Sr. 21
Sullivan, Lee 74
Sullivan, Parker 50
Sullivan, Price 58
Sullivan, Reuben 30
Sumnerhill, William 32, 85,112
Summers, Anthony 43
Sommers, George 108
Summers, James 43,108
Summers, Matthew 43
Sutton, Nicy 32,85
Sutton, Toliver 32,124
Swain, Caleb 5
Swain, Caleb W. 108
Swain, James H. 108
Swain, John 64
Swain, John N. 108
Swain, Williaa H. 108
Swan, Andrew 19
Swan, George 133
Swan, George L. 52
Swan, James 19,52
Swan, James, Jr. 133
Swan, James, Sr. 133
Swan, John 32,52,133
Swan, John, Jr. 52
Swan, John W. 52
Swan, Philip 133
Swan, William 52,133
Swann, Andrew 72
Swann, George 105
Swann. James 72,106
Swann, John 85,106
Swann, Willian 106,133
Swann, William, Jr. 106
Swann, William, Sr. 106
Swanner, John 30.83
Swany, William 120
Sweatt, Asariah 52,106
Sweatt, Edward 52,106, 132

Sweatt, George 52,74
Sweatt, Joseph 52,133
Sweatt, Robert 52,106
Sweatt, V. 132
Sweatt, William 18
Sweatt, William, Jr. 52,132
Sweatt, William, Sr. 106,132
Swift, Clevias W. 90
Swindle, Isaiah 3.56
Suindle, Joel 22,74,120
Swindle, John 120
Swindle, Joseph 120
Swindle, Pillage 3,56
Swindle, William H. 120
Swingley, George 108
Swingley, Jonas 28,81
Swinney, William 53,74
Swinney, John 124
Sypert, A. 112
Sypert, Elison A. 60
Sypert, Hardy 7,112
Sypert, Hardy H. 60
Sypert, Lawrence 6,56,112
Sypert, Robert 32,85,124
Sypert, Sarah 60
Sypert, Thomns 32,60,85,124
Sypert, Thomas, Sr. 7
Sypert, William L. 3,56,112
Tailor, Benjamin 32
Tailor, Paterson 32
Taller, Bird 124
Taller, Poleman 124
Tallow, Benjamin 85
Tallow, Peterson 85
Tally, Archibald 33,86
Tally, Coleman 117
Tally, Ephraim 53,107,132
Tally, Hailey 33
Tally, Haley 86
Tally, Henry 53,107,132
Tally, James 18,71,117
Tally, Payton 33,86
Tally, Richard 33,63
Tally, Spencer W. 10,63
Tapp, John 3,56,112
Tapp, John S. 3,112
Tarier, Thomas 58
Tarpley, H. 63
Tarpley, John 36,89,126
Tarpley, Sterling 36,89,126
Tarpley, Steth 89
Tarpley, Steth T. 126
Tarver, Benjamin 35,87
Tarver, Calvin 60
Tarver, Silas 35,87

Tarver, Thomas B. 5
Tarver, William 7,60
Tate, John W. 50,104
Tate, Richard B. 104
Tate, Richard D. 50
Tate, Robert L. 104
Tate, Robert S. 50
Tate, Zachariah 28,50,104
Tatum, Dabney 16,69
Taylor, Abraham 14,66
Taylor, Caleb 38,90
Taylor, Fanny 47,101,131
Taylor, Henry 131
Taylor, Howard 90
Taylor, Hugh 69
Taylor, Hughey 16
Taylor, Isaac 131
Taylor, Isaiah P. 90
Taylor, J. B. 100,101
Taylor, James 47,85,124
Taylor, James B. 47,131
Taylor, James N. 36
Taylor, John 23,39,47,91,
 92,100,129,131
Taylor, John D. 38
Taylor, John L. 101
Taylor, John M. 120
Taylor, Joseph 47
Taylor, Joshua 47,101
Taylor, Joshua V. 47,131
Taylor, Mary 19,72
Taylor, Robert 47,69,101,
 131
Taylor, Solomon 38,90
Taylor, Thomas 39
Teague, Joshua 45,99
Teague, William 45,99
Telford, Hugh 30,83
Telford, Hugh, Jr. 83
Telford, John 30,83
Telford, Robert 30
Telford, Robertson 83
Telford, Samuel 83
Telford, Thomas 30,83
Terrell, Thomas 114
Terrill, William 30,108
Terry, Elijah 19,72,118
Terry, Jeremiah 118
Terry, Peter G. 19,72
Thaxton, Nathaniel 81
Thomas, Ann 14
Thomas, Anna 66
Thomas, David 14,90
Thomas, Henry 5
Thomas, Jacob 24,77,96,
 122
Thomas, Jacob H. 44,97
Thomas, James 5,44,96
Thomas, James, Sr. 63
Thomas, John 14,66
Thomas, John C. 44
Thomas, John F. 44,97
Thomas, John G. 96
Thomas, Neal 106
Thomas, Robert 18,76,117
Thomas, S. T. 63
Thomas, William 45
Thomas, Wilson B. 44
Thompkins, James 66
Thompson, And R 10
Thompson, Andrew 11
Thompson, Andrew, Jr. 63
Thompson, Andrew, Sr. 63
Thompson, Ausborne 104
Thompson, E. A. 92
Thompson, Eli M. 39
Thompson, Elizabeth 50,104
Thompson, Henry 24,89,126
Thompson, James 11,104
Thompson, James B. 11
Thompson, James, Jr. 10
Thompson, James M. 63
Thompson, James P. 50
Thompson, James, Sr. 10,63
Thompson, John 50,150
Thompson, Margaret 50,150
Thompson, Moses 41,94,128
Thompson, Moses H. 41,94
Thompson, Moses, Jr. 128
Thompson, Osburn 50
Thompson, Samuel 10
Thompson, Swan 36,89,126
Thompson, Thomas J. 3,56,112
Thompson, William 11,50,81,104
Thompson, William A. 41,94
Thompson, William D. 128
Thorn, David 41
Thorn, David K. 94
Thorn, James 128
Thorn, John H. 41,94,128
Thorn, William 94,128
Thornton, Henry 101
Thornton, Seth 30,83
Thrift, A. D. 90
Thrift, Drewry 38
Thrower, Eli 58,114
Thweatt, Elijah 58
Thweatt, Henry 58
Thweatt, Margaret 58
Thweatt, William 11

Tilman, Jacob 28,81
Tinsley, Josiah B. 41
Tippitt, John 76
Tippitt, John C. 23,129
Tipton, Barnaby 14
Tipton, James 16,69
Tipton, Jonathan 69
Tipton, Rus B. 69
Tipton, William 16,69
Tittle, Anthony 43
Tittle, Samuel 61
Todd, John 18
Tolbert, William 109
Tolliver, Zachariah 3,56, 112
Tomlinson, Allen 22,74, 120
Tomlinson, Ervin 74
Tomlinson, Irvin 22
Tomlinson, Major 16
Tomlinson, William 22,28, 74,126
Tompkins, James 16
Toule, Richard 108
Townsend, Onswell 30
Townsend, Ozwell 83
Townsend, Richard 12,64, 115
Tracy, Evans 47,101
Tracy, Thomas 92
Travillian, Edward 32,85, 124
Travillian, James 32
Travis, Solomon 43
Trayler, Edward D. 112
Traylor, Edward 3,56
Trewett, Captain 112
Tribble, Isaiah 10,63
Tribling, William 113
Trice, Edward 94,128
Trigg, A. 91
Trigg, Abraham 79
Trigg, Alanson 79
Trigg, Daniel 45,79
Trigg, Edward 41
Trigg, Haden 79
Trigg, John 79
Trigg, Lancen 112
Trigg, Lucy 45
Trigg, Mary A. 79
Trigg, Nancy 79
Trigg, Samuel 79
Trigg, Stephen 79
Trigg, William 78
Trigg, William H. 45

Trout, Adam 3,112
Trout, John 22,74,132
Trout, Joseph 22,74,132
Truett, Adam 56
Truett, Captain 3
Truett, Elige 114
Truett, Elijah 5
Truett, Henry 5,114
Tubb, John 44,79
Tucker, Abbot 58
Tucker, Andrew 114
Tucker, Benjamin 35,87
Tucker, Green 32,85,124
Tucker, John W. 35,87
Tucker, Priscilla 18
Tulliston, Robert 56
Tunage, Isaac 8
Tune, Thomas 58
Turnage, Isaac 61
Turner, Captain 132
Turner, Elizabeth 76
Turner, James 18,33,76,86,129
Turner, Jeremiah 33,86
Turner, John 7,69
Turner, John G. 69
Turner, Jonathan 8,61,102
Turner, N. G. 129
Turner, Samuel 69
Turner, Thomas 76,129
Turner, Thomas D. 23
Turner, William 52,106,129,133
Underwood, Elisha 83
Underwood, Joel 36,89,126
Underwood, Joseph 48,102
Underwood, Milton 36,89,126
Underwood, Perry 24,83
Underwood, Thomas 36
Upchurch, Abner 26,79
Usry, Henry 56
Vantrease, Jacob 33,86
Vantrease, John 33,86
Vantrease, William 33,86
Vaughan, Abraham 74
Vaughan, Abram 22,126
Vaughan, David 22,74
Vaughan, Edmund 69
Vaughan, James 36,89
Vaughan, John S. 56
Vaughan, Malijah 17
Vaughan, Mary J. 17
Vaughan, Mary T. 69
Vaughan, Mecijah 69
Vaughan, Thomas 17,23,69,76,129
Vaughan, Turner 17,69
Vaught, Elijah 39,92

Vaughter, Ludwich 122
Vaughters, Ludwell 24
Vick, Allen W. 3,56,112
Vick, Samuel 38,91
Vier, Thomas 83
Vinson, David 3,18,56
Violett, Anderson 106
Vivrett, Captain 12,65
Vivrett, Henry 35,87
Vivrett, John 14
Vivrett, John B. 66
Vivrett, Micajah 35,87
Vivrett, William 114
Vowell, James L. 39,95
Vowell, Jesse H. 128
Vowell, Jesse J. 41
Vowell, W. A. 92
Vowell, William A. 41, 95,128
Waddle, John 95
Wade, Allen W. 114
Wade, Charles 5,58,114
Wade, Robert 114
Wade, T. H. 114
Wade, W. W. 63
Wade, Willis W. 11
Wadkins, Joel 88
Wadkins, Reece 120
Wadle, John 128
Walch, James 71
Walch, Norman 71
Walden, Fielden 33
Walden, John 33
Walker, Delila 85,124
Walker, drucilla 66
Walker, Drusila 14
Walker, Elizabeth 85
Walker, H. 123
Walker, Henry 7,85
Walker, James D. 16,69
Walker, John 53
Walker, Kesiah 124
Walker, Mary 28
Walker, Millander 124
Walker, Milner 32,85
Walker, Noah 85,124
Walker, Polly 81
Walker, R. 85
Walker, Radford 32,85,124
Walker, Samuel 28,81
Walker, Tabitha 7,60
Walker, Thomas P. 81
Walker, W. B. 63
Walker, William 32,33,74, 81,85,124
Walker, William, Jr. 32
Wall, Adam 58,114
Wall, Benjamin 5,58,114
Wall, Bird 112,114
Wall, Bird, Jr. 5,58
Wall, Bird, Sr. 5,58
Wall, Burrell 5,58
Wall, Evan 5,58
Wall, Merrett 96
Wallace, Cary 99
Wallis, Gary 46
Walls, Alexander 53,87
Walsh, James 18
Walsh, Norman 18
Walton, A. C. 63
Walton, archibald C. 48
Walton, Harris 124
Walton, James 36,89,126
Wamack, Elijah 39
Wamack, Rachel 39
Wamack, Richard 39
Wanick, James 58
Ward, Andrew 30,82
Ward, Hasa 109
Ward, Henry 20,72
Ward, Hosea 11
Ward, John 11
Ward, John, Jr. 63
Ward, John, Sr. 63
Ware, Dudley 46,99
Warnick, James 5
Warren, Benjamin 20,36,89,126
Warren, Boothe 19,74,118
Warren, Charles 12,65
Warren, Enoch 109
Warren, John 46
Warren, Linsi 65
Warren, Luce 126
Warren, Lucy 20
Warren, Seloma 115
Warren, Sina 12,115
Warren, Solomon 12,65
Warren, William 12,46,64,109,115
Waters, John 47
Waters, Lansy P. 47
Waters, Shelah 47
Waters, Shelah, Jr. 22
Waters, Shelah, Sr. 101
Waters, Shely 75,133
Waters, William 39,47,92,101,133
Waters, Wilson T. 39,92
Watkins, David 74,107
Watkins, Joel 35

Watson, Joseph 38,91
Watson, Thomas 38,91
Weatherly, Abner 97
Weatherly, Denny 46,99
Weatherly, William 99
Weatherly, Wright M. 97
Webb, Anderson 109
Webb, George 11,63
Webb, John 11,16,63,69
Webb, Sarah 14
Webb, Woodson 102
Webber, James 88
Weir, Elizabeth 3
Weir, James 120,132
Weir, James C. 53,132
Weir, James J. 53
Weir, James, Sr. 22
Weir, John 53
Weir, John B. 132
Weir, Joseph 53
Weir, Thomas 120
Welch, John 30,83
Welch, Thomas 30,83
West, James 117
Wheeler, Edward B. 19,72,
  118
Wheeler, Nathan 33,86
Wheer, William 112
Wherry, Simeon 7
Wherry, William A. 56
Whitaker, Mark 30,83
White, Cader 3,56
White, E. 3
White, E. A. 3
White, Edward 35,88
White, George 19,72,118
White, Isaac B. 56
White, J. B. 3
White, James 3
White, Jesse B. 3
White, John 112
White, John W. 3,56,74,
  120
White, Little B. 56
White, Littleberry 3
White, Samuel 19,72
White, W. L. 112
White, William 35,88
Whitehead, James 19,72,
  118
Whitehead, William 118
Whitlock, Henry 11
Whitlock, James 11,63
Whitlock, John 11

Whitlock, Thomas 11,63,109
Whitlock, Thomas, Jr. 11
Whitlow, Henry 109
Whitson, Abram 16,69
Whitson, John 16,69
Whitson, John D. 14
Whitton, Jonathan 46
Whitton, Robert J. 46
Whitworth, Daniel 51
Whitworth, James 23,76
Whorton, Joseph 18,71
Wier, Absolum 60
Wier, James 107
Wier, James C. 107
Wier, James J. 74
Wier, James, Sr. 74
Wier, Joseph 107
Wiley, James 41
Wiley, Mary J. 41
Wilie, Mary A. 95
Wilkerson, Meredith 50
Wilkinson, Meredith 104
Wilkinson, William 69
Willard, Alfred 71
Willard, Alligood 71
Willard, Beverly 8
Willard, John 43,61,96
Williams, A. S. 92
Williams, Allen 91
Williams, Anderson 39
Williams, Argales 109
Williams, Barnett 48
Williams, Burnett 102
Williams, Edward 46,109
Williams, Elbert 46,79
Williams, Elijah 18,66
Williams, George 19,72
Williams, Henry B. 46
Williams, Isaac 11,63
Williams, James 66
Williams, James J. 11
Williams, James, Jr. 63
Williams, Jeptha 46,109
Williams, Jeremiah 14,91
Williams, John 20,72,128
Williams, Jonathan 46
Williams, Joseph 11,63
Williams, Julias H. 46,99
Williams, Mahala 44,79
Williams, Martha 39
Williams, Mas 11
Williams, Moses 109
Williams, Nathaniel 14,41,48,61,
  91,95

Williams, Robert 53,107, 132
Williams, Roger 66
Williams, Samuel 128
Williams, Thomas 14,38, 66,79,91,99
Williams, Thomas E. 41
Williams, Thomas G. 44
Williams, Thomas J. 102
Williams, Thomas R. 128
Williams, Turner P. 14
Williams, Washington 46,99
Williams, William 26,79,124
Williams, Williamson 99
Williamson, Auston 8,61
Williamson, George 50,104
Williamson, James 28
Williamson, John 50
Williamson, John A. 50,104
Williamson, Joseph 51,104
Williamson, Littleberry 20
Williamson, Margaret 50,104
Williamson, Margaret, Jr. 104
Williamson, Nancy 104
Williamson, Robert 48,102
Williamson, Thomas 50,102, 104
Williamson, William 50,61, 104
Williamson, William H. 8
Williamson, Zachariah 8, 102
Williford, George 76
Williford, George A. 23,129
Williford, James C. 76
Williford, Wiley 43
Williford, William H. 23,76
Williford, William, Jr. 129
Willis, Edward 28,81
Willis, James 66
Willis, James M. 28
Willis, Thomas 17,66,69
Willis, William 38,90
Willy, Ezekiel C. 44
Wilson, Allen 48,102
Wilson, Captain 7,60,91
Wilson, Charles 43,96
Wilson, J. R. 63
Wilson, James 8,50,61,104
Wilson, James R. 11
Wilson, John 50
Wilson, John R. 102,104
Wilson, Joseph L. 3,56,112

Wilson, Matthew 8,61
Wilson, Robert 8,61
Wilson, W. 112
Wilson, William 22,75,102,120
Winford, Alexander 35,129
Winford, Alexander S. 88
Winford, Benjamin 87
Winford, William 35
Winford, William W. 87
Winston, Ann 79
Winston, Isaac 26
Winston, Isaac, Sr. 79
Winston, John 79
Winston, John J. 26
Winter, Ambrose V. 35,88
Winter, Wilborn R. 88
Winter, William 35
Winters, John 77
Witherspoon, Alexander 43,96
Witherspoon, Enos 96
Witty, Ezekiel C. 97
Womack, Elijah 92
Womack, Richard 101
Womack, Robert 99
Wood, A. C. 79
Wood, Archer 104
Wood, Archibald 50
Wood, Benton 109
Wood, Isham 16,69
Wood, James 24,33,77,107,132
Wood, Jesse 39,92
Wood, John 16,26,69
Wood, Josiah 16,69
Wood, Reuben 30,83
Wood, Tandy 58
Wood, Thomas 16,69
Wood, William 26
Woodall, George W. 126
Woodall, Henry H. 89
Woodard, Baker 79
Woodard, Hezekiah 19
Woodcock, Henry 19,72
Woodcock, Jesse 20,72,118
Woodcock, Mary 19,72,118
Wooden, Fielden 86
Wooden, John 86
Woodrell, George 36
Woodrell, Henry 36
Woodrill, H. H. 112
Woodrum, Jacob 30,83
Woodrum, William 83
Woods, James 3,86
Woodson, Washington M. 28
Woodward, Baker 26

Woodward, H. W. 20
Woodward, Hezekiah 72,118
Woodward, John 26
Woody, James 86
Woolard, Alfred 18,117
Woolard, Alligood 18
Woolard, Allison 71
Woolard, Godfrey 117
Woolard, John 56,112
Woolard, John B. 3
Woolard, Simeon 56
Woolen, Edward 24,77
Woolen, Joshua 24,77,122
Woolen, Luvina 122
Woolen, Moses 24,77,122
Word, Fanny 46
Word, Henry B. 99
Word, James 11,63
Word, John 99
Word, William 79
Wortham, W. H. 79
Wrae, Hiram S. 11
Wray, Thomas 28
Wrice, David 77
Wright, Anderson 69
Wright, Berry 85,124
Wright, Captain 49
Wright, Charles 50
Wright, Charles, Jr. 104
Wright, Charles, Sr. 104
Wright, E. 38
Wright, Ellis G. 91
Wright, Isaac 69
Wright, James 85,124
Wright, John 69,122
Wright, Jonathan 51,104
Wright, Joseph 51,104
Wright, Lemuel 51
Wright, Lewis 51,104
Wright, Samuel, Jr. 104
Wright, Samuel, Sr. 104
Wright, Solomon D. 51,104
Wright, Thomas 50,104
Wright, Thomas A. 66
Wroe, H. L. 63
Wynne, A. H. 35
Wynne, Alason G. 88
Wynne, Albert H. 87
Wynne, Cetiva 16
Wynne, Daniel 14
Wynne, James 30
Wynne, John 117
Wynne, John K. 35
Wynne, John R. 88

Wynne, Joseph D. 69
Wynne, Manerva 124
Wynne, Minerva 56
Wynne, Ridley 30
Wynne, Ridley B. 83
Wynne, William 18,71,117
Yandle, James 83
Yandle, William 83
Yates, John B. 18,71
Yeargin, James 91
Yerger, Michael 3,56
Yerger, Samuel 3
Yonce, Patrick 32
York, Edmund 38,91
York, James 14
York, Robert 66
Young, Adnah 14
Young, Beverly 14,66
Young, Captain 43,96
Young, Charles 44,97
Young, David 22,75,120
Young, David, Jr. 120
Young, Delia 66
Young, Demetrius 14
Young, Doak 39
Young, Francis 108
Young, Gilbert 108
Young, J. D. 11
Young, James 47,101
Young, James H. 66
Young, John 41,95,128
Young, Joseph 17,66
Young, Joseph D. 86
Young, Robert 69
Young, Samuel 30
Young, Sarah 86
Young, Stacy 108
Young, Stephen 14,66
Young, William 14,66,81
Young, William, Jr. 66
Young, William L. 28
Young, William, Sr. 28
Yourie, patrick 85,124
Zachery, Allen 77,122
Zachery, Hartwell 122
Zachry, Allen 24
Zachry, Stokes 24

www.ingramcontent.com/pod-product-compliance
Lightning Source LLC
Chambersburg PA
CBHW020652300426
44112CB00007B/343